THE CHAUCERIAN APOCRYPHA:
A SELECTION

The Middle English Texts Series is designed for classroom use. Its goal is to make available to teachers and students texts that occupy an important place in the literary and cultural canon but have not been readily available in student editions. The series does not include those authors, such as Chaucer, Langland, or Malory, whose English works are normally in print in good student editions. The focus is, instead, upon Middle English literature adjacent to those authors that teachers need in compiling the syllabuses they wish to teach. The editions maintain the linguistic integrity of the original work but within the parameters of modern reading conventions. The texts are printed in the modern alphabet and follow the practices of modern capitalization, word formation, and punctuation. Manuscript abbreviations are silently expanded, and *u/v* and *j/i* spellings are regularized according to modern orthography. Yogh (3) is transcribed as *g*, *gh*, *y*, or *s*, according to the sound in Modern English spelling to which it corresponds; thorn (þ) and eth (ð) are transcribed as *th*. Distinction between the second person pronoun and the definite article is made by spelling the one *thee* and the other *the*, and final *-e* that receives full syllabic value is accented (e.g., *charité*). Hard words, difficult phrases, and unusual idioms are glossed on the page, either in the right margin or at the foot of the page. Explanatory and textual notes appear at the end of the text, often along with a glossary. The editions include short introductions on the history of the work, its merits and points of topical interest, and brief working bibliographies.

THE CHAUCERIAN APOCRYPHA: A SELECTION

Edited by
Kathleen Forni

Published for TEAMS
(The Consortium for the Teaching of the Middle Ages)
in Association with the University of Rochester

by

MEDIEVAL INSTITUTE PUBLICATIONS
Kalamazoo, Michigan
2005

Library of Congress Cataloging-in-Publication Data

The Chaucerian apocrypha : a selection / edited by Kathleen Forni.
    p. cm. -- (Middle English texts series)
 "Published for TEAMS (The Consortium for the Teaching of the Middle Ages) in association with the University of Rochester."
 Includes bibliographical references (p.).
 ISBN 1-58044-096-7 (pbk. : alk. paper)
 1. English poetry--Middle English, 1100-1500. 2. Chaucer, Geoffrey, d. 1400--Authorship. I. Forni, Kathleen. II. Consortium for the Teaching of the Middle Ages. III. Middle English texts (Kalamazoo, Mich.)
 PR1898.C47 2005
 821'.1--dc22

                                   2005025269

ISBN 1-58044-096-7

Printed in the United States of America

❧ CONTENTS

 # ACKNOWLEDGMENTS

This volume would not have been possible without Russell Peck's early interest in my proposal and his support over the last three years. Both he and the assistant editor of the series, Michael Livingston, thoroughly edited my manuscript (both text and gloss), and the final version is a much better book. N. M. Heckel, also of the series, initially formatted the manuscript and helped to check the texts against the manuscripts; Emily Rebekah Huber helped to reformat the volume into the new look of the series. Thanks are also due to Patricia Hollahan and her staff at Medieval Institute Publications for their help in bringing this book to fruition. Any errors are my own fault.

Joseph Dane, who first inspired my own interest in the Chaucerian apocrypha long ago, yet once again generously contributed his expertise and advice at several critical junctures. Tom McCreight provided invaluable and inspired tips on translating Gower's Latin. I am especially grateful to Loyola College in Maryland for providing me with a sabbatical and the financial means to consult the manuscript sources for these poems, and to the various archivists (at the British Library, Trinity College, Cambridge, and the Bodleian Library, Oxford) for allowing me to transcribe or photocopy their materials. Special thanks are due to Father Nicholas Hudson and Sister Mary Joseph McManamon at the Venerable English College in Rome for helping me locate, and allowing me to use here, their MS 1405. Finally, for tolerating my occasional compulsion to work when he wants to play (especially on our honeymoon!), this book is for my husband, Wes.

GENERAL INTRODUCTION

The poems in this volume were prized and preserved because of their association with Chaucer's name and have been, paradoxically, almost entirely ignored by modern readers for the same reason. The so-called Chaucerian apocrypha — suggesting works that are uncanonical, inauthentic, forged, and false — has come to refer to a somewhat ill-defined, diffuse, and amorphous body of poetry and prose. Bibliographers and editors have most often referred to the apocrypha as those presumably spurious works (approximately fifty in number) that were printed with or as Chaucer's authoritative work in the large folio editions by William Thynne (1532, 1545, 1550), John Stow (1561), Thomas Speght (1598, 1602, 1687), and John Urry (1721). These works were ostensibly mistaken as Chaucer's own productions, influencing the poet's reception history until the nineteenth century. The Chaucerian apocrypha is not, however, necessarily limited to those texts that circulated under the rubric "The Workes of Geffrey Chaucer." Eleanor Hammond, for instance, in addition to the spurious works in the printed folio editions, also includes those (now rejected) works that nineteenth-century editors and scholars introduced to the canon as well as verses that the fifteenth-century scribe John Shirley ascribed to Chaucer. Aage Brusendorff includes only those poems erroneously ascribed to Chaucer in fifteenth-century manuscripts. And perhaps most influentially, in his bibliographical essay "The Chaucerian Apocrypha," Rossell Hope Robbins defines the apocrypha as "[s]ome one hundred miscellaneous poems [that] have been either ascribed to Chaucer in fifteenth- and sixteenth-century manuscripts, or printed with or as Chaucer's in the black-letter editions of the sixteenth century, or linked to Chaucer by later scholars in the eighteenth and nineteenth centuries."[1] Robbins includes works that accompanied Chaucer's poetry in fifteenth-century manuscripts, Chaucerian imitations, works that were presumably inspired by Chaucer or that contain allusions to Chaucer or his poetry, as well as several works associated with or indebted to Chaucer's literary successor, John Lydgate.

The vague and inclusive term *apocrypha*, therefore, seems to encompass texts that were not only mistaken for Chaucer's or falsely attributed to Chaucer in both manuscript and print, but also works that were inspired by or associated with Chaucer's poetry. The term is worth considering because since the early fifteenth century the apocrypha has been a defining feature of the Chaucer canon. Rather than collecting Chaucer's minor poems into single authoritative editions, scribal editors habitually contextualized Chaucer's poetry in manuscript anthologies and miscellanies (distinguished by the perceived presence or absence of an editorial intelligence or thematic coherence) of courtly verse. Seth Lerer calls this "anthologistic impulse" a defining feature of English medieval literary culture.[2] The

---

[1] Robbins, "Chaucerian Apocrypha," p. 1061.

[2] Lerer, "Medieval English Literature," p. 1253.

Chaucerian contents of these manuscript collections were often anonymous as were the contributions of authors such as Lydgate, Hoccleve, and Clanvowe. Chaucer's sixteenth-century print editors drew their materials from these manuscript collections and continued the century-old practice of supplementing and complementing Chaucer's poetry with what they advertised on their title pages as "dyvers workes." Although Chaucer's print editors appear to have been intent upon preserving a canon of his genuine poetry, at the same time the appearance of new "diverse" works — especially those "never in print before" — seems to have been an equally compelling editorial and commercial incentive. Indeed, David Carlson suggests that the printed folio editions were marketed as authorial collections ("The Workes of Geffrey Chaucer") because in so-called print culture, Chaucer appears to have had value as a "brand name": "Chaucer's name, even attached to things he did not write, made books saleable, for it was his name, not the work, that moved the stock."[3]

While one would be naive, I think, to dismiss the commercial incentive of Chaucer's early editors, these manuscript and print collections obviously did not develop in a political vacuum. Several scholars have suggested that Chaucer's (and his imitators') poetic use of the vernacular was valued by both the Lancastrians and the Tudors as a form of linguistic capital, a crucial foundation for English nationalism. In John Fisher's view, for instance, Henry IV and V encouraged the dissemination of Chaucer's poetry in order to promote English as a national language and to acquire popular acceptance for their "usurpation and taxes": "If the Lancastrian administration was in any way consciously seeking popular sup-port by strengthening the use of the vernacular, it needed socially accepted models of English . . . the royal establishment appears to have undertaken a program to elevate the prestige of English."[4] Similarly, John Watkins surmises that the sixteenth-century Chau-cerian anthologies played an important role in the larger dynastic, political, and ideological context of Tudor centralization and reform, "casting Chaucer as a champion of the King against the conflicting claims of Church and nobility."[5] Although the thematic idiom of the manuscript and print anthologies is fundamentally courtly, invoking a feudal past in which ritualized and hierarchical social relations provided a cultural and ideological cement, the early Chaucer canon is peppered with anti-ecclesiastical works, such as the *Plowman's Tale* and *Jack Upland*, which not only complemented the anti-clerical satires in *The Canterbury Tales*, but also perhaps contributed to the ideology of imperial kingship and the prerogative rights of monarchs (Chaucer's *Retraction*, which softens the blow of his invective, was not printed for over two hundred years). Similarly, a poem like Gower's *In Praise of Peace* affirms the legitimacy of sacral monarchy, and the various short poems of wisdom and advice re-inforce a conservative, authoritarian social and cosmic hierarchy. The Chaucer that emerges from these early collections is sometimes a very different authorial and ideological product from the poet valued today, but it is important to remember that his early canonization was, in part, dependent upon these royalist, reformist, and sententious accretions.

It was not until the late eighteenth century, which saw the renewed valuation of the English literary past and the emergence of a national literary canon, that Thomas Tyrwhitt, in the interest of compiling a glossary of Chaucer's language for his 1775 edition of *The Canterbury Tales*, became the first critic to compile a list of what he considered Chaucer's

---

[3] Carlson, "Chaucer, Humanism, and Printing," p. 279.

[4] Fisher, *Importance of Chaucer*, p. 144.

[5] Watkins, "'Wrastling for this world,'" p. 23.

"genuine productions." It would take another one hundred years, however, before the apocrypha was first omitted from Chaucer editions. Walter Skeat's *Complete Works of Geoffrey Chaucer* (1894–97) can be considered the first manifestation of the modern Chaucer canon. Skeat included, as a seventh volume, *Chaucerian and Other Pieces*, the only modern edition of the apocrypha. Skeat includes thirty-one of these texts, relying heavily on the first printed folio of Chaucer's works (edited by William Thynne in 1532) and on works by known authors (Lydgate, Hoccleve, Gower, Clanvowe). He seems to have eschewed those poems that he did not consider "worthy" of association with Chaucer's name or consonant with Chaucer's status as a laureate poet, omitting for instance, most of the scabrous antifeminist works printed by John Stow in 1561, four of which are included here.

Although several spurious works, including Henryson's *Testament of Cresseid*, Usk's *Testament of Love*, the Prologue to the *Tale of Beryn*, and *The Floure and the Leafe*, are known to modern readers, most works of the Chaucerian apocrypha have received relatively little critical attention since their exclusion from the Chaucer canon. Yet many of these pieces are worthy of study, not only in the context of Chaucerian reception, but also as specimens of the kinds of vernacular poetry that circulated in late-medieval manuscripts and that remained in print, largely by the accidental virtue of their association with Chaucer, throughout the Renaissance and well into the nineteenth century. The various genres represented in this sampler — the dream vision, good counsel, female panegyric, mass parody, proverbial wisdom, lovers' dialogue, prophecy, advice to princes, elegiac complaint, courtly parody, and anti-feminist satire — attest to the diversity of late-medieval literary tastes and to the flexibility of the courtly idiom. These poems derive from a variety of manuscript sources, largely anthologies and miscellanies of secular, vernacular verse (what Robbins calls "aureate collections"), usually professionally prepared and presumably purchased by the affluent: members of the landed gentry, prosperous bourgeois businessmen, and prominent clergy. Although such collections are often labeled "courtly," that is, produced for those with some courtly connections or pretensions, and concerned with amorous courtship, social courtesy, and political courtiership, the contents sometimes can exercise our assumptions about this broad and inclusive category. For instance, several apocryphal poems appearing in this sampler (*The Craft of Lovers, Of Theyre Nature, In February, O Merciful, I Have a Lady, O Mosy Quince, Beware, The Court of Love*) are extant in Cambridge, Trinity College MS R.3.19, a secular miscellany consisting of forty-six poems and one prose work dating from the third quarter of the fifteenth century, after the advent of print in England. Although lacking the illuminations and decorated capitals often found in deluxe or so-called bespoke manuscripts (such as Bodleian Library, Fairfax 16), the manuscript appears to have been professionally prepared, probably from a number of unbound fascicles (short booklets) from which either the scriptorium (on speculation) or a customer could compile a collection of verse to suit their tastes.[6] Bradford Fletcher quite accurately describes the contents as "eclectic" (p. xv): a few of Chaucer's works appear — *The Parliament of Fowls, The Legend of Good Women, The Complaint to Pity*, and extracts from The Monk's Tale copied from Caxton's first edition of *The Canterbury Tales* — in addition to several works by Lydgate, folk traditions, satires on women, an explanation of the four humors, courtly complaints, proverbs, a pedigree of English royalty, and a meditation on bad habits. For modern readers who may find little courtliness or rational coherence in such variety, Julia Boffey reminds us that such

---

[6] See Mooney, "Scribes and Booklets," pp. 241–66.

collections were not solely literary but fulfilled a variety of functions: "social, musical . . . biographical and purely practical."[7]

Similarly, in the sixteenth century both Chaucer's poetry and the diverse works with which it circulated appear to have continued to have been valued for their perceived courtly qualities. Paul Strohm is not alone in lamenting what he sees as a "narrowing" of critical appreciation for Chaucer's "incomparably rich" poetic legacy and an inordinate "affection or nostalgia for the courtly style."[8] However, it appears that the printed Chaucer folio editions of the sixteenth century were not valued simply as collections of Chaucer's poetry but also may have had a more utilitarian function, acting, in part, as courtesy books. Wendy Wall argues that similar printed courtly anthologies (such as *Tottel's Miscellany*) served as "conduct books" and were intended to market "exclusivity" by demonstrating "to more common audiences the poetic practices entertained by graceful courtly readers and writers."[9] Most of the apocryphal poems either concern the theory and practice of *fin amours* (including sophisticated parodies of courtly genres and conventions) or offer both public and domestic codes of behavior in the form of princely advice, moral instruction, and proverbial wisdom. Arthur Marotti suggests that the audience for similar collections included "the universities, the Inns of Court, the court, and the household or the family . . . both aristocratic and middle-class individuals."[10] These readers purchased printed poetry collections partly to gain access to what what was perceived as the "socially restricted communications" of a privileged elite, but also for intellectual and moral self-improvement, or to participate in the "traditional fictional world of love experience."[11] In other words, such works presumably provide both rhetorical and practical models of courtship, courtiership, and courtesy and represent, in Pierre Bourdieu's formulation, forms of cultural knowledge or competence readers may have deemed necessary for social advancement and distinction.

For modern readers, perhaps the most striking characteristic of some of these poems, second only to their anonymity, is the frequency of unacknowledged quotation. Patchworks, poems which are composed of extracts borrowed from other poems, seem to be examples of unimaginative plagiarism and have been treated as such by many literary critics. But Walter Benjamin once said that the literature of the future would not be original works, but assemblies of multiple texts; and readers may be familiar with the eclectic approach of artists such as Robert Rauschenberg whose paintings are composed of found objects, or hip-hop lyrics which are based on sampling. Indeed, Seth Lerer observes: "What seems to many distinctive of the postmodern textual condition — the fascination with pastiche, with the quoted quality of any utterance . . . seems also to some distinctive of the medieval textual condition."[12] The practice of extrapolating memorable or pithy lines from longer works was quite common in the late Middle Ages and both Chaucer and Lydgate's poetry were especially susceptible to these peculiar acts of homage. Addressing the charge of plagiarism in Gower's work, R. F. Yeager warns: "Plagiarism is a hard charge; but it is also a rather

[7] Boffey, "Manuscripts of Courtly Love Lyrics," p. 11.

[8] Strohm, "Chaucer's Fifteenth-Century Audience," p. 20.

[9] Wall, *Imprint of Gender*, p. 97.

[10] Marotti, *Manuscript, Print, and the English Renaissance*, p. 30.

[11] Marotti, *Manuscript, Print, and the English Renaissance*, p. 218.

[12] Lerer, "Medieval English Literature," p. 1255.

anachronistic — and hence inappropriate — one to level against most medieval poets. . . . The term presupposes distinct ideas of artistic originality and literary property unfamiliar to most medieval writers."[13] A full appreciation of such poems comes with a broad knowledge of medieval literature, and, perhaps, the aesthetic pleasure is (and was) derived less from the quality of the poetry than from the recognition of the original context of the extracted lyric.

None of the poems in this collection will be reclaimed as Chaucer's any time soon and readers steeped in Chaucer's poetics may find it puzzling that any of these pieces once circulated under his name. Indeed, some critics once worried that the apocrypha harmed Chaucer's early literary reputation, tainting the correct evaluation of his aesthetic achievement. Although the title of this book suggests that Foucault's notion of the "author-function" is still operative, giving these texts some degree of coherence and cultural status,[14] these poems were also, in turn, operative in establishing Chaucer's own historical literary reputation. While a different authorial product (courtly, monarchical, anticlerical, misogynist) from the one valued today may emerge from the early manuscript and print collections, the spurious works found in these books would not have been canonized if they did not have some perceived cultural, political, ideological, or commercial value. Today Chaucer is valued for what he presumably wrote (enshrined in *The Riverside Chaucer*) but Chaucer's early scribal and print editors also appear to have prized his sphere of influence (attested to by imitation, continuation, and emendation) and his adaptability to contemporary social and political needs. The ostensibly rigorous distinction we make today between the genuine and the spurious appears to have had less conceptual validity before the early eighteenth century and the formation of Chaucer's canon confirms Jerome McGann's consensus that literary production is fundamentally "a social and an institutional event."[15] The renewed critical attention to the Chaucerian apocrypha is, I believe, in response to both an interest in the material, institutional and cultural forces that shape canonicity as well as the related recognition of this socialized concept of literary production.

COMMONLY USED ABBREVIATIONS

CA	Gower, *Confessio Amantis*
CT	Chaucer, *Canterbury Tales*
IMEV	Brown and Robbins, *Index of Middle English Verse*
MED	*Middle English Dictionary*
OED	*Oxford English Dictionary*
RR	*Roman de la Rose*
SIMEV	Robbins and Cutler, *Supplement to the Index of Middle English Verse*

---

[13] Yeager, *John Gower's Poetic*, p. 46.

[14] See Foucault, "What Is an Author?"

[15] McGann, *Critique of Modern Textual Criticism*, p. 100.

 THE COURT OF LOVE

INTRODUCTION

The Court of Love — a deft and humorous treatment of courtly genres, images, and conventions — deserves more critical attention than it has received. Although it is usually categorized as a dream vision, the lover, Philogenet, does not fall asleep, and the poem perhaps can better be described as a rhetorical primer of courtly erotic desire. For readers conversant with the allegorical love-vision there is much here that is familiar — the lover-poet, the guide, the rules of love, allegorical personages, personified abstractions, the birds' Matins on May Day — and the poet's primary achievement seems to be his easy ability to incorporate all of these literary motifs, as well as the attendant genres — the *complaint d'amours*, the lovers' dialogue, and the courtly panegyric — into a single, engaging, and coherent narrative. Indeed, although the poem has sometimes been seen as simply a compendium or patchwork of careworn courtly literary motifs, these familiar conventions are nonetheless treated with an invention and wry humor that revivifies the genre of love allegory.

Frances McNeely Leonard accurately suggests that "[t]he poet constructs the court out of places, personages, and rules drawn almost at random from the literature of love and stitched together with a cheerful disregard for their earlier allegorical significance."[1] After the customary apology for his poetic ineptitude, the eighteen-year-old lover (later identified as Philogenet), says that when he has attained "ripe corage" (line 45, meaning either psychological or sexual maturity) he is compelled to visit Love's Court (lines 1–112). There he meets the king and queen of Love — Admetus and Alceste — borrowed from Chaucer's *Legend of Good Women*. Chaucer's chaste and charitable Alceste is here disdainful and somewhat "straunge" (line 734) and presides over a venal and chaotic collection of miserable devotees. Not knowing how to conduct himself, Philogenet is provided with a female guide, Philobone, who gives him a tour of the spectacular glass temple where Venus and Cupid preside over an eclectic mix of mostly unhappy lovers, including a large contingent of malcontent religious (lines 113–301). The lover is then enjoined to follow the twenty statutes reserved for lovers, which include, among other familiar restraints, secrecy, fidelity, misery, patience, humility, discretion, deception, and starvation, in addition to the rigorous sixteenth statute which demands extraordinary sexual fortitude (lines 302–630). With a billion (!) other supplicants the lover then offers his own prayer, a light parody of Marian panegyrics, to Venus' golden icon (lines 631–86). He is then introduced to Pity's tomb and Philobone secretly confesses that Pity is indeed dead and that women accept their lovers' advances only to satisfy their own desires.

---

[1] Leonard, *Laughter*, p. 101.

Somewhat absurdly, Philogenet loves but knows not whom; he finally learns that his own lover is named Rosiall (after her tendency to blush). After the requisite Vinsaufian portrait cataloguing the details of her exceptional physical beauty (lines 778–819), he presents her with a lengthy "bille" or formal petition to receive his service as her lover. There then ensues the familiar lovers' dialogue, reminscent of both *The Craft of Lovers* and *La Belle Dame sans Merci*, in which the commonsensical (or "daungerous," in courtly parlance) Rosiall presses for more particulars ("Whate is youre name?" — line 904) and insists that a few glib, formulaic compliments will not win her heart (lines 820–994). As a reliable sign of his sincerity, Philogenet swoons; he is then accepted, provided he uphold the rigorous twenty statutes (with some leeway granted in fulfilling the demanding sixteenth) (lines 995–1024). He must, however, be instructed in the more advanced "guyse" ("customs," line 954) of the court, and Philobone introduces him to some of the usual personified suspects (borrowed ultimately from *The Romance of the Rose*) representing the less salient features of sensual pursuits: Despair, Hope, Lust, Liar, Envy, and Flattery (lines 1025–92). A gap in the text here opens on a large group of disgruntled clerics and nuns (borrowed from Lydgate's *Temple of Glass*) who lament their enforced service to Diana, the goddess of chastity (lines 1093–1190). More personified abstractions appear — Dissemble, Shamefastness, Avaunter ("Boaster"), and Private Thought — representing the familiar vicissitudes of human courtship (lines 1191–1316). Following another textual lacuna, Rosiall agrees to accept Philogenet, following the dictates of the resurrected Pity (lines 1317–51). The poem concludes with a macaronic choir of birds on May Day, appropriating the language of Matins and Lauds, singing in praise of love (lines 1352–1442).

Paradoxically, *The Court of Love* has been largely ignored by modern readers by virtue of its association with Chaucer. John Stow was the first to print the poem with Chaucer's works in 1561. The poem continued to appear both with Chaucer's works and, in a popular translated version by Arthur Maynwarning, with Ovid's *Art of Love*, until the nineteenth century. Indeed, it was Swinburne's passing admiration for the poem in a discussion of Blake's lyrical poems that, in part, sparked the infamous and acrimonious exchange with Frederick Furnivall who, on the basis of new language and rhyme tests, had insisted that the poem was spurious. Ejecting the poem from Chaucer's canon was not without controversy, and Skeat settled the debate by demonstrating, at considerable length, that its language was much later than the time of Chaucer, although the text is not as late (c. 1535) as he had hoped to establish.

Indeed, in his zeal to disassociate the poem from Chaucer's canon, Skeat, perhaps inadvertently, sealed its critical fate for most of the twentieth century. Although Skeat says he has "nothing to say against" the poem itself, his treatment is consistently pejorative, so that the author's ignorance of Middle English becomes not simply linguistic, but, rather, a sequence of literary "offenses."[2] I believe that for Skeat the poem was a canonical anomaly, a derivative, anachronistic, and deliberately archaized product of the sixteenth century, stupidly accepted as Chaucer's by generations of readers (and editors). Subsequent commentators, including William Neilson and Josef Schick, read the poem as a tapestry of literary allusions, inspired primarily by Lydgate's *Temple of Glass*, but also by Chaucer's love poetry, Ovid's *Metamorphoses*, and *The Romance of the Rose*. C. S. Lewis suggests that the poem is largely a "pastiche," perhaps intended as a forgery, although he does praise the poem as "light," "graceful," and "sophis-

---

[2] Skeat, *Chaucer Canon*, p. 133.

ticated," especially compared to other literary efforts of the "Drab Age."[3] Lewis is also the first to read *The Court of Love* as a parody of courtly genres, an approach that has proven quite popular with the few modern critics who have considered the text. Although in her survey of Chaucerian imitations Alice Miskimin dismisses the poem as an "interminable," "turgid and mindless" allegory,[4] for Frances Leonard "it is a thoroughgoing parody of the courtly convention at the same time that it is made up of bits and pieces taken from earlier poems in the convention."[5] Assuming the poem is a product of the Renaissance, Leonard suggests that "the Court of Love stands finally for nothing but inactive rigidity";[6] the lover's success represents an "elevation of the active life," a "new world," without moral dilemma, which rejoices in the "fallen life, exults in the sexual drive."[7] Finally, Bonita Friedman felicitously describes the piece as "a swan song to the medieval English love allegory" and as a "celebration of a fading genre and a compendium of the stereotypes and sophistical clichés of that genre."[8] Friedman reads the allegory as a form of "ironic cautionary verse," which is intended to "mock humorously" both the misguided devotion of the erotic lover and the various motifs borrowed from other allegorical love visions. I would suggest, however, that although the numerous exaggerations are obviously meant to be parodic, the poem is more accurately a parody by virtue of its imitation of well-known conventions rather than because of its mockery or derision of courtly literary traditions.

The Text

The Court of Love is extant in one manuscript — Cambridge, Trinity College MS R.3.19 (fols. 217r–234r) (**T**) — and the copy is both incomplete and sometimes careless. The poet has clearly attempted to archaize his text, using, for instance, the problematical final -*e* in unlikely, and incorrect, forms (*whate*, *thowe*), and Bradford Y. Fletcher is correct in his assessment that "it will only scan if one assumes extensive deterioration of ME inflections."[9] However, in plurals and genitives, the final -*e* and -*es* are both retained and usually sounded: *loves* (lines 67 and 91), *estates* (line 84), *armes* (line 86), *tales* (line 412), *woundes* (line 390). Skeat's edition of the poem (which silently incorporates many of Bell's readings), although by virtue of vigorous conjectural emendation is a highly readable and coherent text, is nonetheless schizophrenic by modern conventions of textual editing; he somewhat inconsistently both modernizes spelling and grammar (for instance, he deletes the final -*e* when it is not sounded although it is grammatically correct) but also sometimes restores Middle English forms and spelling. My editorial approach has been to present the text, warts and all, as it appears in the manuscript, only correcting what seem to me to be obvious scribal errors that interfere with sense. All emendations follow those previously established by Stow, Bell, or Skeat, and are accounted for in the Textual Notes.

---

[3] Lewis, *English Literature in the Sixteenth Century*, p. 240.

[4] Miskimin, *Renaissance Chaucer*, p. 231.

[5] Leonard, *Laughter*, p. 98.

[6] Leonard, *Laughter*, p. 99.

[7] Leonard, *Laughter*, p. 103.

[8] Friedman, "In Love's Thrall," p. 173.

[9] Fletcher, "Edition of MS R.3.19," p. 536.

The Court of Love

1	With tymeros hert and tremlyng hand of drede,	*timorous heart; trembling*
	Of cunnyng naked, bare of eloquence,	*lacking wit, stripped*
	Unto the flour of poort in womanhede[1]	
	I write, as he that none intelligence	*no knowledge*
5	Of metres hath, ne floures of sentence,	*nor flourishes of learning*
	Sauf that me list my writing to convey,	*Except; I wish*
	In that I can to please her hygh nobley.	*nobility*
	The blosmes fresshe of Tullius garden soote	*Cicero's; sweet*
	Present thaim not, my matere forto borne;	*adorn*
10	Poemys of Virgile taken here no rote,	*root*
	Ne crafte of Galfride may not here sojorne.	*Nor the abilities of Geoffrey*
	Why nam I cunnyng? O well may I morne,	*Why am I not clever?*
	For lak of science, that I can not write,	*learning*
	Unto the princes of my life aright,	
15	No termys digne unto her excellence,	*worthy*
	So is she sprong of noble stripe and high;	*lineage*
	A world of honoure and of reverence	
	There is in her, this wille I testifie.	
	Callyope, thowe sister wise and sly,	
20	And thowe, Mynerva, guyde me with thy grace,	
	That langage rude my mater not deface.	
	Thy suger dropes swete of Elicone	
	Distill in me, thowe gentle muse I pray;	
	And thee, Melpomene, I calle anone,	
25	Of ignoraunce, the miste to chace away,	
	And give me grace so forto write and sey,	
	That she, my lady, of her worthinesse,	
	Accepte in gree this litill short tretesse,	*favorably; treatise*
	That is entitled thus *The Courte of Love*.	
30	And ye that bene metriciens me excuse,	*poets*

---

[1] *To the paragon (flower) of feminine deportment*

10

I you beseche for Venus sake above;
For whate I mene in this ye nede not muse.
And yf so be my lady it refuse
For lak of ornat speche, I wolde be woo,   *literary; woeful*
35 That I presume to her to writen soo.

But myne entent and all my besy cure   *anxious care*
Is forto write this tretesse, as I can,
Unto my lady, stable, true, and sure,
Feithfull and kynde, sith first that she began   *since*
40 Me to accept in service as her man;   *servant*
To her be all the pleasure of this boke,
That when her like, she may it rede and loke.   *whenever she wants to*

When I was yong, at eighteen yere of age,
Lusty and light, desirous of plesaunce,   *pleasure*
45 Approchyng on full sadde and ripe corage,   *mature disposition*
Love arted me to do myn observaunce   *compelled*
To his astate, and doon hym obeysaunce,   *office*
Commaundyng me the Courte of Love to see,
A lite beside the mounte of Citharee,   *Close beside*

50 There Citherea goddesse was and quene,   *Venus*
Honowred highly for her majestie;
And eke her sonne, the myghty god, I wene,   *believe*
Cupyde the blynde, that for his dignyté
A mille lovers worship on theire kne.   *thousand; knees*
55 There was I bidde, in payn of deth, to pere   *appear*
By Marcury, the wynged messengere.

So than I went be straunge and ferre contrees,   *far*
Enquiryng ay whate costes that it drewe,   *coasts; inhabited*
The Courte of Love; and thiderward as bees,
60 At last I se the peple gan pursue.
Anon me thought som wight was there that knewe   *person*
Where that the courte was holden, ferre or nye,   *far or near*
And aftir thaim full faste I gan me hie.   *hurry*

Anone as I theim overtoke, I seide,
65 "Haile frendes, whider purpose ye to wende?"   *where; go*
"For sothe," quod one, that aunswered lich a mayde,   *Truly; like*
"To Loves Courte nowe goo we, gentill frend."
"Where is that place," quod I, "my felowe hend?"   *gentle*
"At Citheron, sir," seid he, "withoute dowte,
70 The Kyng of Love and all his noble rowte,   *company*

Dwellyng withynne a castell ryally."   *royally*
So than apace I jorned forth among,   *promptly*
And as he seid, so fond I there truly:
For I behelde the towres high and strong,
75 And high pynacles, large of hight and long,   *spires*
With plate of gold bespredde on every side,
And presious stone the stonewerke forto hide.   *masonry*

No saphir Ind, no rubé riche of price,   *Indian sapphire; ruby*
There lakked thaime, nor emerawd so grene,   *emerald*
80 Bales, turkes, ne thing to my devise,   *Baleis (ruby), turquoise*
That may the castell maken forto shene;   *shine*
All was as bright as sterres in wynter bene.
And Phebus shone, to make his pease agayne,
For trespace doon to high estates tweyne —

85 Venus and Mars, the god and goddesse clere —
When he theim founde in armes cheyned faste.
Venus was than full sad of harte and chere,
But Phebus bemes, streight as is the maste,   *Phebus' (i.e., the sun's) beams*
Upon the castell gynith he to cast,   *begins*
90 To please the lady, princesse of that place,
In signe he loketh aftir loves grace.

For there nys god in Heven or Helle, iwis,   *is not; certainly*
But he hath ben right soget unto love: *subject*
Jove, Pluto, or whatesoever he is,   *whoever*
95 Ne creature in erth, or yet above;
Of thise the revers may no wight approve.
But furthermore, the castell to discrive,   *describe*
Yet sawe I never none so large and high,

For unto Heven it streccheth, I suppose.
100 Withynne and oute depeynted wonderly,   *painted*
With many a thousand daisy, rede as rose,
And white also, this sawe I verely;   *truly*
But whate tho deyses myght do signifie,   *those; symbolize*
Can I not tell, sauf that the quenes floure,
105 Alceste yit was, that kepte there her sojoure,   *residence*

Which under Venus lady was and quene,   *Who*
And Admete kyng and soverayn of that place,
To whom obeide the ladyes gode nineteen,
With many a thowsand other, bright of face.
110 And yong men fele came forth with lusty pace,   *many*
And aged eke, theire homage to dispose;   *apply*
But whate thay were, I cowde not well disclose.

	Yet nere and nere furth in I gan me dresse,	*forward*
	Into an halle of noble apparayle,	*furnishings*
115	With arras spred and cloth of gold, I gesse,	*tapestries*
	And other silke of esier availe;	*of less value*
	Under the cloth of theire estate, saunz faile,	*without fail*
	The kyng and quene ther sat, as I beheld;	
	It passed joye of Helise the feld.	*the Elysian field*

120	There saintes have theire commyng and resort	
	To seen the kyng, so ryally beseen,	*adorned*
	In purple clad, and eke the quene, in sort;	*suitably*
	And on theire hedes sawe I crownes twayn,	
	With stones frett so that it was no payne,	*ornamented*
125	Withouten mete and drynke, to stand and see	*food*
	The kynges honor and the ryaltie.	

	And forto trete of states with the kyng,	*business*
	That bene of councell chief, and with the quene,	
	The kyng had Daunger nere to hym standyng,	*Resistance*
130	The Quene of Love, Disdeyne, and that was seen;	*appropriate*
	For by the feith I shall to God, I wene,	*believe*
	Was never straunger in her degree	
	Than was the quene in castyng of her ye.	*eye*

	And as I stode perceyvyng her apart,	
135	And eke the bemes shynyng of her yen,	*eyes*
	Me thought thay were shapyn liche a darte,	
	Sherpe and persyng, smale, and streight as lyne.	
	And all her here, it shone as gold so fyne,	*hair*
	Disshivill, crispe, downe hyngyng at her bak	*Loose, curled*
140	A yarde in length; and southly, than I spake:	*truly*

	"O bright Regina who made thee so faire?	*Queen*
	Who made thy colour vermelet and white?	*red*
	Where woneth that god? Howe fer above the eyre?	*lives*
	Grete was his crafte, and grete was his delite.	
145	Now marvel I nothing that ye do hight	*are called*
	The Quene of Love, and occupie the place	
	Of Citharé; nowe, swete lady, thi grace."	*[give me] your grace*

	In mewet spake I, so that nought astert,	*silence; escaped*
	By no condicion, worde that myght be harde;	*heard*
150	But in myne inward thought I gan adverte	*contemplate*
	And oft I seid, "My witte is dulle and harde!"	
	For with her bewtie thus, God wot, I ferde	*fared*
	As doth the man i-ravisshed with sight,	
	Whenne I beheld her cristall yen so bright,	*eyes*

155   No respect havyng whate was best to doon.
        Till right anon, beholding here and there,
        I spied a frend of myne, and that full sone;
        A gentil woman was the chamberer
        Unto the quene, that hote, as ye shall here,   *was called*
160   Philobone, that loved all her life.
        Whan she me sey she led me furth as blyfe,   *saw; at once*

        And me demaunded howe, and in whate wise,
        I thider come and whate myne erand was.
        "To sene the courte," quod I, "and all the guyse,   *custom*
165   And eke to sue for pardon and for grace,   *also*
        And mercy aske for all my grete trespace,
        That I none erst come to the Courte of Love;   *no sooner*
        Forgeve me this ye goddes all above."

        "That is well seid," quod Philobone, "in dede;
170   But were ye not assomaned to apere   *summoned*
        By Mercurius? For that is all my drede."
        "Yis, gentill feire," quod I, "nowe am I here.   *companion*
        Ye, yit whate thowe, though that be true, my dere?" *yet what if it were true*
        "Of youre fre wille ye shuld have come unsent;
175   For ye dide not I deme ye wille be shent.   *Because; disgraced*

        "For ye that reigne in youth and lustynesse,
        Pampired with ease, and joylof in youre age,
        Youre dewtie is, as ferre as I canne gesse,
        To Loves Courte to dressen youre viage,   *direct; journey*
180   As sone as nature maketh you so sage,
        That ye may knowe a woman from a swan,
        Or whanne youre fote is growen half a spanne.   *hand's breadth*

        "But sith that ye, be wilfull necgligence,   *since*
        This eighteen yere have kepte youre self at large, *at liberty*
185   The gretter is youre trespace and offence,
        And in youre nek ye motte bere all the charge;   *must*
        For better were ye ben withouten barge,   *boat*
        A midde se in tempest and in rayne,
        Than byden here receyvyng woo and payne,

190   "That ordeyned is for suche as thaim absente
        Fro Loves Courte by yeres long and fele.   *many*
        I ley my lyf ye shall full sone repent,
        For Love wille reyve youre coloure, lust, and hele; *seize; health*
        Eke ye most bayte on many an hevy mel.   *feast; meal*
195   No force, iwis, I stired you long agoone   *No matter*
        To drawe to courte," quod litell Philobon.

"Ye shall well se howe rowhe and angry face   *rough*
The Kyng of Love will shewe when ye hym se.
By myne advyse, knele downe and aske hym grace,
200   Eschewing perell and adversitee;
For welle I wot it wolle none other be,   *know*
Comforte is none, ne councell to youre ease.
Why wille ye thanne the Kyng of Love displese?"

"O mercy god," quod iche, "I me repent;
205   Caytif and wrecche, in hert, in wille, and thought.   *Miserable; wretched*
And aftir this shall be myne hole entent
To serve and please, howe dere that love be bought;   *however*
Yit sith I have myne owen penaunce i-sought,   *since*
With humble sprite shall I it receyve,
210   Though that the Kyng of Love my life bereyve.   *take away*

"And though the fervent loves qualité   *burning*
In me did never worche truly, yit I,
With all obeysaunce and humilité,   *submissiveness*
And benigne harte, shall serve hym till I dye.
215   And he, that lord of myghtes, grete and high,   *mighty one*
Right as hym lyste, me chastice and correcte,   *pleases*
And punyssh me with trespace thus enfecte."   *corrupted*

Thise wordes seid, she caught me by the lap,   *sleeve*
And led me furth intill a temple round,   *into*
220   Large, and wyde; and as my blessed hap   *luck*
And gode aventure was, right sone I founde
A tabernacle reised from the grounde,   *pavilion*
Where Venus sat, and Cupide by her side;
Yit half for drede I gan my visage hide.   *face*

225   And eft agayn I loked and behild,
Seyng full sundry peple in the place,
And myster folke, and som that myght not wild   *skilled; control (wield)*
Theire lymmes wele, me thought a wounder case;   *strange*
The temple shone with wyndowes all of glasse,
230   Bright as the day, with many a feire ymage.
And there I sey the fressh quene of Cartage,   *saw*

Dydo, that brent her bewtie for the love   *who burned*
Of fals Eneas; and the weymyntyng   *lamenting*
Of hir Anelida, true as turtill dove,
235   To Arcite fals; and there was in peynting
Of many a prince and many a doughty kyng   *worthy*
Whose marterdom was shewed aboute the walles;
And howe that feale for love had suffred falles.   *many; treachery*

	But sore I was abasshed and stonyed	*astonished*
240	Of all thoo folke that there were in that tide;	*at that time*
	And than I asked where thay hade woned:	*lived*
	"In dyvers courtes," quod she, "here beside."	
	In sondry clothing, mantilwise full wide,	*with wide robes*
	They were arrayed, and did theire sacrifice	
245	Unto the god and goddesse in theire guyse.	*customary manner*

	"Lo, yonder folke," quod she, "that knele in blewe,	
	Thay were the coloure ay, and ever shall,	
	In signe thay were, and ever will be true,	
	Withouten chaunge; and southly, yonder all	*truly*
250	That ben in blak with mornyng, cry and calle	
	Unto the goddes, for theire loves bene	
	Some ferre, some dede, some all to sherpe and kene."	*far; cruel*

	"Ye than," quod I, "whate done thise prestes here,	
	Nonnes, and hermytes, freres, and all thoo	*those*
255	That sit in white, in russet, and in grene?"	*Who; brown*
	"For soth," quod she, "thay waylen of theire woo:	*wail about their woe*
	'O mercy lord, may thay so come and goo	
	Frely to court, and have suche libertie?'	
	Ye, men of eche condicion and degree,	

	"And women eke; for truly there is none	*also*
260	Excepcion made ne never was, ne may:	
	This courte is ope and fre for everychone.	*open*
	The Kyng of Love, he wille nat say thaim nay;	
	He takith all, in poore or riche arraye,	
265	That mekely sewe unto his excellence	*attend*
	With all theire harte and all theire reverence."	

	And walkyng thus aboute with Philobone,	
	I se where come a messengere in high,	*saw; in haste*
	Streight from the kyng, which let commaunde anon,	
270	Throughoute the courte to make an ho and crye:	*an outcry*
	"A! Newe come folke, abide! And wote ye whye?	
	The kynges luste is forto seen youe sone.	*king's desire is to see you soon*
	Come nere, let se! His wille mote nede be done."	*must*

	Than gan I me present tofore the kyng,	*before*
275	Tremelyng for fere, with visage pale of hewe;	*Trembling from fear*
	And many a lover with me was knelyng,	
	Abasshed sore, till unto the tyme thay knewe	
	The sentence gove of his entent full trewe.	*given*
	And at the laste the kyng hath me behold,	
280	With sterne visage, and seid, "Whate doth this old,	*Why does this old [person]*

"Thus ferre i-stope in yeres, come so late   *So far advanced*
Unto the courte?" "For soth, my liege," quod I,
"An hundred tyme I have ben at the gate
Afore this tyme, yit coude I never espye   *Before; see*
285 Of myne acqueyntaunce eny with myne ye,
And shamefastnes away me gane to chace,
But nowe I me submytte unto your grace."   *submit myself*

"Well, all is perdoned, with condicion:
That thowe be trewe from hensforth to thy myght,
290 And serven love in thyne entencion.
Swere this and thanne, as fer as it is right,
Thowe shalte have grace here in my quenes sight."
"Yis, by the feith I owe youre crowne, I swere,
Though Deth therfore me thirlith with his spere."   *pierce*

295 And whan the kyng had sene us everychone,
He let commaunde an officer in hie   *at once*
To take oure feith, and shewe us, one by one,
The statutis of the courte full besyly.   *carefully*
Anon the boke was leide before her ye,   *their eyes*
300 To rede and se whate thyng we most observe   *must*
In Loves Courte, till that we dye and sterve.   *decay*

And, for that I was lettred, there I redde   *because; literate; read*
The statutis hole of Loves Courte and halle.
The firste statute that on the boke was spred,
305 Was to be true, in thought and dedes all,
Unto the Kyng of Love, the lord ryall,   *royal*
And to the quene, as feithfull and as kynde,
As I coude thynke, with harte, and wille, and mynde.

The secunde statute: Secretely to kepe
310 Councell of love, nat blowyng everywhere   *proclaiming*
All that I knowe, and let it synk and flete,   *float*
It may not sowne in every wightes ere;   *sound; person's ear*
Exilyng slaunder ay for dred and fere,
And to my lady, which I love and serve,
315 Be true and kynde, her grace forto deserve.

The thridde statute was clerely write also:
Withouten chaunge, to lyve and dye same,   *together*
None other love to take, for wele ne woo,
For brynde delite, for ernest nor for game,   *burning desire*
320 Withoute repent, for laughyng or for grame;   *grief*
To biden still in full perseveraunce —   *persist*
All this was hole the kynges ordynaunce.

The fourth statute: To purchace ever to here,   *cause [folk] perpetually to pay heed*
And stiren folke to love, and beten fire   *to kindle*
325   On Venus awter, here aboute and there,   *altar*
And preche to thaym of love and hote desire,
And tell howe love will quyten well theire hire;   *repay them*
This must be kepte — and loth me to displease —
Yf love be wroth, passe forby is an ease.[2]

330   The fifth statute: Not to be daungerous,   *reluctant*
Yf that a thought wold reyve me of my slepe,   *deprive*
Nor of a sight to be oversquymouse;   *overly squeamish*
And so verely this statute was to kepe,   *faithfully*
To turne and walowe in my bed and wepe,
335   When that my lady, of her crueltie,
Wold from her harte exilyn all pyté.

The sixte statute (it was for me to use):   *sixth; to follow*
Alone to wander, voyde of company,
And on my ladys bewtie forto muse,
340   And to thinke no force to lyve or dye;   *no matter*
And eft agayn to thynke the remedy,
Howe to her grace I myght anon attayn,
And tell my woo unto my souverayn.   *woe*

The seventh statute was to be pacient,
345   Whether my lady joyfull were or wroth,
For wordes glad or hevy; dilygent,   *persistent*
Wheder that she me helden lefe or loth;   *friend or foe*
And hereupon I put was to myn othe,
Hir forto serve, and lowly to obey,
350   And shewing my chere, ye, twenty sith aday.   *times*

The eighth statute, to my remembraunce,
Was to speke and pray my lady dere
With hourely laboure, and grete attendaunce,
Me forto love with all her harte entier,   *entire*
355   And me desire, and make me joyfull chere,
Right as she is, surmountyng every faire,   *fair [thing]*
Of bewtie well, and gentill debonayre.

The ninth statute, with lettres writ of gold:
This was the sentence how that I, and all,
360   Shuld ever dred to be to over bolde
Her to displease — and truly so I shall —

---

[2] *If my love is angry, [to] get away is a relief*

But ben content for thyng that may falle,
And mekely take her chastisement and yerde,   *rod (punishment)*
And to offende her ever ben aferd.   *afraid*

365   The tenth statute was egally discerne   *[to] justly distinguish*
       Bytwene thy lady and thyn abilitee,   *worthiness*
       And thynke thyself arte never like to yerne,   *earn*
       By right, her mercy, nor of equité,   *fairness*
       But of her grace and womanly pitee;
370   For though thyself be noble in thy strene,   *lineage*
       A thowsand-fold more nobill is thy quene,

       Thy lives lady and thy souverayn,
       That hath thyne harte all hole in governaunce.
       Thow maist no wise hit taken to disdayne,
375   To put thee humbly at her ordynaunce,
       And yf her free the reyne of her plesaunce;   *give*
       For libertie ys thing that woman loke,   *seek*
       And truly ellis the mater is acroke.   *or else; awry*

       The eleventh statute: Thy signes forto knowe,   *covert signals*
380   With ie, and fynger, and with smyles soft,   *eye*
       And lowe to kowigh, and always forto shon,   *cough; shun*
       For dred of spies, forto wynken ofte;
       But secretly to bring up a sigh aloft,
       And eke beware of over moche resorte,   *coming together too often*
385   For that, peraventure, spilleth all thy sporte.   *perhaps, ruins*

       The twelfth statute remember to observe:
       For all the payne thow haste for love and wo,
       All is to lite her mercy to deserve,   *too little*
       Thow must thou thynke where ever thow ride or goo;
390   And mortall woundes suffer thow also,
       All for her sake, and thynke it well beset
       Upon thy love, for it may be no bette.   *no better*

       The thirteenth statute, whilom is to thynke,   *frequently*
       Whate thyng may best thy lady lyke and please,
395   And in thyne hartes botom let it synke;
       Som think devise, and take for thyne ease,   *Some thing*
       And sent it her, that may her harte pease: *send; appease*
       Some hert, or ryng, or lettre, or devise,   *heart-shaped jewelry; ornament*
       Or precious stone — but spare not for no price!

400   The fourteenth statute eke thou shalte assay   *attempt*
       Formely to kepe the most parte of thy life: *Correctly*
       Wisshe that thy lady in thyne armes lay,

And nyghtly dreme thow hast thy hartes wife
Swetely in armes, straynyng her as blife;   *embracing; busily*
405   And whanne thou seest it is but fantasy,
Se that thow syng not over merely,   *too merrily*

For to moche joye hath oft a wofull end.   *too much*
It longith eke, this statute forto hold: *It is also befitting*
To deme thy lady evermore thy frende,   *consider*
410   And thynke thyself in nowise a cocold.   *cuckold*
In every thing she doth but as she shuld;
Construe the beste, beleve no tales newe,
For many a lie is told that semyth full trewe.

But thinke that she, so bounteous and fayre,   *Instead; virtuous*
415   Cowde not be fals; imagyne this algate.   *always*
And thinke that tonges wykked wold her appaier,   *damage*
Sklaunderyng her name and worshipfull estate,
And lovers true to setten at debate;
And though thow seest a fawte right at thyne ye,   *fault; eye*
420   Excuse it blive and glose it pretily.   *quickly; interpret*

The fifteenth statute: Use to swere and stare,   *Be accustomed*
And counterfete a lesyng hardely,   *lie readily*
To save thy ladys honoure everywhare,
And put thyself to fight boldely.
425   Sey she is gode, vertuous, and gostely,   *spiritual*
Clere of entent, and harte, and thought, and wille;   *Pure*
And argue not, for reson ne for skille,

Agayne thy ladys plesire ne entent,   *Against*
For love wille not be counterpleted, in dede.   *disputed*
430   Sey as she seith, than shalte thowe not be shent: *scorned*
"The crowe is white"; "Ye, truly, so I rede!"
And ay whate thyng that she thee wille forbidde,
Eschewe all that, and give her soverentie;   *Avoid*
Hir appetide felawe in all degree.   *desire join*

435   The sixteenth statute, kepe it yf thow may!
Seven sith at nyght thy lady forto please,   *times*
And seven at mydnyght, seven at moroweday;
And drynke a cawdell erly for thyne ease.   *fortified drink; benefit*
Do this, and kepe thyne hede from all dyssease,
440   And wynne the garland here of lovers alle,
That ever come in courte, or ever shalle.

Full fewe, thynke I, this statute hold and kepe!
But truly, this, my reason giveth me fele: *awareness*

That som lovers shuld rather fall aslepe,
445   Than take on hand to please so ofte and wele.
There lay none othe to this statute adele,
But kepe who myght, as gave hym his corage.
Nowe get this garlant lusty folke of age;

Nowe wynne whoo may, ye lusty folke of youth,
450   This garland fressh, of floures rede and white,
Purpill and blewe, and colours fel uncowth,   *many unfamiliar*
And I shall crowne hym kyng of all delite!
In all the courte there was not, to my sight,
A lover trewe, that he ne was adrede,   *afraid*
455   Whan he expresse hath hard the statute redde.   *heard*

The seventeenth statute: When age approchith on,
And lust is leide, and all the fire is queynt,   *calmed; quenched*
As fresshly than thowe shalte begyn to fonne,   *be foolish*
And dote in love, and all her ymage paynte
460   In the remembraunce till thow begyn to faynte,
As in the firste season thyne hart beganne.
And her desire, though thowe ne may ne can

Perfourme thy lyvyng actuell, and lust,
Regester this in thy remembraunce.
465   Eke whan thow maist not kepe thy thing from rust,
It speke and talke of plesaunt dalyaunce,   *Yet*
For that shall make thyne harte rejoyse and daunce;
And when thou maist no more the gam assay,   *game practice*
The statute bidde thee pray for hem that may.

470   The eighteenth statute, holy to commende
To please thy lady, is that thow eschewe   *forego*
With sluttishnesse thyself forto offend;   *slovenliness*
Be jolif, fresshe, and fete with thinges newe,   *decked out*
Courtly with maner — this is all thy due —   *duty*
475   Gentill of porte, and loving clenlynesse,   *behavior*
This is the thing that liketh thi mastresse.   *pleases your mistress*

And not to wander liche a dulled asse,   *dull-witted*
Ragged and torn, disguysed in array,
Rybaude in speche, or oute of mesure passe,   *Ribald; moderation*
480   Thy bounde excedyng; thynk on this always.
For women been of tender hartes aye,   *always*
And lightly set theire plesire in a place;
When they misthinke, they lightly let it passe.

The nineteenth statute: Mete and drynke forgete!   *Food*
485   Eche other day, se that thow fast for love,
       For in the courte thei live withouten mete,
       Sauf suche as comyth from Venus all above;   *Save*
       Thei take none hede, in payne of grete reprove,   *no heed*
       Of mete and drynke, for that is all in vayn;
490   Only they live be sight of theire soverain.

       The twentieth statute, last of everychone,
       Enrolle it in thyn harte privité: *secretly*
       To wring and waile, to turne, and sigh, and grone,
       When that thy lady absent is from thee;
495   And eke renewe the wordes that she
       Bitwene you twayn hath seid, and all the chere
       That thee hath made, thy lives lady dere.

       And se thyne harte, in quiete ne in rest,
       Sojorne to tyme thowe sene thy lady eft;[3]
500   But where she wonne be south, or est, or west,   *wherever she lives*
       With all thy force, nowe se it be not left.   *neglected*
       Be diligent, till tyme thy life be reft,   *is taken away*
       In that thowe maist, thy lady forto see;
       This statute was of old antiquité.

505   An officer of high auctorité,
       Cleped Rigour, made us swere anon   *Hardness-of-heart (obduracy)*
       (He nas corrupt with parcialyté,
       Favor, prayer, ne gold that cherely shone):   *Bias; luxuriously*
       "Ye shall," quod he, "nowe sweren here ecchone,   *each one*
510   Yong and old, to kepe in that they may,
       The statutes truly all aftir this day."

       O god, thought I, hard is to make this oth;   *oath*
       But to my power shall I thaim observe.
       In all this world nas mater half so loth,   *troublesome*
515   To swere for all; for though my body sterve,   *die*
       I have no myght the hole forto reserve.
       But herkyn nowe the cace how it befell: *listen*
       Aftir my othe was made, the trouth to telle,

       I turned leaves, lokyng on this boke,
520   Where other statutes were of women shene;   *excellent*
       And right furthwith, Rigour on me gan loke

---

[3] Lines 498–99: *And see [to it that] your heart, [neither] in repose nor in rest, / [Does not] passively await until the time that you see your lady again*

Full angrily, and seid unto the quene
I traitour was, and charged me let bene.   *to desist*
"There may no man," quod he, "the statute know,
525   That long to woman, hie degree ne low.   *belongs*

"In secrete wise thay kepten ben full close,
They sowne ecchone to Libertie, my frend;   *speak each one*
Pleasaunt thay be, and to theire owen purpose.
There wot no wight of thaim but God and fend,   *knows; fiend*
530   Ne naught shall witte, unto the worldes ende.   *none; know*
The quene hath gove me charge, in payne to dye,   *has given; on pain of death*
Never to rede ne sen thaim with myne ye.   *nor see; eye*

"For men shall not so nere of councell ben
With womanhode, ne knowen of her guyse,   *customs*
535   Ne whate they thinke, ne of there wit th'engene;   *the mechanism of their wit*
I me reporte to Salamon the wise,
And mighty Sampson, which begyled thries   *beguiled thrice*
With Dalida was; he wot that, in a throwe,   *knew; short time*
There may no man statute of women knowe.

540   "For it paraventure may right so befalle,   *perchance*
That they be bounde be nature to disceyve,
And spynne, and wepe, and sugre strewe on gall,   *bitterness*
The hart of man to ravissh and to reyve,   *pierce*
And whet theire tong as sharpe as swerd or gleyve;   *spear*
545   It may betide, this is theire ordynaunce.
So must thei lowly done the observaunce,   *humbly*

"And kepe the statute goven thaim of kynde,   *given [to them] by nature*
Or suche as love hath gove hem in theire life.
Men may not wete why turneth every wynde,   *know; change*
550   Nor waxen wise, nor ben inquisytyf
To knowe secret of mayde, widue, or wife.   *widow*
For thai theire statutes have to thaim reserved,
And never man to knowe thaim hath deserved.

"Now dresse you furth, the god of love you guyde!"
555   Quod Rigour than, "and sike the temple bright   *seek*
Of Cithera, goddes here beside.   *Venus*
Beseche her, by enfluence and myght
Of all her vertue, you to teche aright
How forto serve youre ladis, and to please,
560   Ye that ben sped, and set your hart in ease.

"And ye that ben unpurveied, pray her eke,   *unprovided for*
Comforte you sone with grace and destiné,

That ye may set youre hart there ye may like,
In suche a place, that it to love may be
565 Honoure, and worship, and filicité   *happiness*
To you for ay. Now goth, by one assent."   *forever; go*
"Graunt mercy, sir," quod we, and furth we went

Devoutly, soft and esy pace, to se   *slow*
Venus the goddes ymage, all of gold;
570 And there we founde a thousand on theire kne,
Sum fressh and feire, som dedely to behold,
In sondry mantils newe, and some were old,   *cloaks*
Som paynted were with flames rede as fire,
Outeward to shewe theire inwarde hote desire:

575 With dolefull chere, full feele in theire complaynt   *fierce*
Cried, "Lady Venus, rewe upon oure sore!   *have pity*
Receyve oure billes with teres all bedreynte;
We may not wepe, there is no more in store,
But woo and payne us frettith more and more.   *consumes*
580 Thow blessedfull planet, lovers sterre so shene,   *lover's star (Venus); bright*
Have rowth on us, that sigh and carefull bene.   *compassion*

"And ponysshe, lady, grevously, we pray,   *punish*
The false untrew with counterfete plesaunce,   *pleasantness*
That made theire othe, be trewe to live or dye,
585 With chere assured, and with countenaunce;   *composure*
And falsely now thay foten loves daunce,   *execute the steps of*
Baron of rewth, untrue of that they seid,   *Barren*
Now that theire lust and plesire is alleide."   *alleviated*

Yit eft again, a mille milion,   *thousand million*
590 Rejoysing love, ledyng theire life in blisse,
Thay seid: "Venus, redresse of all divysion,   *redresser*
Goddes eternel, thy name i-hired is!   *praised*
By loves bond is knyt all thing, iwis: *indeed*
Best unto best, the erth to water wanne,   *pale*
595 Birde unto bird, and woman unto man.

"This is the life of joye that we ben in,
Resemblyng life of hevenly paradyse.
Love is exiler ay of vice and synne;
Love maketh hartes lusty to devise.   *perform [good deeds]*
600 Honoure and grace have thay in every wise,
That ben to loves lawe obedyent.
Love makith folke benigne and diligent,

"Ay steryng theim to drede vice and shame.   *moving them to fear*
In theire degree it maketh thaim honorable,
605 And swete it is of love to bere the name,
So that his love be feithfull, true, and stable.
Love prunyth hym to semen amyable;   *grooms*
Love hath no faute there it is excercised,   *flaw*
But sole with theim that have all love dispised.   *only*

610 "Honoure to thee, celestiall and clere
Goddes of love, and to thi celcitude,   *loftiness*
That gevest us light so ferre downe from thi spere,   *gives; sphere*
Persing our hartes with thi pulcritude.   *Piercing; beauty*
Compersion none of similitude   *No similar comparison*
615 May to thi grace be made in no degré,
That hast us set with love in unité.

"Grete cause have we to prayse thy name and thee,
For through thee we live in joye and blisse.
Blessed be thowe, most souverayn to se.
620 Thi holy courte of gladnesse may not mysse:
A thousand sith we may rejoise in this,   *times*
That we ben thyne with harte and all i-fere,   *together*
Enflamed with thi grace and hevynly fere."   *fire*

Musyng of tho that spakyn in this wise,   *Considering those*
625 I me bethought, in my remembraunce,
Myne oryson right godely to devise,   *prayer*
And pleasauntly, with hartes obeysaunce,
Beseche the goddes voiden my grevaunce: *[I] beseeched; to void*
For I loved eke, sauf that I wist nat where.   *also, except; knew not*
630 Yet downe I set and seid as ye shall here:

"Feirest of all that ever were or be,
Lucerne and light to pensif creature,   *Lamp; melancholy*
Myne hole affiaunce and my lady fre,
My goddes bright, my fortune, and my ure,   *fate*
635 I geve and yeld my harte to thee, full sure,   *give and yield*
Humbly beseching lady, of thi grace,
Me to bestowe into som blissed place.

"And here I vowe me feithfull, true, and kynde,
Withoute offence of mutabilité,   *inconstancy*
Humbly to serve, while I have witte and mynde,
640 Myne hole affiaunce, and my lady free,   *trust*
In thilke place there ye me signe to be.   *where; assign*
And sith this thing, of newe, is gove to me,   *given*
To love and serve, and nedely, most I obey.   *earnestly*

645   "Be merciable with thi fire of grace,
       And fix myne harte there bewtie is, and routh.   *pity*
       For hote I love, determyne in no place,
       Sauf only this, be God and by my trouth: *Except; by*
       Trowbled I was with slomber, slepe, and slouth
650   This other nyght, and in a vision
       I se a woman romen up and downe —   *saw*

       "Of mene stature, and semly to behold,   *moderate; becoming*
       Lusty and fressh, demure of countynaunce,
       Yong and wel shap, with here that shone as gold,   *well-shaped; hair*
655   With yen as cristall fercid with plesaunce —   *eyes; filled*
       And she gan stir myne harte alite to daunce;   *caused; to dance a little*
       But sodenly, she vanyssh gan right there.
       Thus I may sey I love and wot not where!

       "For whate she is, ne her dwellyng, I note,   *I know not*
660   And yit I fele that love distrayneth me;   *constrains*
       Might iche her knowe, that wold I fayne, God wot,   *[If] I might; then would I desire*
       Serve and obey with all benignité.   *[To] serve*
       And yf that other by my destiné,   *another [girl is to] be*
       So that nowise I shall hir never see,
665   Than graunte me her that best may liken me,

       "With glad rejoyse to live in parfite hele,   *perfect happiness*
       Devoide of wrath, repent, or variaunce.   *sorrow, or infidelity*
       And able me to do that may be wele   *enable*
       Unto my lady, with hartes hie plesaunce.
670   And, myghty goddes, through thy purviaunce,   *providence*
       My witte, my thought, my lust, and love so guyde,
       That to thyne honoure I may me provyde

       "To set myne harte in place there I may like,
       And gladly serve with all affeccion.
675   Grete is the payn which at myne hart doth styke,
       Till I be sped by thyne eleccion.   *advanced; selection*
       Helpe, lady goddes, that possession
       I might of her have, that in all my life
       I clepen shall my quene and hartes wife.   *call*

680   "And in the Courte of Love to dwell, for aye,   *forever*
       My wille it is, and done thee sacryfice
       Dayly, with Diane eke, forto fight and fraye,   *also; attack*
       And holden werre as myght well me suffice.

That goddes chaste I kepen in no wise[4]
685 To serve; a figge for all her chastité!
Hir lawe is for religiosité!"   *the religious-minded*

And thus gan fynyssh prerer, lawde, and preice   *praise*
Which that I gove to Venus on my kne;   *gave*
And in myne harte to ponder and to peice,   *weigh*
690 I gave anon hir ymage fressh bewtie:
"Heile to that figure swete, and heile to thee,   *Hail*
Cupide," quod I, and rose and yede my way.   *went*
And in the temple as I yede I sey   *saw*

A shryne sormownting all in stones riche,   *exceeding*
695 Of which the force was plesaunce to myne ye;   *effect*
With diamant or saphire nevir liche
I have none seyen, ne wrought so wounderly.   *marvelously*
So whan I met with Philobone, in hie   *immediately*
I gan demaund, "Who is this sepulture?"   *Whose*
700 "Forsoth," quod she, "a tender creature

"Ys shryned there, and Pité is her name.
She saw an egle wreke hym on a flye,   *avenge himself*
And pluk his wynge, and ete hym in his game;
And tender harte of that hath made her dye.
705 Eke she wold wepe and morne right piteously,
To sene a lover suffre grete destresse.
In all the courte nas none that, as I gesse,

"That coude a lover have so well availe,   *half; help*
Ne of his woo, the torment or the rage,
710 Aslake, for he was sure, withouten faile,   *Alleviate*
That of his gryfe she coude the hete aswage.   *relieve*
Insted of Pité, spedeth hote corage,   *desire*
The maters all of courte, now she is dede;   *[In] all the matters*
I me report in this to womanhode.

715 "For weile and wepe, and crye, and speke, and pray —
Women wold not have pité on thi playnt;
Ne by that meane to ease thyne hart convey,
But thee receyven for theire owen talent,   *desire*
And sey that Pité causith thee, in consent
720 Of rewth, to take thy service and thy payne
In that thow maist, to please thy souverayn.

---

[4] *[For] that chaste goddess (i.e., Diana) I care in no way*

"But this is councell, kepe it secretly,"   *confidential*
Quod she, "I nold for all the world abowte,
The Quene of Love it wist. And witte ye why?
725   For yf, by me, this mater spryngen oute,
In courte no lenger shuld I, owte of dowte,
Dwellen, but shame in all my life endry.   *endure*
Nowe kepe it close," quod she, "this hardely.   *firmly*

"Well, all is well nowe, shall ye sene," she seid,   *you shall see*
730   "The feirest lady under sonne that is!
Come on with me, demeane you liche a mayde,   *govern*
With shamefast drede, for ye shall spede, iwis,   *succeed; indeed*
With her that is the mirth, and joye, and blisse —
But sumwhate straunge and sad of her demeane   *bearing*
735   She is — beware youre countenaunce be sene,

"Nor over light, ne rechelesse, ne to bold,
Ne malapert, ne rymyng with your tong.   *impudent*
For she will you abeisen and behold,   *abash; inspect*
And you demaund why ye were hens so long   *away*
740   Oute of this courte, withouten resorte among;
An Rosiall her name is hote aright,   *called*
Whose harte is yet goven to no wight.   *given*

"And ye also ben, as I understond,
With love but light avaunced, by your worde;
745   Might ye, be happe, youre fredome maken bond,   *constrain*
And fall in grace with her, and wele accorde,
Well myght ye thank the god of love and lord.
For she that ye sawe in youre dreme appere,
To love suche one, whate ar thee than the nere?

750   "Yit wote ye whate? As my remembraunce
Me gevith nowe, ye fayne where that ye sey   *dissemble*
That ye with love had never acqueyntaunce,
Sauf in your dreme right late this other day.
Why, yis, pardé! my life — that durst I lay —   *dare*
755   That ye were caught opon an heth, when I   *heath*
Saw you complayn and sigh full piteously.

"Withynne an erber and a garden faier,   *herb garden*
With floures growe and herbes vertuse,   *wholesome*
Of which the savour swete was and the heire,   *smell; fumes*
760   There were youre self full hote and amerous:
Iwis, ye ben to nyse and daungerouce.   *fussy; reserved*
A! Wold ye nowe repent, and love some newe?"
"Nay, by my trouth," I seid, "I never knewe

"The godely wight, whoes I shall be for aye.
765 Guyde me the lord that love hath made and me."
But furth we went intill a chambre gay: *into*
There was Rosiall, womanly to se,
Whose stremes, sotell persyng, of her ye   *rays, subtly piercing*
Myne harte gann thrill for bewtie in the stound.   *in an instant*
770 "Alas," quod I, "whoo hath me gove this wounde?"   *given*

And than I dred to speke, till at the laste
I grete the lady reverently and wele,
Whan that my sigh was gon and over past;
And downe on knees full humbly gan I knele,
775 Beseching her my fervent woo to kele,   *cool*
For there I toke full purpose, in my mynde,
Unto her grace my paynfull harte to bynde.

For yf I shall all fully her discryve,
Her hede was rounde, by compace of nature;   *contrivance*
780 Here here as gold — she passed all on live —   *surpassed*
And lylly forhede had this creature,
With loveliessh browes, flawe, of coloure pure,   *yellowish*
Bytwene the whiche was mene disseveraunce   *moderate distance*
From every browe, to shewe a distaunce.

785 Her nose, directed streight and even as lyne
With fourme and shap therto convenient,   *appropriate*
In which the goddes mylke white path doth shyne;
And eke her yen ben bright and orient   *eyes; brilliant*
As is the smaragde, unto my juggement,   *emerald*
790 Or yet thise sterres hevenly, smale, and bright.
Hir visage is of lovely rede and white,

Her mouth is shorte and shitte in litill space,   *small; enclosed*
Flamyng somdele, not over rede, I mene,   *blazing*
With prengnaunte lippes, and thik to kisse, percas!   *full; perchance*
795 For lippes thynne, not fatte, but ever lene,
They serve of naught, thay be not worth a bene.
For yf the basse ben full, there is delite,   *kiss*
Maximyan truly thus doth be write.

But to my purpose: I sey, white as snowe
800 Ben all her teth, and in order thay stand
Of one stature; and eke her breth, I trowe,
Surmounteth all oders, that ever I found,
In switnesse; and her body, face, and hond
Ben sharply slender, so that from the hede
805 Unto the fote, all is but womanhede.

I hold my pease of other thinges hidde:
Here shall my soule, and not my tong, bewry.   *divulge*
But how she was arrayed, yf ye me bidde,   *clothed, if you ask me [to say]*
That shall I well discover you and say: *reveal [to] you*
810   A bend of gold and silke, full fressh and gay,   *ribbon*
With her in tresse, browdered full well,   *tresses, braided*
Right smothly kepte and shynyng every dele.

Aboute her nec a floure of fressh devise   *vivid design*
With rubies set, that lusty were to sene;   *delightful*
815   And she in gowne was, light and somerwise,
Shapen full wele, the coloure was of grene,
With awreat seint aboute her sides clene,   *gold sash; shapely sides*
With dyvers stones, precious and riche:
Thus was she raied, yit saugh I never her liche.   *arrayed; like*

820   For yf that Jove had this lady seyn,
Tho Calixto ne Alcenia,
Thay never hadden in his armes leyne;[5]
Ne he had loved the faire Europa,
Ye, ne yit Dane, ne Antiopa!   *Danae*
825   For all theire bewtie stode in Rosiall;
She semed lich a thyng celestiall

In bownté, favor, porte, and semlynesse,[6]
Plesaunt of figure, myrroure of delite,
Gracious to sene, and rote of gentilnesse,
830   With angell visage, lusty, rede and white.
There was not lak, sauf Daunger had, a lite,   *Disdain*
This godely fressh in rule and governaunce;   *delightful person*
And somdele straunge she was, for her plesaunce.

And, truly, sone I toke my leve and went
835   Whanne she had me enquired whate I was;
For more and more impressen gan the dent
Of loves darte, while I beheld her face;
And eft agayn I com to seken grace,   *came*
And up I put my bille, with sentence clere,   *formal petition; purport*
840   That folowith aftir; rede and ye shall here:

"O ye fressh, of bewtie the rote,
That nature hath fourmed so wele and made
Pryncesse and quene! And ye that may do bote   *provide a remedy*

---

[5] Lines 821–22: *Then [neither] Callisto nor Alcmene / [Would] have ever lain in his arms*
[6] *In virtue, disposition, deportment, and graciousness*

	Of all my langoure with youre wordes glad!	
845	Ye wounded me, ye made me wo bestad;	*beset with woe*
	Of grace, redresse my mortall grief, as ye,	
	Of all myne harm, the verrey causer be.	

"Now am I caught, and unware sodenly,
With persant stremes of your yen clere,   *piercing beams; eyes*
850 Subjecte to ben, and serven you mekely,
And all youre man, iwis, my lady dere;
Abidyng grace, of which I you require,   *Awaiting*
That merciles ye cause me not to sterve,   *die*
But guerdon me liche as I may deserve.   *reward*

855 "For, by my trouth, the dayes of my breth,
I am and wille be youre in wille and harte,
Pacient and meke, for you to suffree dethe
If it require; nowe rewe upon my smert!   *pity; pain*
And this I swere: I never shall oute sterte   *run out*
860 From Loves Courte for none adversité,
So ye wold rewe on my distresse and me.

"My destiné, and me fate, and ure, i-blisse,   *fortune (luck), [God] bless me*
That have me set to ben obedient
Only to you, the floure of all, iwis;
865 I truste to Venus never to repent —
Forever redy glad and dyligent
Ye shall me fynde, in service to your grace,
Tyll deth my life oute of my body rase.   *tear*

"Humble unto your excellence so digne,   *noble*
870 Enforcyng ay my wittes and delite   *Exerting*
To serve and please with glad harte and benigne,
And ben as Troylus, Troyes knyghte,
Or Antony for Cleapatre bright,
And never you me thynkes to reney: *renounce*
875 This shall I kepe unto myne endyng day.

"Enprint my speche in youre memoriall   *memory*
Sadly, my princes, salve of all my sore!   *Fully; princess, remedy*
And think that, for I wold becommen thrall,   *enslaved*
And ben youre owyn, as I have seid before,
880 Ye most of pité cherissh more and more
Youre man, and tender aftir his deserte,   *merit*
And yf hym corage forto ben expert.   *And give; experienced (in love)*

"For where that one hath sette his harte on fire,
And fyndeth nether refute, ne plesaunce,   *refuge*

885   Ne worde of comforte, deth will quite his hire.   *render his due*
       Allas, that there is none allegaunce   *mitigation*
       Of all theire woo! Allas, the grete grevaunce
       To love unloved! But ye, my lady dere,
       In other wise may governe this matere."

890   "Truly, gramercy, frende, of your gode wille,   *great thanks*
       And of youre profer, in youre humble wise.   *offer*
       But for youre service, take and kepe it stille;
       And where ye say, I ought you well cheryssh,
       And of youre gref the remedy devise,
895   I knowe not why: I nam acqueynted well
       With you ne wote not, southly, where ye dwell."   *know; truly*

       "In arte of love I write, and songes make,
       That may be song in honour of the Kyng
       And Quene of Love; and than I undertake,
900   He that is sadde shall than full mery syng.
       And daungerus not ben in everything   *disdainful*
       Beseche I you, but sene my wille and rede,
       And let your aunswere put me oute of drede."

       "Whate is youre name? Reherse it here, I pray,
905   Of whens, and where, of whate condicion,   *station*
       That ye ben of. Let se, com of, and say!   *be quick*
       Fayne wold I knowe your dysposicioun;   *frame of mind*
       Ye have putte uppon youre old entencioun,
       But whate ye meane to serve me I nete,   *don't know*
910   Sauf that ye say ye love me wounder hete."   *hotly*

       "My name, allas, my hart, why make it straunge?
       Philogenet I cald am, fer and nere,
       Of Cambrige clerke, that never think to chaunge
       For you, that with youre hevenly stremes clere,
915   Ravissh myne harte and goste and all in fere.   *soul; together*
       This is the firste I write my bille for grace;
       Me thynke I se som mercy in youre face.

       "And whate I mene, by goddes that all hath wrought,
       My bille, that maketh fynall mencion,
920   That ye bene, lady, in myne inward thought,
       Of all myne harte withouten offencion,   *transgression*
       That I beste love, and have, sith I beganne
       To drawe to courte. Lo thanne, whate myght I say?
       I yeld me here unto youre nobly.   *yield; nobility*

925	"And yf that I offend, or wilfully,	
	Be pompe of harte, youre precepte disobey,	*Through pride*
	Or done agayn youre wille unskyllfully,	*act against*
	Or greven you, for ernest or for play,	*aggrieve*
	Correcte ye me right sharply than, I pray,	
930	As it is sene unto youre womanhede,`	*As seems appropriate*
	And rewe on me, or ellis I nam but dede."	
	"Nay, god forbede to feffe you so with grace,	*invest*
	And for a worde of sugred eloquence,	
	To have compassion in so litell space!	
935	Than were it tyme that som of us were hens!	
	Ye shall not fynde in me suche insolence.	*misbehavior*
	Ay, whate is this? May ye not suffer sight?	
	How may ye loke upon the candill lyght	
	"That clere is and hatter than myn ye?	*hotter; eye*
940	And yet ye seid the bemes perse and frete;	*burn*
	Howe shall ye thanne the candelight endry?	*endure*
	For well wotte ye, that hath the sharper hete.	
	And there ye bidde me you correcte and bete	
	Yf ye offende; nay, that may not be done!	
945	There come but fewe that speden here so sone.	*succeed*
	"Withdrawe youre ye, withdrawe from presens eke;	*eye; [my] presence*
	Hurte not youreself, thrugh foly, with a loke!	
	I wold be sorry so to make you syke.	
	A woman shuld beware eke whom she toke.	*attracts*
950	Ye beth a clarke — go serch ynne my boke —	
	Yf any women ben so light to wynne.	
	Nay, abide a while; thowe ye were all my kynne,	*though*
	"So sone ye may not wynne myne harte, in trouth;	
	The guyse of courte wille sene youre stedfastnesse,	
955	And as ye done, to have upon you rewth.	*pity*
	Youre owen deserte and lawly gentilnesse —	*humble*
	That wille reward you, joy for hevynesse.	
	And thowe ye waxen pale, and grene, and dede,	
	Ye most it use a while, withouten drede,	*endure*
960	"And it accept, and grucchen in no wise.	*grumble*
	But where as ye me hastily desire	
	To bene to love, me thynke ye be not wise.	
	Cease of youre language, cease, I you require!	
	For he, that hath this twenty yere bene here,	
965	May not optayne; than marveile I that ye	*be successful*
	Be nowe so bold, of love to trete with me."	

"A! Mercy, hart, my lady, and my love,
My rightwose princesse and my lives guyde!   *rightful*
Nowe may I playn to Venus all above,   *complain*
970   That, rewthles, ye may gife this wounde wide!   *merciless; give*
Whate have I done? Why may it not betide,
That for my trouth I may receyved be?
Allas thanne, youre daunger and your crueltie!

"In wofull howre I gote was, welaway!   *hour; conceived*
975   In wofull oure fostered and i-fedde,
In wofull oure i-borne, that I ne may
My supplicacion swetely have i-spedde.   *succeed*
The frosty grave and cold miste be my bedde,
Withoute ye list youre grace and mercy shewe,   *Unless*
980   Deth with his axe so faste on me doth hewe.

"So grete disease and in so litell while,
So litell joy, that felte I never yet;
And at my wo fortune gynnyth to smyle,   *begins*
That never arst I felte so harde a fitte.   *erstwhile*
985   Confounded ben my spiritis and my witte,   *Troubled*
Tylle that my lady take me to her cure,
Which I love best of erthely creature.

"But that I like, that may I not com by;
Of that I playn, that have I habondaunce
990   Sorowe and thought; thay sit me wounder nye.   *near*
Me is withhold that myght be my plesaunce;
Yet turne agayn my worldly suffisaunce,   *satisfaction*
O lady bright, and sauf your feithfull true,   *save*
And, ar I dye, yet ons upon me rewe."   *before; once*

995   With that I fell in sounde, and dede as stone,   *a swoon*
With coloure slayn and wanne as assh pale;   *extinguished; gray*
And by the hande she caught me up anon:
"Aryse anon," quod she, "whate, have ye dronken dwale?   *(a narcotic)*
Why slepen ye? It is no nytirtale!"   *not night*
1000   "Now mercy, swete," quod I, iwis affraied.
"What thyng," quod she, "hath made you so dysmayed?

"Now wote I well that ye a lover be —
Youre hewe is witnesse in this thyng," she seid.
"Yf ye were secrete, ye might knowe," quod she,   *discreet*
1005   "Curteise and kynde, all this shuld be aleyde.   *alleviated*
And nowe, myne harte, all that I have mysseide
I shall amend, and set youre harte in ease."
"That worde, it is," quod I, "that doth me please."

	"But this I charge — that ye the statutes kepe —	
1010	And breke thaym not for slouth nor ignoraunce."	*laziness*
	With that she gan to smyle and laughen depe.	*passionately*
	"Iwis," quod I, "I wille do youre plesaunce.	
	The sixteenth statute doth me grete grevaunce:	
	But ye most that relesse or modifie!"	
1015	"I graunte," quod she, "and so I wille, truly."	

And softly thanne her coloure gan appeire,
As rose so rede, throughoute her visage all;
Wherefore me thynke that it is accordyng here,   *appropriate*
That she of right be cleped Rosyall.
1020 Thus have I wonne, with wordes grete and small,
Some godely worde of hir that I love best,
And trust she shall yit sette myne harte in rest.

"Goth on," she seid to Phelobone, "and take
This man with you, and lede hym all abowte
1025 Withynne the courte, and shewe hym, for my sake,
Whate lovers dwell withynne, and all the rowte   *company*
Of officers him shewe; for he is, oute of dowte,
A straunger yit." "Come on," quod Philobone,
"Philogenet, with me nowe must ye gon."

1030 And stalkyng softe with easy pase, I sawe
Aboute the kyng stonden environ,   *around*
Attendaunce, Diligence, and theire felowe   *Attention*
Fortherer, Asperaunce, and many one.   *Assistance, Hope*
Dred-to-Offende there stode, and not alone;
1035 For there was eke the cruell adversary,
The lovers foo, that cleped is Dispaire,

Which unto me spak angrely and felle,   *cruelly*
And seid my lady me dysseyvene shall: *deceive*
"Throwest thowe," quod he, "that all that she did tell   *Trust*
1040 Ys true? Nay, nay, but under hony gall!
Thy birth and hers be nothing egall;   *equivalent*
Caste of thyne harte for all her wordes white,   *fair*
For, gode faith, she lovith thee but alite.

"And eke remember, thyne habilité   *worthiness*
1045 May not compare with hir, this well thowe wote."   *know*
Ye, than came Hope and seid, "My frende, let be!
Beleve hym not; Dispaire, he gynneth dote."   *begins to act foolishly*
"Alas," quod I, "here is both cold and hote:
The tone me biddeth love, the toder nay.   *one; other*
1050 Thus wote I not whate me is best to say.

"But well wote I, my lady graunted me,
Truly to be my woundes remedy.
Her gentilnesse may not infected be
With doblenesse; this trust I till I dye.
1055   So cast I voide Dispaires company,
And taken Hope to councell and to frande."
"Ye, kepe that wele," quod Phelibone, "in mynde."

And there beside, withyn a bay wyndowe,
Stode one in grene, full large of brede and length,   *width*
1060   His berd as blak as fethers of the crowe:
His name was Lust, of wounder might and strength.   *extraordinary*
And with Delite to argue there he thynketh,
For this was all his opynyon,
That love was synne; and so he hath begonne

1065   To reason faste and legge auctorité.   *[to] appeal to*
"Nay," quod Delite, "love is a vertue clere,
And from the soule his progresse holdeth he;
Blynd appityde of lust doth often stirre,
And that is synne, for reason lakketh there.
1070   For thowe thinke thi neighbours wife do wyn,
Yit thynk it well that love may not be synne.

"For God and seint, thay love right verely,
Voide of all synne and vise, this knowe I wele;
Affeccion of flessh is synne, truly,   *Desire*
1075   But verray love is vertue, as I fele,   *true*
For love may not thy freyle desire akkele: *cool*
For verray love is love withouten synne."
"Nowe stynte," quod Lust, "thow spekest not worth a pynne."   *stop*

And there I left thaim in theire arguyng,
1080   Romyng ferther in the castell wide,
And in a corner Lier stode talkyng
Of lesinges fast, with Flatery there beside: *falsehoods*
He seid that women were attire of pride,   *equipped with*
And men were founde of nature variaunte
1085   And coude be false, and shewen beawe semblaunt.   *fair appearance*

Than Flatery bespake and seid, iwis:
"Se, so she goth on patens faire and fete,   *wooden clogs*
Hit doth right wele; whate prety man is this
That rometh her? Nowe truly, drynke ne mete   *Who reaches [for] her*
1090   Nede I not have; myne harte for joye doth bete,
Hym to behold, so is he godely fressh.
It semeth for love his harte is tender nessh."   *softened*

[text missing]

"This is the courte of lusty folke and glad,
And welbecometh theire abite and arraye."   *clothing*
1095   "O why be som so sory and so sadde,
Complaynyng thus in blak and white and gray?"
"Freres thay ben, and monkes, in gode fay.   *in good faith (i.e., truly)*
Alas, for rewth, grete dole it is to sene,   *it is distressing to behold*
To se thaim thus bewaile and sory bene.

1100   "Se howe thei crye and wryng theire handes white,
For thei so sone went to religion!   *too soon*
And eke the nonnes, with vaile and wymple plight,   *fastened*
There thought that thei ben in confusion:
'Alas,' thay sayn, 'we fayn perfeccion,
1105   In clothes wide, and lake oure libertie;
But all the synne mote on oure frendes be.   *must*

"'For Venus wote, we wold, as fayne as ye   *knows; would*
That bene attired here and welbesene,   *good-looking*
Desiren man and love in oure degree,
1110   Ferme and feithfull, right as wold the quene.
Oure frendes wikke, in tender youth and grene,   *wicked*
Agenst oure wille made us religious;
That is the cause we morne and waylen thus.'"

Than seid the monke and freres in the tide,   *at the same time*
1115   "Well may we course oure abbes and our place,   *curse; abbacy*
Oure statutes sharpe: to syng in copes wide,   *cowls*
Chastly to kepe us oute of loves grace,
And never to fele comforte ne solace.
Yit suffre we the hete of loves fire,
1120   And aftir than other happly we desire.

"O Fortune cursed, why nowe and wherefore
Hast thowe," thay seid, "berafte us libartie,   *denied*
Sith nature gave us instrument in store,   *Since*
And appetide to love and lovers be?
1125   Why mot we suffer suche adversité,   *must*
Dyane to serve and Venus to refuse?
Full often sith this matier doth us muse.   *times; ponder*

"We serve and honour sore agenst oure wille,   *against*
Of chastité the goddes and the quene;
1130   Us leffer were with Venus biden stille,   *We would rather*
And have reward for love, and soget bene   *subject*
Unto thise women courtly, fressh, and shene.   *beautiful*

Fortune, we curse thi whele of variaunce!   *wheel*
There we were wele thou revist our plesaunce."   *turn back*

1135   Thus leve I thaym, with voice of pleint and care,   *complaint*
        In ragyng woo crying full petiously;
        And as I yede, full naked and full bare   *went*
        Some I beholde, lokyng dispiteously
        On Poverté, that dedely cast theire ye;   *mournfully*
1140   And "Welaway!" thei cried, and were not fayne,   *happy*
        For they ne myght theire glad desire attayne.

        For lak of richesse worldely and of gold,
        Thay banne and curse, and wepe, and seyn, "Allas,   *condemn*
        That Poverté hath us hent that whilom stode   *captured; once*
1145   At hartis eas, and fre, and in gode case!
        But now we dare not shew ourself in place,
        Ne us embolde to duelle in company,
        There as oure harte wolde love right faithfully."

        And yit agaynewarde shryked every nonne,   *shrieked*
1150   The prange of love so strayneth thaym to crye: *agony*
        "Nowe woo the tyme," quod thay, "that we be boune!   *were bound [to religion]*
        This hatefull ordre nyse will done us dye!   *strict; cause us [to] die*
        We sigh and sobbe and bleden inwardly,
        Fretyng oureself with thought and hard complaynt,   *Devouring*
1155   Than nay, for love, we waxen wode and faynt."   *nearly; distracted*

        And as I stode beholdyng here and there,
        I was ware of a sorte full languysshyng,   *fully*
        Savage and wilde of lokyng and of chere,
        Theire mantaylles and theire clothes ay teryng;   *robes; tearing*
1160   And ofte thay were of nature complaynyng,
        For they there membres lakked, fote and hand,
        With visage wry and blynde, I understand.   *twisted*

        They lakked shap and beautie to preferre   *advance*
        Theymself in love, and seid that God and Kynde   *Nature*
1165   Hath forged thaym to worshippen the sterre,
        Venus the bright, and leften all behynde
        His other werkes clene and oute of mynde:
        "For other have theire full shappe and bewtie,
        And we," quod thay, "ben in deformyté."

1170   And nye to thaym there was a company,   *near*
        That have the susters waried and mysseid;   *cursed; slandered*
        I mene, the thre of fatall destyné,
        That be our wordes. And sone, in a brayde   *weirds (fates); outburst*

	Oute gan thay crye as thay had ben affrayed:	*disturbed*
1175	"We curse," quod thay, "that ever hath nature	
	I-formed us this wofull life to endure!"	

	And there he was contrite and gan repent,	*(see note)*
	Confessyng hole the wounde that Citheré	*Venus*
	Hath with the darte of hote desire hym sent,	
1180	And howe that he to love muste subjet be;	
	Thanne held he all his skornes vanyté,	
	And seid, that lovers lede a blissedfull life,	
	Yong men and old, and widue, maide, and wife.	

	"Bereve, my goddesse," quod he, "thi myght,	*Take away*
1185	My skornes all and skoffes, that I have	
	No power forth to mokken any wight	
	That in thi service dwell; for I ded rave,	
	This knowe I welle right nowe, so God me save.	
	And I shal be the chife post of thy feith,	
1190	And love uphold, the revers who so seith."[7]	

	Dissemble stode not ferre from hym, in trouth,	*Concealment; far*
	With party mantill, party hode and hose;	*multi-colored mantle*
	And seid, he had upon his lady rowth,	*pity*
	And thus he wounde hym in, and gan to glose	*gloss*
1195	Of his entent full doble, I suppose.	*double*
	And all the world, he seid, he lovid it wele;	
	But ay, me thoughte, he loved hir nere adele.	*not at all*

	Eke Shamefastnesse was there, as I toke hede,	
	That blasshed rede and darst nat ben a knowe	*blushed; dared not be revealed*
1200	She lover was, for therof had she drede.	
	She stode and hyng her visage downe alowe.	*hung*
	But suche a sight it was to sene, I trowe,	*trust*
	As of thise roses rody on theire stalke;	*ruddy*
	There cowde no wight her spy to speke or talke	

1205	In loves arte, so gan she to abasshe,	*be embarassed*
	Ne durst not utter all her previté.	*dared; intimacies*
	Many a stripe and many a grevouse lasshe	
	She gaven to thaym that wolden lovers be,	
	And hindered sore the sympill comonaltie,	*people*
1210	That in nowise durste grace and mercy crave.	
	For were not she, thei nede but aske and have,	

---

[7] *And [to] uphold love, regardless of what others say*

Where yf thay nowe approchyn forto speke,
Thanne Shamefastnesse returnyth thaym agayn:
Thay thynke if thay oure secrites councell breke,

1215 Oure ladys wille have scorne on us certen,
And, aventure, thynken grete disdayne.
Thus Shamefastnesse may bryngyn in Dispeire;
When she is dede, the toder will be heire.   *other*

Com forth, Avaunter, nowe I ryng thy bell!   *Boaster*
1220 I spied hym sone; to God I make a vowe,
He loked blak as fendes doth in Hell.
"The firste," quod he, "that ever I ded wowe,   *seduce*
Withynne a worde she com, I wotte not howe,   *know*
So that in armes was my lady fre;
1225 And so hath ben a thousand mo than she.

"In Englond, Bretayn, Spayn, and Pycardie,
Artyes, and Fraunce, and up in hie Holand,   *Artois*
In Burgoyne, Naples, and Italy,
Naverne, and Grece, and up in hethen lond,   *Navarre*
1230 Was never woman yit that wold withstond
To ben at myne commaundement, whan I wold!
I lakked neither silver coyne ne gold,

"And there I met with this estate and that,
And here I broched her, and here, I trowe;   *pierced*
1235 Lo, there goith one of myne; and wotte ye whate?
Yonne fressh attired have I leyde full lowe,
And suche one yonder eke right well I knowe —
I kepte the statute whan we lay i-fere,   *together*
And yet yon same hath made me right goode chere."

1240 Thus hath Avaunter blowen everywhere   *boasted*
All that he knowith, and more, a thousand fold.
His auncetrye of kynne was to Lier,   *forefather*
For first he makith promyse forto hold
His ladys councell, and it not unfold;   *reveal*
1245 Wherefore, the secrete when he doth unshitte,   *disclose*
Than lieth he, that all the world may witte.   *know*

For falsing so his promyse and beheste,   *betraying; oath*
I wounder sore he hath suche fantasie;
He lakketh witte, I trowe, or is a beste,   *beast*
1250 That canne no bette hymself with reason guy.   *guide*
Be myne advice, love shal be contrarie
To his avayle, and hym eke dishonoure,   *advantage*
So that in courte he shall no more sojorne.   *reside*

       "Take hede," quod she, this litell Philobone,

1255   "Where Envye rokketh in the cornor yonde,

       And sitteth dirke; and ye shall se anone   *obscured*

       His lene bodie, fading face and hond;

       Hymself he fretteth, as I understond.   *devours*

       Witnesse of Ovide *Methamorphosees*;

1260   The lovers foo he is, I will not gloose.   *deceive*

       "For where a lover thinketh hym promote,

       Envye will grucche, repynyng at his wele;   *grieving; prosperity*

       Hit swelleth sore aboute his hartes rote,   *core*

       That in no wise he canne not live in hele.   *comfort*

1265   And yf the feithfull to his lady stele,   *comes secretly*

       Envye will noise and ryng it rounde aboute,

       And sey moche worse than done is, oute of dowte."

       And Prevye Thought, rejoysing of hymself,

       Stode not ferre thens in abite mervelous;   *clothing*

1270   Yonne is, thought I, som sprite or some elf,   *spirit*

       His sotill image is so corious.   *subtle*

       "Howe is," quod I, "that he is shaded thus

       With yonder cloth, I note of whate coloure?"   *know not*

       And nere I went, and gan to lere and pore,[8]

1275   And frayned hym question full hard: *asked*

       "Whate is," quod I, "the thyng thou lovest beste?

       Or whate is bote unto thi paynes hard?   *relief*

       Me think thowe liveste here in grete unreste;

       Thowe wandrest ay from south to est and weste,

1280   And eft to north: as ferre as I canne see,

       There is no place in courte may holden thee.

       "Whom folowest thowe? Where is thi harte i-set?

       But my demaunde asoile, I thee require."   *answer*

       "Me thought," quod he, "no creature may lette,   *My; hinder*

1285   Nowe to ben here, and where, as I desire;

       For where as absence hath done oute the fire,

       My mery thought it kyndelith yet agayne,

       That bodely, me thinke, with my souverayne   *physically*

       "I stand, and speke, and laugh, and kisse, and halse, *embrace*

1290   So that my thought comforteth me full oft.

       I think, God wote, though all the world be false,

       I wille be trewe; I think also howe softe

---

[8] *And nearer I went, and began to stare [at him] and examine [him]*

My lady is in speche, and this on lofte   *up high*
Bryngeth myne harte to joye and gladnesse;
1295   This prevey thought alayeth myne hevynesse.   *allays*

"And whate I thinke, or where to be, no man
In all this erth can tell, iwis, but I.
And eke there nys no swalowe swifte, ne swan
So wight of wyng ne half so yerne can flye;   *nimble; swiftly*
1300   For I canne ben, and that right sodenly,
In Heven, in Helle, in Paradise, and here,
And with my laday, whan I wylle desire.

"I am of councell ferre and wide, I wote,   *believe*
With lord and lady and there previté,   *secrets*
1305   I wotte it all, and be it cold or hoote,   *know*
Thay shall not speke withouten licence of me —
I mene in suche as sesonable bee —
For firste the thing is thought withynne the harte,
Er any worde oute from the mouth astarte."

1310   And with that worde Thought bad farewell and yeede.   *went*
Eke furth went I to sene the cortis guyse;   *affairs*
And at the dore came in, so God me spede,
Twey courteours, of age and of assise,   *Two; feature*
Liche high and brode; and as I me advise,
1315   The Golden Love and Leden Love, thay hight: *Leaden; are called*
The tone was sad the toder glad and light.   *one; other*

[text missing]

"Yis, drawe youre harte, with all your force and myght,
To lustynesse, and bene as ye have seid.
And thinke that I no drope of favour hight,   *promised*
1320   Ne never hade unto youre desire obeide,
Tille sodenly, me thought me was affrayed
To sene you wax so dede of countenaunce,
And Pité bade me done you som plesaunce.

"Oute of her shryne she rose from deth to live,
1325   And in myne ere full prively she spake: *ear; privately*
'Doth not youre servaunte hens a way to drive,
Rosiall,' quod she; and than myn harte brak
For tender reuth. And where I founde moche lak   *pity*
In youre personne, than I me bethought,
1330   And seid, 'thus is the man myne harte hath sought.'"

      "Gramercy, Pité! Myght I but suffice   *be capable*

      To yeve the lawde unto thy shryne of gold,   *give; praise*

      God wotte, I wold, for sitth that thou dide rise

      From deth to live for me, I am behold   *duty-bound*

1335   To thanken you a mille tymes told,   *thousand*

      And eke my lady Rosyall the shene,   *beautiful*

      Which hath in comforte set myne harte, I wene.   *believe*

      "And here I make myne protestacion,

      And depely swere, as myne power, to bene

1340   Feithfull, devoide of variacion,   *fickleness*

      And here forbere in anger or in tene,   *adversity*

      And serviceable to my worldes quene,

      With all my reason and intelligence,

      To done her honoure high and reverence."

1345   I had not spoke so sone the worde, but she,

      My souverayn, dyde thanke me hartily,

      And seid, "Abide, ye shall dwelle stille with me

      Tylle season come of May; for than, truly,

      The Kyng of Love and all his company

1350   Shalle hold his feste full ryally and welle."   *celebration*

      And there I bode till that the season felle.   *remained*

      On May day when the larke began to ryse,

      To matens went the lusty nithingale,   *morning service*

      Withyn a temple shapen hawthorne wise.   *like a hawthorn tree*

1355   He myght not slepe in all the nyghtertale,   *night*

      But "*Domine, labia*" gan he crye and gale,   *shout*

      "My lippes open, lord of love, I crye,

      And let my mouth thi prysing nowe bewrey."   *praising; reveal*

      The egle sang "*Venite*, bodies all,

1360   And let us joye to love that is oure helth."

      And to the deske anon thay gan to falle,   *lectern*

      And who come late, he preced in by stelth.

      Than seide the fawcon, "Oure owen hartis welth,   *falcon*

      Domine, dominus noster, I wote,   *believe*

1365   Ye be the god that done us brenne thus hote."   *makes us burn*

      "*Cely enarant*," seid the popyngay,   *parrot*

      "Youre myght is told in heven and firmament!"

      And than came inne the gold fynche fresh and gay,

      And seid this psalme with hartily glad intent:

1370   "*Domini este terra*, this Laten intent,   *Latin means*

      The god of love hath erth in governaunce."

      And than the wren gan skippen and to daunce,

"*Jube, domine*, lorde of love, I pray,
Commaunde me well this lesson forto rede:
1375   This legend is of all that wolden dye
Marters for love; god yf the sowles spede!   *Martyrs; give; success*
And to thee, Venus, singe we oute of drede,   *without doubt*
By influence of all thy vertue greate,
Beseching thee to kepe us in oure hete."

1380   The seconde lesson Robyn Redebreste sang:
"Hayle to thee, god and goddes of oure lay!"   *song*
And to the lectorn amoryly he sprong: *ardently*
"Haile," quod he eke, "O fresshe season of May,
Oure moneth glad that syngen on the spray.   *bough*
1385   Haile to the floures rede, and white, and blewe,
Which by theire vertue maketh oure lustes newe!"

The thridde lesson the turtill dove toke up,
And therat lough the mavis in scorne.   *laughed; song thrush*
He seid, "O god, as mut I dyene or suppe,   *must; dine*
1390   This folissh dove wille gife us all an horne!   *(i.e., mock us)*
There ben right here a mille better borne   *thousand*
To rede this lesson, which, as welle as he
And eke as hote, can love in all degree."

The turtylle dove seid, "Welcom, welcom May,
1395   Gladsom and light to lovers that ben trewe!
I thanke thee, lord of love, that doth purvey   *provide*
For me to rede this lesson all of dewe;   *in due form*
For in gode south, of corage I purpose   *truth, with all my heart*
To serve my make till deth us most departe."   *mate*
1400   And than *tue autem* sang he all aparte.   *"but you"*

"*Te deum amoris*," sang the thrustell cok;   *"You, lord of love"; blackbird*
Tuball hymself, the firste musician,
With key of armony coude not onlok
So swete tewne as that the thrustill can:
1405   "The lord of love we praysen," quod he than,
"And so done all the fowles, grete and light,   *little*
Honoure we May, in fals lovers dispite."

"*Dominus regnavit*," seid the pecok there,
"The lord of love, that myghty prynce, iwis,
1410   He hath receyved her and everywhere;
Nowe *Jubilate* sing!" "Whate meneth this?"
Seid than the lynette, "welcom, lord of blisse!"
Oute sterte the owle with "*Benedicité*,
What meneth all this mery fare?" quod he.

1415   "*Laudaté*," sang the larke with voice full shirll;   *"Praise you"; shrill*
        And eke the kight, "*O admirabile,*   *kite*
        This quere will throwe myne eris pers and thrille.   *choir; pierce*
        But whate? Welcom this May season," quod he,
        "And honoure to the lord of love mot be,   *must*
1420   That hath this feeste so solempne and so high."
        "*Amen,*" seid all, and so seid eke the pye.   *magpie*

        And furth the cokkowe gan procede anon,
        With "*Benedictus,*" thankyng god in hast,
        That in this May wold visite thaim echon,
1425   And gladden thaym all while the feste shall lest.   *last*
        And therewithall a loughter oute he braste,   *in laughter he burst out*
        "I thanke it god that I shuld end the song,
        And all the service which hath ben so long."

        Thus sang thay all the service of the feste,
1430   And that was done right erly, to my dome;   *in my judgment*
        And furth goith all the courte, both most and lest,
        To feche the floures fressh, and braunche, and blome;   *blossom*
        And namly hawthorn brought both page and grome,
        With fressh garlantis partie blewe and white,   *parti-colored*
1435   And thaim rejoyson in theire grete delite.

        Eke eche at other threwe the floures bright,
        The prymerose, the violet, the gold;   *marigold*
        So than as I beheld the riall sight,
        My lady gan me sodenly behold,
1440   And with a trewe love, plited many fold,   *pleated*
        She smote me thrugh the harte as blive;   *at once*
        And Venus yet I thanke I am alive!

EXPLANATORY NOTES TO *THE COURT OF LOVE*

2–12   *of cunnyng naked . . . Why nam I cunnyng?* The opening represents the common
         modesty topos — the writer's claim of poetic ineptitude — which is usually
         belied, as in this case, by his knowledge of the chief authorities on the "flowers"
         of rhetoric. Both the *De Inventione* of *Tullius* (line 8, Marcus Tullius Cicero) and
         the *Poetria Nova* of *Galfride* (line 11, Geoffrey de Vinsauf) were influential
         sources on medieval rhetoric. See Murphy, *Rhetoric in the Middle Ages.*

19–24   *Callyope . . . Mynerva . . . Melpomene.* In Greek mythology, Calliope is the muse
         of eloquence and epic poetry, and Melpomene is the muse of tragedy; in
         Roman mythology, Minerva is the goddess of wisdom and invention.

22   *Elicone.* Mount Helicon on the Gulf of Corinth, sacred to Apollo and home to
         the Muses. According to Ovid (*Metamorphoses* 5.250–63) a blow from the hoof
         of Pegasus created a miraculous and sacred stream on the mount, a stream later
         interpreted as a font of poetic inspiration (Hippocrene).

45   *full sadde and ripe corage.* Suggesting both psychological and sexual maturity.

46   *Love arted me.* Friedman detects a pun here: "The poet is constrained by Love to
         create his art, to write this poem, his 'observauance,' for his lady's pleasure" ("In
         Love's Thrall," p. 176). Chaucer uses the verb in a similar way in *Troilus and
         Criseyde*: "And over al this, yet muchel more he thoughte / What for to speke, and
         what to holden inne; / And what to arten hire to love he soughte" (1.386–88).

48   *Courte of Love.* John Stevens suggests that courts of love in medieval literature
         (such as those found here and in *The Kingis Quair*) have four principal mean-
         ings: 1) they are social courts, "in which the lover is at school and receives
         instruction in polite behavior"; 2) they resemble courts of law, "with its statutes,
         presided over by a judge"; 3) they invoke the image of the feudal court, "in
         which the subject pays homage to a sovereign"; and 4) because love is a reli-
         gion, the court is a "congregation of the faithful" (*Music and Poetry*, p. 164).

49–50   *Citharee.* Skeat (*Chaucerian*, p. 541) points out that this is a common confusion
         (found also in Chaucer) of the mountain Cithaeron and the island Cythera (Ceri-
         go), where Venus was thought to have risen from the foam of the sea. *Citherea*
         (line 50) is another name for Venus based on her association with the island.

66   *lich a mayde.* The description calls into question the gender of the speaker. Is it
         a woman who speaks like a youthful girl? Or is it a man whom love has made
         effeminate? The one interpretation might speak well of love, but which is
         meant is unclear until line 69, where the speaker is finally identified as male.

80   *turkes*. Skeat (*Chaucerian*, p. 542) suggests the adjective "Turkish"; similarly, Friedman states that the Turkish ruby represents infidelity, "as in other works" ("In Love's Thrall," p. 177), but I have been unable to find any supporting references. I have therefore suggested the noun "turkes," or turquoise, considered a semiprecious stone in the Middle Ages: "*Turtogis*, þat hatte turkeys also, is a white ȝelow stoon and haþ þat name of þe contre of Turkeys þer it is ybred. Þis stoon kepeþ and saveþ þe sight and bredeþ gladnesse and confort" (Trevisa, *On the Properties of Things*, 2.878 [xvi.lxxxxvi]).

83–91   *Phebus shone, to make his pease . . . aftir loves grace*. Following Ovid and Chaucer (*Complaint of Mars*), it is Phoebus (the sun) that is faulted for discovering the adultery of Venus and Mars, those "high estates tweyne" (line 84) caught in Vulcan's net ("in armes cheyned faste" — line 86). Friedman suggests that since Phoebus is in the service of Venus, "light and wisdom are subservient to sensuality in this place" ("In Love's Thrall," p. 177).

94   *Jove, Pluto*. Jove is another name for the Roman god Jupiter, renowned for his extramarital sexual exploits; Pluto (also known as Hades or Dis) is the god of the underworld. Both usually resort to kidnap and rape rather than laborious courtship.

99   *unto Heven it streccheth*. The idea of a building so high that it reaches for Heaven itself might remind readers of the tower of Babel in Genesis 11:1–9. Associating the court of love with that which gave rise to the confusion of tongues (and perhaps also with the vanity and egotism behind it) is another means of subtly undercutting the subject matter.

104–05 *the quenes floure / Alceste*. The flower of Queen Alceste (i.e., the daisy). Although the story of Alceste and Admetus is also found in Gower (*Confessio Amantis* 7.1917–43), the allusion is probably more directly to Chaucer's *Legend of Good Women* in which Alceste is the paragon of wifely fidelity who "for hire housbonde chees to dye, / And eke to goon to helle, rather than he" (F 513–14). She is later transformed into a daisy. The speaker's ignorance of what "tho deyses myght do signifie" is perhaps meant to be facetious given not only Chaucer's own ruminations on the flower but also the corpus of *dits amoreaux* by Machaut (*Dit de la marguerite*), Froissart (*Dittie de la flour de la marguerite*), and Deschamps (*Lay de Franchise*) known as the "marguerite" poems. See Wimsatt, *Chaucer and the French Love Poets*.

108   *the ladyes gode nineteen*. A reference to Chaucer's *Legend of Good Women* (F 283). Chaucer describes ten good women in nine tales, although manuscripts of Chaucer's *Canterbury Tales* variously refer to the number as twenty-five, nineteen, and fifteen. See Hammond, "Chaucer's 'Book,'" pp. 514–16.

119   *Helise*. Elysium, in Greek mythology, the eternal dwelling place of the virtuous, noted chiefly for its clement climate.

129–30 *Daunger . . . Disdeyne*. These two are also paired in Chaucer's *Parliament of Fowls* (line 136), and Lydgate's *Temple of Glass* (line 156). Daunger (Resistance) is the usual foil of Fair Welcoming; see *RR* (lines 2823–3325).

136   *liche a darte*. The queen's eyes being like darts might be an oblique reference to the medieval commonplace that love casts a dart into the heart of the lover. The poet's immediate source here is perhaps Chaucer's Knight's Tale, where Arcite proclaims that Emily has slain him with her eyes (*CT* I[A]1567): "Love hath his firy dart so brennyngly / Ystiked thurgh my trewe, careful herte" (1564–65), though in *RR* Cupid shoots several of his arrows into the lover's eye.

140   *A yarde in length*. In this feature this poet's Alceste resembles Chaucer's Emily in The Knight's Tale, whose "yelow heer was broyded in a tresse / Bihynde hir bak, a yerde long, I gesse" (*CT* I[A]1049–50). See also our poet's description of Rosiall's hair (lines 810–12).

160   *Philobone*. The name suggests either "good to lovers" (Neilson, *Origins and Sources*, p. 240), "love of the good," or the "good of love" (Friedman, "In Love's Thrall," p. 178).

171   *Mercurius*. Mercury, the messenger of the gods. Although he sometimes serves as Jupiter's henchman, his appearance is perhaps a bad omen since in the *Aeneid* Mercury delivers Jove's command that Aeneas fulfill his duty and leave Carthage for Italy (see Chaucer's *Legend of Good Women*, F 1297, and *House of Fame*, lines 427–32).

181   *a woman from a swan*. An allusion to a popular story, adopted by Boccaccio (*Decameron*, Introduction to Fourth Day) and La Fontaine (*Les Oies de Frere Philippe*), in which a boy who has been raised in a cave and shielded from worldly temptations visits Florence and, immediately attracted to some young ladies, is told by his father that they are geese (*papere*). The point is that young men have an innate affection for females, even though they may not be able to name it properly.

182   *spanne*. The distance from the tip of the thumb to the tip of the middle or the little finger when the hand is fully extended.

194   *bayte on many an hevy mel*. Although not listed in Whiting, this sounds proverbial. See also Chaucer's Man of Law's Tale: "On many a sory meel now may she bayte" (*CT* II[B¹]466).

229   *glasse*. Similarly, in both in Chaucer's *House of Fame* and Lydgate's *Temple of Glass*, Venus' temple is made of glass, suggesting, perhaps, not only the privileged nature of courtly erotic desire but also its insubstantiality and impermanence. Painted glass windows depicting faithful (and therefore usually unhappy) lovers are also common in these abodes. But *glasse* also means mirror, thus, narcissism, as one looks about in a house of mirrors to see only oneself. This scene is most closely imitated from Lydgate's *Temple of Glass* (lines 44–142).

232   *Dydo*. Dido is the archetypal betrayed lover; her story is found in Virgil's *Aeneid* 4, Ovid's *Heroides* 7, and Chaucer's *House of Fame* (lines 239–432) and *The Legend of Good Women* (lines 924–1367).

234–35   *Anelida, true . . . Arcite fals*. In Chaucer's *Anelida and Arcite*, Anelida, who was faithful to "fals Arcite" (line 11), describes her ordeal in a long complaint.

255   *in white, in russet, and in grene.* Skeat suggests that white refers to the Carmelites and russet to hermits (*Chaucerian*, p. 543). Bell reads the green garments as alluding to "the unfaithfulness of these ecclesiastics to their religious vows" (*Poetical Works*, p. 140).

266   Another longer lament by cloistered lovers (at lines 1093–1176) somewhat incoherently interrupts Philogenet's introduction to the allegorical denizens of Love's court; although the transition is still rickety, it would make some sense if those twelve stanzas (consisting of two manuscript pages) were inserted here. See my note to line 1092.

270   *an ho and crye.* To make an outcry or clamor; distinct from the legalistic *hue and cry* which is more specifically the alarm raised against criminals (*MED*).

304–504   *The firste statute . . . of old antiquité.* Such statutes are quite common (compare Ovid's *Art of Love*, Capellanus' *De Amore*, and *The Ten Commandments of Love* [*IMEV* 590]); those statutes listed here most closely resemble the rules found in *RR* (lines 2023–2577) and Lydgate's *Temple of Glass* (lines 1152–1213). The more ribald rules (particularly sixteen and seventeen) are apparently the author's invention.

323   *To purchace ever to here.* Bell interprets this difficult phrase as "to acquire, or gain over proselytes" (*Poetical Works*, p. 142).

329   *passe forby is an ease.* Skeat suggests that this line means that "to pass by, i.e. to get out of his [Love's] way" is "a relief, a way of escape" (*Chaucerian*, p. 544). Stow reads, "If love be wroth, passe for there by is an ease" (*Workes*, p. 349v). Even emended, this line makes no sense since the second half of the line should have some bearing on the consequences of love's wrath.

431   *The crowe is white.* In Ovid's *Metamorphoses* (Book 2), in an effort to prevent the raven from revealing to Phoebus his wife's infidelity, the crow relates how his own plumage was changed from white to black for telling tales (i.e., the truth). See also Chaucer's Manciple's Tale: "Whit was this crowe as is a snow-whit swan, / And countrefete the speche of every man / He koude, whan he sholde telle a tale" (*CT* IX[H]133–35). The point of the fifteenth statute is, of course, to tell lies.

506   *Rigour.* Bell suggests that this personified official denotes "the strictness of the obedience required of his subjects" (*Poetical Works*, p. 148). But see note to line 521.

521   *Rigour. MED* n.1a: "Hardness of heart (obdurancy)." Compare *La Belle Dame sans Mercy*, lines 717–20: "O marble hert, and yet more harde . . . What vayleth you to shewe so gret rigoure?" See Symons, ed., *Chaucerian Dream Visions*.

536–37   *Salamon and Sampson.* The standard examples of wisdom and fortitude, neither of which is adequate defense against women's perfidy. For Sampson, see Chaucer's Monk's Tale (*CT* VII[B²]2015–94). Solomon is, of course, proverbially wise; sometimes his sagacity is attributed to his vast experience with women.

629   *sauf that I wist nat where.* The comic futility of the poet's presentation of love is neatly summed up by the speaker's impassioned, honest admission that he

knows that he loves a lady, knows that he must give a fervent prayer for her graces, yet has no idea who she is or where she might be. He is left to request assignment to "som blissid place" (line 637).

647–48   *For hote I love . . . by my trouth.* Left to his own imagination, the would-be lover at last thinks of someone he saw in a dream. He wonders if she might be the object of his desires. There is, perhaps, a pun on the word *hote*, as well. Read one way, the speaker swears (*be God and by my trouth* — line 648) that he calls (*hote* — line 647) love, no matter where it is, nothing but the effects that it has on him (line 649). This reading would neatly parallel the beginning of Chaucer's *Parliament of Fowls*, where the narrator likewise knows love by its reported effects and not "in dede" (line 8). Yet one might also read *hote* as meaning "hotly"; thus the speaker claims that he loves most passionately, even if he does not know anything specific about the object of his love (not even where she is) aside from the mere fact that he swears he was troubled one night.

685   *a figge for all her chastité.* The *OED* lists this as an instance of a construction that conveys the meaning "not at all"; that is, the speaker cares not at all for Diana's chastity. The association with chastity (and thereby with sex), however, could mean that a sexual connotation is also implied. This indecent meaning (usually associated with the phrase "giving the fig" — i.e., making a gesture meant to replicate the female genitalia) is first cited by the *OED* in Fulwell's *Art of Flattery* (1579), over 100 years later than the present poem.

701   *Pité.* Although the personified figure of Pity is commonplace, there is a possible allusion here to Chaucer's *Complaint Unto Pity*, in which, in a "Bill of Complaint," the speaker unsuccessfully attempts to rally the moribund Pity to ward off Cruelty. Our poem's Pity is, of course, a personification *in extremis*, for she dies from pity at an eagle eating a fly (lines 702–03).

778–819 The poet's description of Rosiall, including her round head, golden hair, lily forehead, separated eyebrows, starry eyes, pregnant lips, straight and snowy teeth, sweet breath, and braided hair, closely follows Geoffrey of Vinsauf's rhetorical model for how to describe a beautiful woman found in his *Nova Poetria*. See Murphy, *Three Medieval Rhetorical Arts*, pp. 54–55.

787   *mylke white path.* The Milky Way, also referred to in the Middle Ages as the *galaxye*. Skeat suggests (*Chaucerian*, p. 547) that the poet refers to the "prominent ridge of Rosial's nose"; Seaton suggests the white skin betweeen the eyebrows (*Sir Richard Roos*, p. 452); and Friedman suggests the poet is describing Rosiall's "milk-white nose" ("In Love's Thrall," p. 182). Our poet appears to be following Vinsauf: "let the appearance of her eyebrow be like dark blueberries; let a milk-white path divide those twin arches" (Murphy, *Three Medieval Rhetorical Arts*, p. 54).

798   *Maximyan.* Cornelius Maximianus Gallus. The reference is to his *First Elegy*, lines 97–98: "flammea dilexi modicumque tumentia labra, / quae gustata mihi basia plena darent" ("I loved flaming and somewhat swollen lips, which gave me full kisses when tasted"). See Maximianus, *Elegies of Maximianus*, ed. Webster.

816   *grene.* Green can be an ambiguous color, associated with not only inconstancy, fickleness, and frivolity, but also youth and fecundity. See Chaucer's "Against Women Unconstant," with its refrain "In stede of blew, thus may ye were al grene." The color can also be emblematic of constancy: in Lydgate's *Temple of Glass*, his Lady wears green and white (line 299), and in the *Legend of Good Women*, Chaucer's Alceste is also dressed in green (F 214).

821–24   These lines are lifted from Vinsauf's *Nova Poetria* (Murphy, *Three Medieval Rhetorical Arts*, p. 55). Incidentally, it would, no doubt, be better if one's beauty did not catch Jove's attention. Jove's seduction/rape of each of these ladies, as well as the usually unhappy aftermath (occasioned by the jealous Juno) is described in Ovid's *Metamorphoses*. *Calixto* (Callisto) bore Jove's son and was turned into a bear (Book 2). *Alcenia* (Alcmene), the mother of Hercules, was forced to undergo her own Herculean labor as Juno delayed the birth of her son for a week (Book 9). *Europa* was seduced by Jove in the form of a bull (Book 2). *Dane* (Danae) was impregnated through the form of a golden shower and bore Perseus (Book 4). And Jove seduced *Antiopa* as a satyr; she later delivered twins (Book 6).

862   *ure, i-blisse.* The word *ure* derives from Latin *augurium* through the Old French *eure*, and carries with it the connotations of fortune, destiny, and, as I have glossed it here, luck (see *MED eure* [n]). The term *i-blisse* is idiomatic, meaning something like "may God bless me," or "if I may be so blessed by God."

890–96   The entrance of the lady's voice is abrupt and somewhat jarring. Perhaps we are meant to think of this "dialogue" as an internal debate of sorts, possibly akin to discussions between Amans and Genius in Gower's *Confessio Amantis*.

904–10   The "lady" is understandably confused and concerned. She does not know who this "lover" is, much less what he intends.

912   *Philogenet.* Our lover's name has been variously interpreted: Friedman suggests "he who generates love" or "love of generation" ("In Love's Thrall," p. 183), and Neilson guesses "a lover born" (*Origins and Sources*, p. 240).

995   *in sounde.* Here, the swoon, as in Chaucer's *Troilus and Criseyde*, is an outward sign of the lover's sincerity, and is usually quite efficacious in eliciting the lady's pity.

1016   *her coloure gan appeire.* For Leonard, it is here that the poem has real "allegorical vitality," insofar as Rosiall's blush suggests "not only her namesake, the Rose of the *Roman* [*de la Rose*], but also Christ, the Rose of Sharon, and, more abstractly, Charity, whose symbolic color is red" (*Laughter*, p. 103).

1040   *under hony gall.* Proverbial; see Whiting G7; H505.

1092   *tender nessh. Nessh[e]* (adj.) is often used in conjunction with "tender" to describe a softened, compassionate, or receptive heart, but never as a compound adjective. This reflects the author's practice of sometimes joining two adjectives: e.g., "gentill debonayre" (line 357), "godely fressh" (line 832), "feithfull true" (line 993).

            There appears to be a lacunae in the text here with the transition between Flattery's blandishments and the introduction of the malcontent religious having been lost. It seems to me that at line 1093 Philobone is speaking to Philogenet and I have placed the quotation marks accordingly. In addition, the twelve stanzas (lines 1093–1176) which describe the unhappy clerics and nuns seem out of place, since they interrupt Philogenet's discourse with the various allegorical personifications. Having reached this conclusion independently, I nonetheless agree with Neilson (*Origins and Sources*, pp. 6–7) that it would make some sense if this section followed line 266, where those constrained by religion are first introduced. The three stanzas (lines 1177–90) that follow this section could conceivably be attributed to Flattery, who stands "not ferre" (line 1191) from Dissemble. Neilson suggests that the speaker at line 1177 could be an allegorical figure, Contrite. See note below, line 1177.

1095–1155 The clerical laments are borrowed from Lydgate's *Temple of Glass* (lines 196–208); see Schick, *Lydgate's Temple*, pp. cxxix–cxxxi.

1096 *blak and white and gray.* The colors, respectively, of the Dominican, Carmelite, and Franciscan friars (Skeat, *Chaucerian*, p. 550).

1157 *a sorte full languysshyng.* In a scene reminiscent of Dante's *Inferno*, these grossly deformed lovers may be lepers, who were proverbially thought to be lecherous.

1172 *thre of fatall destyné.* The three fates of Greek myth: Clotho, Lachesis, and Atropos.

1177 *he was contrite.* I.e., one of the company (line 1170) who has slandered the three sisters "of fatall destyné" (line 1172). In order to make sense of this confusing section, Bell (*Poetical Works*, p. 173) and Neilson (*Origins and Sources*, pp. 5–6) suggest that a personified abstraction, Contrite, is the subject of the line. Bell emends to "And there [eek] was Contrite, and gan repent," an emendation that Neilson does not follow.

1192 *party mantill.* Bell suggests that Dissemble's multicolored clothing represents his duplicity (*Poetical Works*, p. 173).

1234 *broched.* Perhaps a double entendre suggesting both pierced and decorated with ornaments.

1259 For the figure of Envy, see Ovid's *Metamorphoses* (Book 2) where, in an attempt to prevent Mercury from seducing Herse, Minerva visits Envy's house in order to arouse the jealousy of Herse's sister, Aglauros. For meddling in the affair, Aglauros is turned into a statue.

1268 *Prevye Thought.* Skeat suggests (*Chaucerian*, p. 551) that this figure is inspired by Douz Penser (Sweet-Thought) in *RR* (lines 2640–68).

1315 Skeat suggests (*Chaucerian*, pp. 551–52) for comparison *RR* (lines 907–85), and Ovid's *Metamorphoses* (1.470–71), where Cupid has two sets of arrows, one gold and the other iron or lead, corresponding, respectively, to attraction and repulsion. See also Gower's *Confessio Amantis* 3.1700–05 and *The Kingis Quair*, stanzas 94–95.

1317 Rosiall is speaking.

1353   *To matens went*. The notion of the birds' songs or matins in spring as a service or office in praise of love is a popular courtly conceit. In this case, opening phrases from Matins and Lauds of the Divine Office are appropriated to praise the power of erotic love. For a similar macaronic use of scripture see the *Birds' Devotions* (*IMEV* 357), Jean de Condé's *La Messe des Oiseaux*, *As I went on a Yol Day* (*IMEV* 377), and *The Lovers' Mass* (*IMEV* 4186). On the tradition of bird poems, see Neilson, *Origins and Sources*, pp. 216–27, and Davenport, "Bird Poems."

1356   *Domine, labia*. From the Oratio or opening prayer of Matins: "Domine, labia mea aperies" ("O Lord, open my lips").

1359   *Venite*. From Vulgate Psalm 94, the Invitatory: "Venite, exsultemus Domino" ("Come, let us give praise to the Lord").

1364   *Domine, dominus noster*. From Vulgate Psalm 8: "Domine, Dominus noster, quam admirabile est nomen tuum in universa terra!" ("Lord our Lord, how admirable is your name in the whole earth!").

1366   *Cely enarant*. From Vulgate Psalm 18: "Caeli enarrant gloriam Dei" ("The heavens show forth the glory of God").

1370   *Domini este terra*. Vulgate Psalm 23: "The earth is the Lord's."

1373   *Jube, domine*. From "Jube, Domine, benedicere" ("Lord, command us to bless"). The versicle of the Absolutio immediately preceeding the first lesson.

1390   *gife us all an horne*. To scorn or mock (Skeat, *Chaucerian*, p. 553). Later, of course, to make a cuckold.

1400   *tue autem*. From "Tu autem, Domine, miserere nobis" ("But you, O Lord, have mercy on us"). The versicle repeated at the conclusion of each lesson.

1401   *Te deum amoris*. A parody of "Te Deum laudamus" ("God, we praise you") recited at the end of Matins.

1402   *Tuball*. Tubal was a metalworker (see Gower, *Confessio Amantis* 4.2425); his brother, Jubal, "was the father of them that play upon the harp and the organs" (Genesis 4:21). Chaucer and others make the same mistake. See *Book of the Duchess*, line 1162.

1408   *Dominus regnavit*. From Vulgate Psalm 92, recited at the beginning of Lauds: "Dominus regnavit, decorem indutus est" ("The Lord hath reigned, he is clothed with beauty").

1411   *Jubilate*. From Vulgate Psalm 99, the second psalm of Lauds: "Jubilate Deo, omnis terra" ("Sing joyfully to God, all the earth").

1413   *Benedicite*. From the "Canticle of the Three Children" (Daniel 3:57–8:56): "Benedicite, omnia opera Domini, Domino" ("All ye works of the Lord, bless the Lord").

1415   *Laudaté*. Vulgate Psalm 148: "Laudate Dominum de caelis" ("Praise ye the Lord from the heavens").

1416   *O admiribile*. The antiphon or refrain following the chapter and hymn.

1423   *Benedictus*. From the Canticle of Zachary (Luke 1:68–79): "Benedictus Dominus,
            Deus Israel" ("Blessed be the Lord God of Israel").

1433   *hawthorn*. In Lydgate's *Temple of Glass* (lines 503–23), the hawthorn represents
            fidelity and constancy in love, even under adverse circumstances; appropriately,
            the hawthorn is an evergreen shrub.

1440   *trewe love*. The herb paris (*Paris quadrifolia*), whose leaves and flowers are ar-
            ranged in whorls of four, and which is usually symbolic of fidelity (*MED*); Skeat
            suggests the term may also refer to a truelove knot of herb paris used for orna-
            mentation (*Chaucerian*, p. 553). See "The Four Leaves of the Truelove" in Fein,
            Moral Love Songs and Laments, pp. 161–254, where the leaf is linked to the
            Trinity and Mary.

1	Marginalia. A later hand (probably Beaupré Bell's) has written "by G. Chaucer" in the right-hand margin. John Stow has provided the title "The courte of love" at the top of the page.
	With. MS: *ith.* Space has been left for a 3-line initial that was never filled in. The same thing occurs at lines 43, 302, 1023, and 1352.
8	*Tullius.* MS: *Tulluis.*
105	A different hand as written in the margin: "Alceste þe dayse."
143	*woneth.* MS: *weneth.*
150	*But.* MS: *B.*
189	*Than.* MS: *That.*
235	*Arcite.* MS: *Artice.*
	in peynting. MS: *inpenytyng.*
246	*Lo.* MS: *To.*
270	*Throughoute.* MS: *Though oute,* with *r* inserted above the line.
333	*verely.* MS: *veryeuly.*
356	*faire.* MS: *fire.*
377	*ys.* MS: *yo.*
386	*remember.* MS: *reve* canceled before.
403	*hartes.* MS: *nyghtes hartes.* See also line 679.
461	*As.* MS: *And.*
481	*been.* MS: *but.*
483	*they.* MS: *the.*
490	*soverain.* MS: *savioure.*
494–95	These lines are transposed in MS, corrected by Stow.
495	*renewe.* MS: *revowe.*
506	*cleped.* MS: *clepes.*
508	*prayer.* MS: *payer.*
519	*leaves.* MS: *loves.*
530	In MS this line appears at the end of the stanza and marginal markings indicate the correct order.
552	*For.* MS: *Or.*
561	*pray her.* MS: *prayer.*
595	*unto man.* MS: *unto woman.*
605	*to.* MS omits.
632	*Lucerne.* MS: *Lucorne.*
634	*ure.* MS: *use.*
639–40	These lines are transposed in MS.

640	This line repeats line 633.
654	*that*. MS: omits.
679	*hartes*. See note to line 403.
684	*I kepen*. MS: *in kepen*.
694	*sormownting*. MS: *sormowting*.
695	*force*. MS: *fore*.
703	*ete*. MS: *eke*.
710	*Aslake*. MS: *Asshke*.
733	*mirth*. MS: *mir*.
747	*thank*. MS: *think*.
760	*hote*. MS: *ote*.
770	*gove*. MS: *you*.
798	*be*. MS: *he*.
823	*Europa*. MS: *Eurosa*.
843	*ye*. MS: *I*.
846	*grief*. MS: *give*.
847	*harm*. MS: *harte*.
853	*not*. Inserted into MS in a later hand.
860	*Loves*. MS: *Love*.
884	*refute*. MS: *refuce*.
897	*I*. MS: *and*.
901	In MS this line occurs out of place, at the end of the stanza.
911	*make it straunge?*. Supplied by Skeat.
928	*greven*. MS: *growen*.
970	*gife*. MS: *gise*.
	wounde. MS: *wounder*.
984	*harde*. Corrected from *harte* in MS.
1004	*ye might*. MS: *might*.
1009	*statutes*. MS: *steutes*.
1012	*I I*. MS: *I*.
1036	*Dispaire*. MS: *Displesire*.
1039	*he*. MS: *she*.
1041	*hers*. MS: *his*.
1076	*love*. MS: *verray love*.
1077	*verray*. MS omits.
1083	*that women*. MS: *thou woman*.
1108	*here*. MS: *hire*.
1116	*copes*. MS: *copies*.
1127	*matier*. MS: *matiers*.
1146	This line is missing from MS; supplied by Stow.
	ourself. Stow: *nor selfe*.
1203	*As*. MS: *And*.
1205	*arte*. MS: *harte*.
1222	*I ded wowe*. MS: *ded vowe*.
1233	*this*. MS: *the*.
1246	*Than lieth*. MS: *That leith*.
1270	*I*. MS omits.

1294	*to.* MS: *from.*
1299	*so.* MS omits.
1305	*cold or hoote.* MS: *hoote or cold.*
1313	*Twey.* MS: *Twenty.*
1324	*shryne.* MS: *shyne.*
1325	*ere.* MS: *eke.*
1326	*servaunte.* MS: *servnte*, with *a* written above the line.
1327	*brak.* MS: *blak.*
1328	*reuth.* MS: *reich.*
1329	*than.* MS: *and.*
1331	*but.* MS: *not.*
1333	*thou.* MS: *she.*
1335	*thanken.* MS: *taken.*
1341	*here.* MS: *heree.*
1369	*this.* MS: *thus.*
1370	*Domini.* MS: *Domine.*
1377	*singe.* MS: *signe.*
1383	*he.* MS omits.
1411	*sing.* MS: *sang.*
1432	*blome.* MS: *bleme.*

LITERATURE OF COURTLY LOVE

INTRODUCTION

Although many different kinds of works circulated with and became attached to Chaucer's name — allegorical, proverbial, monarchical, advisory, anticlerical, and didactic — most of the poems that accompanied Chaucer's works in fifteenth-century manuscripts and sixteenth-century print editions deal in some fashion with what is broadly categorized as *fin amours* or courtly love. The aristocratic amatory idiom is today considered one of the most influential and enduring literary legacies of the Middle Ages and most of the secular manuscript anthologies and miscellanies available in facsimile (particularly those produced by the Variorum Edition of the Works of Geoffrey Chaucer), which are heavily dominated by amorous subjects, suggest that the theory and practice of *fin amours* was a fetishized obsession among fourteenth- and fifteenth-century social elites. Indeed, emphasizing that courtly love was a trivial pursuit — "a pretense, a fiction, a game"[1] — John Stevens suggests that from the late fourteenth until the sixteenth century what he calls the "the game of love," including reading and talking about love, and acting, playing, and emulating the lover, provided a primary form of polite recreation for "social play" and "social *dis*play."[2] Although Richard Firth Green, in *Poets and Princepleasers*, his study of court literature in late medieval England, stresses the "relative unimportance of the literature of idealized love amongst the intellectual preoccupations of the late medieval nobility,"[3] he nonetheless acknowledges that for aristocrats, gentry, and the merchant class, the fiction of courtly love offered a system of etiquette, polite behavior, and good breeding: "Since the capacity to experience exalted human love was, by definition in the middle ages, restricted entirely to the well-born, it followed that one way in which a man might display his gentility was to suggest that he was in love; thus the conventions by which this emotion was defined, originally pure literary hyperbole, became part of a code of polite behavior."[4] Catherine Bates demonstrates that this code remained viable throughout the sixteenth century as "playing the lover" and "being a courtier" came to mean the same thing, especially under Elizabeth's reign.[5] Beyond providing simple models of courtship and courteous behavior, the rhetoric of amorous seduction and compliment, with its emphasis on "flattering, dissembling, deceitful, and tactical discursive strategies," prevailed as an essential feature in the discourse of political courtiership.

---

[1] Stevens, *Music and Poetry*, p. 191.

[2] Stevens, *Music and Poetry*, p. 209.

[3] Green, *Poets and Princepleasers*, pp. 127–28.

[4] Green, *Poets and Princepleasers*, p. 114.

[5] See Bates, *Rhetoric of Courtship*, pp. 6–44.

The various genres represented here, ranging from the serious to the satirical, and the sentimental to the sophisticated, and including the panegyric, valentine, amorous complaint, lovers' dialogue, and sacred parody, attest to the diversity and flexibility of the literature of *fin amours*. Stevens complains that the writers of many love lyrics "have what amounts to a genius for the stilted and colourless," and *In February*, a lover's lament for his disfavor, appears to manifest the "drab lifelessness" he finds common to the genre.[6] Inspired by French "marguerite" poetry and beginning with a panegyric to the daisy, the point of the complaint is not to dazzle the recipient or reader with its insight or originality but to display the writer's familiarity with rhetorical and poetic conventions, or to display what Stevens calls his "sentimental education."

A similar case is found with *O Merciful and O Mercyable*, a lover's plea for mercy from his disgruntled mistress. The first four stanzas are lifted from an unlikely source: an episode allegorizing Christ's atonement and the redemption of mankind found in the didactic dream vision *The Court of Sapience*. In the original poem, a personified Sapience relates to the dreamer the well-known story of the four daughters of God, in which two sisters (Mercy and Peace) plead with Truth and Justice for the release of Adam, God's disobedient and incarcerated servant. Our poet adapts the lines so that it is the lover pleading to Cupid for release from the prison of his love sickness. In keeping with his juristic theme, in which the lover plays the vassal begging for mercy from his sovereign, two other stanzas (lines 57–63 and 78–84) which also appropriate the language of feudal law and hierarchy are taken from *The Craft of Lovers*. Although for some modern readers these poems may seem to be marred by cliché and plagiarism, Stephen Manning reminds us that as with modern pop music, for readers of medieval love lyrics it was the expectation and gratification of the familiar that "creates a peculiar aesthetic pleasure."[7]

The Craft of Lovers, offering a "symilitude" (line 1) or representation of a conversation between a hopeful suitor and his chosen lady, was repeatedly ransacked by later writers. Again, the lover uses conventional rhetoric and tropes — showering his lady with hyperbolic praise, swearing his allegiance and fealty, bemoaning his pain — to express his desire. The lady, although clearly admiring his deft facility with the language of courtly seduction, is nonetheless wary and repeatedly pushes for clarity ("What is your wille?" [line 50]; "What is your name?" [line 80]). Somewhat surprisingly, the lover frankly admits to his carnal intentions, assuring her that she will not be disappointed since he is "Of mannys copulacioun the verray exemplary" (line 89). Even more surprising, given his somewhat crude veracity, the lady accepts his suit: "Unto your plesure I wold be at youre call" (line 137). The poem ends conventionally with the author hoping that his own "love elect" (line 170) will be inspired by the lady's example and will offer a similar remedy for his own amorous distress.

Although the lover's advances may seem somewhat artificial and hyperbolic to the modern reader, Green argues that the poem is a product of what he calls the Continental "second rhetoric" tradition. These "do-it-yourself manuals for the aspiring writer of courtly verse" provided models of "fashionable flirtation" and were characterized by "heavy polysyllabic and Latinate rhymes" and "pretentious classical and biblical name dropping."[8] For the English aristocracy, the poem would have had an "aura of Continental sophistication,"

---

[6] Stevens, *Music and Poetry*, p. 212.

[7] Manning, "Game and Ernest," pp. 225–41.

[8] Green, "*Craft of Lovers*," pp. 106–07.

providing a "pattern-book for fashionable discourse." On the other hand, Arthur K. Moore instead reads the poem as a parody of ornate eloquence which exposes and satirizes the artificial conventions (the "craft") of amorous courtly discourse. For Moore, the poem claims our attention only as "a reaction against insipid courtly verse filled with denatured *amour courtois* and allegorical conceits,"[9] and he contextualizes the dialogue as part of the tradition of antifeminist protest verse that "employs the devices of courtly panegyric ironically." From this approach, the lover's advances should be read as an "indictment of both chivalric pretense and rhetorical excess." In short, the dialogue represents "not only a keen analysis of courtly supplication but also a rejection of that artificial system of love which in the fifteenth century was, like chivalry, largely anachronistic."[10] As such, the poem has a political valence as well, striking at the "pretensions of the nobility, who sought to sustain the faded flower of chivalry at a time when the larger frame that contained it, feudalism, was in rapid decline."[11]

Although one of the purposes of the dialogue is perhaps to contrast the impotent artificiality of the courtly idiom with the rhetorical efficacy of frank sensuality, the poem was nonetheless viewed as a fecund source of amorous diction by other fifteenth-century poets. Green has found no less than seven instances in which lines — and even entire stanzas — all spoken by the lover, were purloined and incorporated into conventional courtly lyrics. Even the lady's skeptical common sense is itself a rhetorical trope, found also, for instance, in *The Court of Love* (lines 841–1015). Nonetheless, the poem does offer an interesting example of the seductive dialogue and is perhaps best contrasted with Alan Chartier's *La Belle Dame sans Merci* in which the unsuccessful lover uses similar tactical rhetoric on his skeptical mistress but who never confesses the frank physical nature of his passion. Believing his own hyperbolic tropes, the lover in *La Belle Dame*, like Chaucer's Troilus, literally dies from his frustrated desire.

John Lydgate's speaker in *The Floure of Curtesye* also appears moribund, experiencing the common symptoms — ranging from listlessness to mortal anguish — elicited by his chosen lady's requisite "daunger." His suffering is exacerbated on the dawn of Valentine's Day as he witnesses the annual, ritualistic avian coupling in which the birds freely choose their mates. The spectacle invokes a lament familiar from Chaucer's *The Parliament of Fowls* that only man, of all species, and apparently against all laws of nature, is constrained to love in one, usually unreceptive, place. Nonetheless, although his case appears hopeless and he lacks literary skill, he composes a lengthy panegyric to his lady in which her beauty and virtues are favorably compared to those of famous women of history and legend. He closes with an encomium, well known to Chaucerians, lamenting his inability to imitate Chaucer's "gay style":

> Chaucer is deed, that had suche a name
> Of fayre makyng, that was, without wene,   *doubt*
> Fayrest in our tonge, as the laurer grene.
> We may assay for to countrefete
> His gay style, but it wyl not be!

---

[9] Moore, "Some Implications," p. 231.

[10] Moore, "Some Implications," p. 234.

[11] Moore, "Some Implications," p. 237.

> The welle is drie with the lycoure swete,
> Bothe of Clye and of Caliopé. (lines 236–42)

In this case, the fount of inspiration refers to the Valentine motif, specifically the association of the eponymous saint with spring, the mating of birds, and human courtship. Both Jack Oruch and H. A. Kelly trace the origins of this tradition — which became popularized in the late fourteenth and early fifteenth centuries and which is found scattered among courtly writers such as Christine de Pisan, Oton de Grandson, John Clanvowe, Charles d'Orleans, and John Gower — to Chaucer's *The Parliament of Fowls*. Lydgate uses the motif in two other poems, *A Kalendar* and *A Valentine to Her That Excelleth All*, and despite his characteristic deprecations of his own literary craft, at least in this case the modesty topos is truly undeserved. Oruch describes Lydgate as the "chief innovator in the treatment of Valentine"; he is both the first to make the "name of the saint a label for a type of poem"[12] and, according to Kelly, the first to use the term "Valentine" as a name for a sweetheart.[13] Indeed, *The Floure of Curtesye*, a "*tour de force*" in Kelly's estimation,[14] represents one of the best examples of early Valentine poetry.

Finally, *The Lovers' Mass* (also known as *Venus' Mass*), a lyrical parody of the first part of the Roman Mass, was once thought to have been by Lydgate, whose amorphous canon in the early twentieth century served as a convenient dumping ground for anonymous verse circulating in courtly anthologies and miscellanies. Although never printed as Chaucer's or attributed to Chaucer, the poem nonetheless has been categorized as a piece of apocrypha by Hartung's *Manual of Writings in Middle English* perhaps on the basis of its allusion to *The Legend of Good Women* or by virtue of its appearance in Bodleian Library, Fairfax 16, a mid-fifteenth-century secular verse anthology concerned "with sophisticated morality and the trials and tribulations of *fin amors* — those concepts and imaginative experiences which reflect the social and literary refinements of the 'lettered chivalry' of the time,"[15] and which includes, in addition to works by Clanvowe, Hoccleve, and Lydgate, an impressive collection of Chaucer's minor poems.

In courtly love lyrics the conflation of profane and spiritual passion is a popular and widespread conceit, and sacred parody comprised of macaronic verse, incorporating Latin tags and phrases from the liturgy, is also quite common (see *The Court of Love*, and Lydgate's *The Floure of Curtesye*). Nonetheless, in the English vernacular tradition there is, to my knowledge, nothing quite like the ambitious and sophisticated parody of Roman liturgy found in *The Lovers' Mass*. Hammond points to some Continental analogues, such as Jean de Condé's *Messe des Oiseaux* ("Birds' Mass") and Suero de Ribera's *Misa de Amores* ("Lovers' Mass"). Sacred parody is found in ecclesiastical vocal music[16] and individual prayers and hymns, such as the *Kyrie Alison* (*IMEV* 377) or the "Ave formosissima" ("Hail, most beautiful one"), a parody of the *Ave Maria*,[17] are often adapted to secular, amorous themes. And in

---

[12] Oruch, "St. Valentine," p. 559.

[13] Kelly, *Chaucer and the Cult of St. Valentine*, pp. 145–46.

[14] Kelly, *Chaucer and the Cult of St. Valentine*, p. 144.

[15] Norton-Smith, *Bodleian Library, MS Fairfax 16*, p. vii.

[16] See Huot, *Allegorical Play*.

[17] See Walsh, *Love Lyrics*.

Parody in the Middle Ages, Martha Bayless describes a long and flourishing tradition of litur-gical parody in Latin, especially Drinkers' and Gamblers' Masses. Many of these texts involve social parody, ridiculing vice or folly. *The Lovers' Mass*, however, which adapts its lyrics to the tone and mood of the Ordinary of the Mass, is closer to what Bayless calls textual parody, which achieves its effects by "imitating and distorting the distinguishing characteristics . . . of specific texts."[18] In this case, Hammond notes that "[i]ts author is not merely dexterous and graceful in the complexities of the Kyrie, and aware of the clear singing quality of the Gloria-stanza, but he is sufficiently sensitive to make the change to the deeper slower seriousness of the Orison."[19] Bayless finds that medieval parody is often not "the tool of the reformer, literary or social," and is "more often entertainment than polemic."[20] And, indeed, the intent of *The Lovers' Mass* is less to ridicule the solemnity of the Mass than to humorously mock those who have made eroticism their religion.

THE TEXTS AND MANUSCRIPTS

In February (*IMEV* 1562) and *O Merciful and O Mercyable* (*IMEV* 2510), both first printed in John Stow's *Workes of Geffrey Chaucer* (1561), are based on the manuscript which he used as copy text: Cambridge, Trinity College MS R.3.19 (fols. 160r, 161r–v).

The Craft of Lovers (*IMEV* 3761), also first printed in John Stow's *Workes of Geffrey Chaucer* (1561), is found in three manuscripts: **H** (British Library, MS Harley 2251, fols. 52r–54v); **A** (British Library, MS Additional 34360, fols. 73v–77r); and **T** (Cambridge, Trinity College MS R.3.19, fols. 154v–156r). Stow's edition is based on T (see Edwards and Hedley, "John Stowe"). H and A, both dated 1460–70, are believed to have been written by the same scribe and copied from the same exemplar (see Hammond, "Two British Museum Manuscripts"). Although Bradford Fletcher suggests that "the readings of T[rinity] should be given the greater weight over those of HA" ("Edition of MS R.3.19," p. 346), it seems to me that the Trinity scribe often emends for clarity and simplicity (e.g., lines 18, 39, 57, 73, 101, 139, 161) although he does also manifest what appear to be superior readings (e.g., 46, 103). Since T is available in Fletcher's facsimile, I have used H (which seems to have fewer errors than A) as my base text for spelling and substantives, while substituting a few readings from T. A complete list of variants is found in the Textual Notes.

Lydgate's *The Floure of Curtesy* is based on the earliest extant text found in William Thynne's *Workes of Geffray Chaucer* (1532). The two previous editors of the poem, Henry Noble MacCracken and Walter Skeat, emend both substantives and accidentals for the sake of sense and meter. MacCracken's text is far more conservative; Skeat, for instance, restores earlier forms although he also drops the final *-e* when it is not sounded. I have adopted their emendations only to correct what appear to be clear substantive errors in Thynne's text.

The Lovers' Mass (*SIMEV* 4186) is edited from the only extant manuscript, Oxford, Bodleian Library, MS Fairfax 16 (fols. 314r–317v). See Norton-Smith, *Bodleian Library, MS Fairfax 16*, introduction.

---

[18] Bayless, *Parody in the Middle Ages*, p. 3.

[19] Hammond, *English Verse*, p. 208.

[20] Bayless, *Parody in the Middle Ages*, p. 7.

 # In February

1	In the season of Feverer, when hit was full colde,	*February*
	Frost and snowe, hayle, rayne hath dominacion,	
	Wyth chaungeable elementes and wyndys manyfolde,	*intense*
	Whyche hath ground flour and herbe, undyr jurysdiccion	
5	For a tyme, to dyspose aftyr theyr correccion;	
	And yet Apryll, wyth hys plesaunt showres,	
	Dyssolveth the snow and bryngeth forthe hys flowres.	

	Of whos invencion ye lovers may be glad,	*action*
	For they bryng yn the kalendes of May;	*beginning*
10	And ye, wyth countenaunce demure, meke and sad,	*serious*
	Owe forto worshyp the lusty flowres all way,	*delightful*
	And inespeciall oone whyche ys callyd see of the day,	*eye of the day*
	The daysé, a flowre whyte and rede,	
	And in frensshe callyd *la bele margarete*.	

15	O commendable flour and most on mynde!	
	O flour and gracious of excellence!	
	O amyable Margaret, exaltyd of natyf kynd,	*native species*
	Unto whom I must resorte, wyth all my diligence,	*adhere*
	Wyth hert, wylle, and thought, wyth most lowly obedience,	
20	I to be your servaunt, and ye my regent,	*ruler*
	For lyfe ne dethe, never to repent.	

	Of thys processe now forth wyll I procede,	*course of events*
	Whyche happeth me wyth gret dysdayne,	
	As for the tyme therof I take leste hede,	*little heed*
25	For unto me was brought the soore payne.	
	Therfore, my cause was the more to complayne;	
	Yet unto me my grevaunce was the lesse,	*injury*
	That I was so nygh my lady and maystresse,	*near*

	There where she was present in thys place.	
30	I, havyng in hert gret adversyté,	
	Except only the fortune and good grace	
	Of hyr whos I am, the whyche relevyed me;	
	And my gret dures unlasyed hath she,	*released*

And brought me out of that ferefull grevaunce.
35   Yef hit were her ease, hit were to me gret plesaunce.   *If; pleasure*

As for the whyche woo I dyd endure,
Hyt was to me a verrey plesaunt payne,
Seying hit was for that fayre creature,
Whyche ys my lady and soverayn,
40   In whos presence I wold be passyng fayne,   *very happy*
So that I wyst hit were hir plesure,   *knew*
For she ys from all distaunce my protecture.   *protector*

Though unto me dredefull were the chaunce,   *event*
No maner of gentylnes oweth me to blame;
45   For I had levyr suffre of deth the penaunce   *rather*
Then she shuld for me have dyshonour or shame,
Or in any wyse lese oo drope of hyr good name;   *one*
So wysely God for Hys endelese mercy
Graunt every trew lover to have joy of his lady!

ABBREVIATIONS: see p. 63.

12   *whyche*. Stow omits.

     see of the day. The daisy is popularly known as the "eye of the day" or the "day's eye" (OE *daeges ēage*) because it closes at evening. See Chaucer, *LGW* F184–86: "men it calle may / The 'daysye,' or elles the 'ye of day,' / The emperice and flour of floures alle."

13   *a flowre whyte and rede*. The European daisy (*bellis perennis*) has pink-tipped petals.

14   *la bele margarete*. On the tradition of French marguerite poetry, see Wimsatt, *Marguerite Poetry*, pp. 30–39; Nouvet, "'Marguerite,'" pp. 251–76; and Huot, "Daisy and the Laurel," pp. 240–51.

15   *on*. Stow: *in*.

18   *diligence*. T: *dilig*. Due to cropping here and at lines 18, 19, 32, 34, 35, 43, 44, 46, 47, and 49, the final words are truncated or missing; the readings are supplied from Stow. Fletcher judiciously cautions that "there is only a reasonable presumption that the page was whole in Stow's time" ("Edition of MS R.3.19," p. 357).

47   *drope*. T: *drape*.

O MERCIFUL AND O MERCYABLE

1	O Merciful and O Mercyable,	
	Kyng of Kynges, and Fadyr of Pité,	
	Whos myght mercy ys incomperable;	*mighty*
	O Prynce Eterne, O Myghty Lord sey we,	
5	To whom mercy ys gevyn of propurté,	*by nature*
	On Thy servaunt that lythe in pryson bounde,	
	Have Thou mercy or that hys hert wounde.	*before*

And that Thou wylt graunte to hym, Thy prisonere,
Fre liberté and loose hym out of payne,   *release*
10 All hys desyres and all hys hevy chere,   *vexed spirits*
To all gladnes they were restoryd agayne;
Thy hygh vengeaunce, why shuld Thou nat refrayne
And shew mercy, syth he ys penitent?
Now helpe hym Lord, and let hym nat be shent.   *destroyed*

15 But syth hit ys so, ther ys a trespas doon,
Unto Mercy late yelde the trespassour.   *yield*
Hyt ys her offyce to redresse hit soon,   *duty*
For trespas to Mercy ys a myrrour,
And lyke as the sweete hath the price by sowre,   *sour*
20 So by trespas Mercy hath all her myght:
Wythout trespas, Mercy hath lak of lyght.   *light (i.e., power)*

What shuld physyk do, but yef sekenes were?   *medicine; unless*
What nedeth salve, but yef ther were sore?   *ointment*
What nedeth drynke wher thurst hath no powere?
25 What shuld Mercy do, but trespas go afore?
But trespas be, Mercy woll be lytyll store;   *of little value*
Wythout trespas, noon execusion   *execution (realization)*
May Mercy have, ne chyef perfeccion.   *highest*

The cause at thys tyme of my wrytyng
30 And towchyng Mercy, to whom I make mone,
Ys for fere lest my soverayn and swetyng,   *sweetheart*
I meane her that lovelyer ys none,
Wyth me ys dysplesyd for causys more then one;

What causes they be, that knoweth God and she,
35   But so do nat I; allas, hit forthynketh me.   *displeases*

What sy she in me, what defaute or offence?   *sees; fault*
What have I do that she on me dysdayne?   *done*
Howe myght I do come to her presence
To tell my complaynt, wherof I were fayne?   *eager*
40   I drede to loke, to speke, or to complayne
To her that hath my hert every dele;   *entirely*
So helpe me God, I wold all thyng were wele!

For in thys case came I never, or now,   *before*
In loves daunce so fer in the trace;   *tressure (confining braids, harness)*
45   For wyth myn ese skape I ne mow   *I may not*
Out of thys daunger, except her good grace.
For though my contenaunce be mery in her face,
As semeth to hyr, by worde or by chere,   *expression*
Yet her good grace sytteth myn hert nere.

50   And yef that my soverayne have any mervayle   *wonder*
Why I to her now and afore wrote,   *before*
She may well thynke hit ys no gret travayle   *labor*
To hym that ys in love brought so hote;
Hit ys a simple tre that falleth wyth oon stroke —   *one*
55   That meane I — though that my soverayne toforne   *before*
Me hath denyed, yet grace may come tomorne!   *tomorrow*

Let never the love of trew loveres be losyd,   *loosened*
My soverayn masteras, in no maner wyse;
In your confydence my wordes I have closyd.
60   My hertes love, to yow I do promyse,
So that ye kynt the knot of exercise,   *conclude the activity*
Bothe lok and key ye have in governaunce,
Wherfore enprynt me in your remembraunce.

But, masteras, for the good wyll that I have yow ought   *owed*
65   And evermore shall, as long as my lyfe dureth,
Have pyté on your servaunt and kepe hym in your thought,
And yeve hym som comfort or medycyn that cureth
Hys fervent agu that encreseth and reneweth,   *fever*
So grevous byn hys peynes and hys syghes soore,
70   That wythout your mercy hys dayes byn all forlore.   *lost*

Go lytyll byll, go forthe and hye thee fast,   *hurry*
And recommaund me, and excuse me as thou can;
For verray febylnes thus am I at the last,   *end [of life]*
My penne ys woren, my hew ys pale and wan,   *worn*

75   My eyen byn sonkyn, dysfiguryd lyke no man,   *eyes are sunken*
      Tyll dethe hys dart that causeth forto smert,   *hurt*
      My corps have consumyd, then farewell swetehert.

      O doughter of Phebus in vertuous apparence,
      My love elect in my remembraunce,
80   My carefull hert, dystreynyd cause of absence,   *tormented because*
      Tyll ye meynprise me and relese my grevaunce;   *you release*
      Uppon yow ys set my lyfe and myn attendaunce,   *attention*
      Wythout recure, ywys, untyll   *remedy*
      Ye graunt trew hert to have hys wyll.

85   Thus, my dere swetyng, in a traunce I do ly,   *sweetheart*
      And shall tyll som dropys of pyté from yow spryng,
      I mene yowre mercy, that lyeth my hert ny,   *near*
      That me may rejoyse and cause me forto syng
      These termys of love: loo, I have won the ryng!
90   My goodly masteras, thus of her good grace,
      God graunt hys blysse in Heven to have a place.
             Amen.

NOTES TO *O MERCIFUL AND O MERCYABLE*

ABBREVIATIONS: see p. 63.

1–28	The first four stanzas are borrowed from *The Court of Sapience* (lines 197–203, 218–24, 365–78). Lines 1–14 adapt Mercy's plea to God for the release of Adam; Mercy is unsuccessful in moving her sisters, Truth and Justice, and Peace takes up her case (lines 15–28), arguing that just as Peace, Truth, and Justice have "no properté" without war, falsehood, and injury, Mercy can only be realized through trespass. See *Court of Sapience*, ed. Harvey.
3	*myght*. Stow: *might and*.
19	*sweete hath the price by sowre*. Proverbial; see Whiting S943.
27	*noon*. Stow: *never*.
57–63	This stanza as well as lines 78–84 are from *The Craft of Lovers* (lines 127–33 and 169–75). The poet appears to have been attracted to juridical metaphors describing the rigors of love.
64	*ought* T: *ou*. The manuscript is cropped here; reading supplied from Stow.
66	*Have pyté on your*. Stow: *Pitie your*.
67	*that*. Stow: *and*.
68	*and*. Stow: *that*.
78	*doughter of Phebus*. Phoebus has no daughter; the allusion may either suggest that his lady has the attributes of the sun god (brilliance, beauty), or it may be a blunder. See note to line 15 of *The Craft of Lovers*.
81	*and*. Stow omits.
89	*loo, I have won the ryng!* To "win the ring" presumably means to become betrothed, as the ring was then, as now, a symbol of matrimony, though a certain sexual connotation might also be understood. The context here seems to imply that these are the initial words to a song, but no such item is listed in the *IMEV* or *SIMEV*.

THE CRAFT OF LOVERS

1	To moralise a symilitude — who list — these balettes sewe	*desires; follow*
	The craft of lovyers curyous argument;	*subtle reasoning*
	For some ben false, and som ben triewe,	
	And som ben double of entendement.	*meaning*
5	These lovyers, with theyre moral document	*correct training*
	And eloquent langage, can exemplefye	*demonstrate*
	The craft of love, what it doth signifye.	*mean*
	Who list these balettes have inspeccioun,	*wishes*
	Think that loves lordshippe excellent	*power*
10	Is remedy for disease and correccioun	
	To woful hert and body impotent,	*weak*
	Suppose that the maker be nat necligent	*careless*
	In his compilyng — hold hym excusable —	*composing*
	Because his spirites be sory and lamentable.	*sad and mournful*

[Lover] "Moste soveraigne lady, surmountyng in noblesse,   *exceeding; nobility*
16   O intemerate jenypere and daysie delicious,   *unblemished juniper*
    My trust, myn helth, my cordial founderesse,   *reviving source*
    O medicyne sanatyf to myn infirmynat langoures,   *enfeebling afflictions*
    O comfortable creature of lovyers amours,   *comforting; affections*
20   O excelent herber of lovely countenaunce,   *herb*
    Ye registre my love in your remembraunce."   *record*

[Lady] "Certes, syr, youre peynted eloquence,   *Certainly; colorful*
    So gay, so fressh, and eke so talkatyve,   *splendid; verbose*
    It doth transcende the wit of Dame Prudence;
25   For to declare your thought or to discryve,   *describe*
    So curiously your eloquence ye contryve.   *cunningly*
    Of youre conceyt, youre thought and your entent,   *plan*
    I wil be ware or than I be shent."   *be careful; disgraced*

[Lover] "O rubicunde rose and white as the lilye,   *red*
30   O korven figure of worldly portrature,   *carved; animate appearance*
    O clarified cristal, resplendent of glorye,   *illuminating; radiant with*
    O gemme of beauté or charbuncle shyneng pure,   *carbuncle*
    Youre fairenesse excedith the craft of Dame Nature,

| | Most wommanly behavyng in countenaunce; | *conduct* |
| 35 | Wherfor ye do registre my love in your remembraunce." | *record* |

[Lady]	"What availeth, syr, suche demonstracioun	*What is the use of*
	Of curious talkyng nat touchyng to sadnesse?	*seriousness*
	It is but wynd, flatteryng, and adulacioun,	*insincere praise*
	Unmesurable cogitaciouns of worldly wieldnesse,	*Immoderate; wantonness*
40	Whiche is chief cause of gostly distresse.	*spiritual*
	Youre wille, youre thought, youre double entendement,	*ambiguous intention*
	I wil be ware for drede that I be shent."	*disgraced*

[Lover]	"My wit, my thought, and myn entencioun	*intention*
	Is for to please yow, lady soveraygne;	
45	And, for youre love, thurgh many a regyoun	
	I wold be exiled, so that ye wold nat disdayne	
	To have pité on me whan I compleyne;	*lament*
	In wele and woo to suffre perturbaunce,	*happiness; trouble*
	So that ye wold have me in your remembraunce."	

[Lady]	"What is your wille? Plainly that ye expresse,	
51	That maketh this curious glosed supplicacion.	*specious plea*
	Sey on syr, briefly, on hertly tenderesse!	*genuine compassion*
	Be right wele advised of vayne delectacioun;	*idle delight*
	At youre begynnyng, thynk on the termynacon.	*end*
55	Passe nat youre boundis, be nat to necligent,	*limits*
	And ever be ware in lesse that ye be shent."	*lest*

[Lover]	"Youre goodely behavyng, your beauté in substaunce,	*innate*
	Makith me to enclyne to do yow reverence;	*to be disposed*
	Youre lovely lokyng, youre wommanly governaunce,	*appearance*
60	Overcomyth my spirit, my wyt, and my prudence.	*Overwhelms*
	Som drope of grace of youre magnificence	
	Unto your suppliaunt, ye shewe attendaunce;	*attention*
	And ones, registre my love in your remembraunce."	*At once*

[Lady]	"O combrous thought of mannes fragilité!	*troubling*
65	O fervent wille of lustis furious!	*ardent; unrestrained*
	O cruel corage causyng adversité!	*desire*
	O Vulcanus corrupcion and erbe contrarious	*herb harmful*
	To helth of man! A chaunce most perilous,	*event*
	To breke the virginité of the virgynal innocent!	
70	Wherfor be ware, mankynd, lesse that ye be shent."	*lest*

[Lover]	"My peyne is prevy, impossible to discerne;	*secret*
	My lamentable thoughtis be cast in mournyng.	*sorrowful*
	O general juge, whiche sittith superne,	*above*
	Graciously conveyeth the love of this lady yeng!	*direct; young*

75	O amyable lady, gracious and benyngne,	*kind*
	I put me holy in youre governaunce;	*wholly; control*
	Exile me nat out of youre remembraunce."	

[Lady]	"Me semes by your langage ye be some potestate,	*[It] seems [to] me [that]; lord*
	Or ellis som curious gloser deceyvable;	*deceptive flatterer*
80	What is your name, mekely, I make regrate,	*request*
	Or of what science or craftes commendable?	*knowledge or skills*
	I am a lady, excelent and honurable;	
	He must be gay that please shuld myn entent.	*charming*
	Wherfor beware, in lesse that ye be shent."	

[Lover]	"O lord God, this is a sharp examynacioun,	
86	Of hir that most is in my memory!	
	Unto yow, lady, I make certificacioun,	*guarantee*
	My name is Triewe Love of Carnal Desidery,	*desire*
	Of mannys copulacioun the verray exemplary,	*joining; model of conduct*
90	Whiche am one of your servaunts of plesaunce;	*pleasure*
	Wherfor I must be registred in your remembraunce."	

[Lady]	"I have sought Triewe Love yeeres grete excesse,	
	Yit found I hym never, but for a season.	
	Som men be dyverse and know no gentilnesse,	*unkind*
95	And som lakkith both wisdam and reason;	*lack*
	In som men is trust, in som is treason.	
	Wherfor I wil conclude, by avisement,	*decide*
	And also beware, in lesse that I be shent."	

[Lover]	"The rectour Tullius, so gay of eloquence,	*rhetorician Cicero*
100	And Ovide that shewith the craft of love expresse,	*describes; explicitly*
	With habundaunce of Salamons sapience,	*wisdom*
	And pulcritude of Absolons fairenesse,	*beauty*
	And I were possessid with Jobis grete riches,	*Job's*
	Manly as Sampson my persone to avaunce —	*promote*
105	Yit wold I submyt me in your remembraunce."	

[Lady]	"Now, syr, if it please youre noblenesse	
	To gyve advertence to my questioun:	*attention*
	What thyng is plesure of worldly swetnesse	
	And is most bitter in fynal successioun?	*in process of time*
110	Or what thyng gevith man occasioun	*gives; cause*
	In tendre age for to be concupiscent?	*lustful*
	Resolve this questioun and ye shul nat be shent."	*reproached*

[Lover]	"My soverayne lady, Ovide, in his writyng,	
	Seyth that desire of worldly concupiscence,	*lust*
115	As for a tyme is swete in his wirchyng,	*effect*

And in his end he causith grete offence.　　*harm*
Nat withstandyng my lady Dame Prudence,　　*In spite of*
Grene flowryng age and manly countenaunce　　*(see note)*
Causith ladyes to have hem in remembraunce."

[Lady] "Yowre goodly answers, so benyngne in substaunce,　　*salubrious*
121　Wold cause the hert of wommanheed convert
Unto delite of natural plesaunce.　　*physical pleasure*
But of oo thyng I wold be expert:　　*one; informed*
Why mannes langage wil procure and transvert　　*seduce; overturn*
125　The wille of wymmen and virgyns innocent?
Wherfor I stonde in feere lesse that I be shent."　　*ruined*

[Lover] "Late never the love of triewe lovers be losed,　　*loosened*
My soverayne lady, in no maner wise.
In youre confidence my wordis have I closed;　　*enclosed*
130　My cordial love to yow I do promyse,　　*sincere*
So that ye knyt the knot of excersise.　　*end this trial*
Both lok and key, ye have in governaunce;　　*control*
Wherfor, emprinte me in your remembraunce."　　*imprint*

[Lady] "Of verray trust and I were certifyed,　　*Truthfully, if I were assured of*
135　The pleyne intencioun of your hert cordiall,　　*clear; sincere*
Me semes in blisse; than were I glorifyed:　　*transformed*
Unto your plesure I wold be at youre call.
But ever I feere me of chauncis casuall,　　*uncertain events*
Of froward disceyt and langage insolent;　　*perverse; improper*
140　Than were I sure my virgynité were shent."　　*destroyed*

[Lover] "Ther was never tresour of terestral richesse,
Nor precious stones rekened innumerable,　　*incapable of being counted*
To be of comparison unto youre high goodenesse,
Of al creatures, to me most amyable.　　*pleasing*
145　Trust nat the contrary; I was never disceyvable.　　*deceptive*
Kepe wele Triewe Love, forge no resemblaunce;　　*invent*
And, fynally, registre and take me in your remembraunce."

[Lady] "Me semes by feture of manly propirté,　　*appearance; nature*
Ye shud be trusty and triewe of compromyse.　　*should; promise*
150　I fynde in yow no false duplicité;
Wherfor, Triew Love, ye have myn herte, iwisse,　　*certainly*
And evermor shal, so have I blisse.
This confederacy made by goode avisement,　　*alliance; consideration*
God grant grace that nother of us be shent."　　*neither; harmed*

155　Whan Phebus first was in his chare splendent,　　*bright chariot*
In the moneth of May, erly in a mornyng,

I herd two lovers dispute this argument,
In the yeere of God a mille by rekenyng,   *a thousand*
Four hundred fifty and nine yere folowyng.   *(i.e., 1459)*
160   O prepotent princesse, conserve triewe lovers all,   *preeminent; preserve*
And graunt of this terestry vale the blisse celestial!   *terrestrial*

[Envoy] Go litel balettis, submyttyng everywhere,
To diew correccioun of benyvolence.   *proper; from*
But where that envye is, loke ye come nat there;
165   For any thyng, kepe youre balettes thens.   *away*
For envy is ful of froward reprehens,   *perverse censure*
And how to hurte, lyth ever in awayte;
Kepe ye thens, that ye be nat theyr bayte.   *enticement*

O doughter of Phebus in vertuous apparence,
170   My love elect in my remembraunce,   *chosen*
My careful hert distreyned cause of absence,   *constrained because of*
Til ye maynprise me and relese my grevaunce;   *release; complaint*
Upon yow is set my lyf and myn attendaunce,   *service*
Without recure, iwisse, untill   *remedy; certainly*
175   Ye graunt Triew Hert to have his will.

Salamon, distressed for love, in loves daunce
Sang in his trace with woful compleynt,   *dance steps*
"Come deere hert," without cessaunce.
Releve my paynes, that in teres am spreynt;   *sprinkled*
180   *Quia amore langueo*, late me nat spil for feynt!   *perish; faintness*
Com on, my deere spowse, joy ye me till   *delight*
Triew Hert, of me, shal have his wyll.

EXPLANATORY NOTES TO *THE CRAFT OF LOVERS*

ABBREVIATIONS: see p. 63.

1–4   Kooper ("Slack Water Poetry," p. 484) accurately describes these lines as "confused and confusing." "To moralise" is to interpret morally or symbolically and a "symilitude" is a reproduction or resemblance (a similarity). These lines can be roughly paraphrased as "Whoever chooses to interpret the moral or spiritual significance of this representation, these stanzas show the craft of lovers' subtle arguments, since some are false, some true, and some have double meanings." Skeat reasonably suggests that the phrase "a symilitude" was in the margin in the exemplar but was incorporated into the text by subsequent scribes (*Chaucerian*, p. xii). The poem offers a similitude, that is, a representation or image of the craft of love. Moore points out that Stephen Hawes uses the phrase to "moralyse the semelytude" (*Pastime of Pleasure* 1.808) in the sense of finding the moral or spiritual significance in a "far-fetched resemblance": "Since . . . no similitude is actually moralized, the phrase may mean only to 'explain' — in this instance, the hidden meaning of the 'curious arguments' of love" ("Some Implications," pp. 233–34).

    balettes. Rhyme royal stanzas (*ababbcc*).

12   *nat*. H and T omit "not." It makes more sense to me, however, that the *maker* claims that he is *not* careless in his composition; any defects in his work can be attributed to his depressed spirits.

15   A designates the speakers as "Cupido" and "Diana," corresponding to sensuality and chastity. Kooper suggests that the A scribe has confused the dedicatee, described as "doughter of Phebus" (line 169), with Diana, the sister of Phoebus ("Slack Water Poetry," p. 489).

    Moore notes that this stanza is "freighted with aureate forms" including *exclamatio, pronominatio, dissolutio, repetitio* and *translatio* ("Some Implications," p. 234). Note also the medicinal theme that runs throughout.

    This stanza, and lines 43–49, 71–77, and 99–105, derived from a separate exemplar, are incorporated in *Lady of Pité* (*IMEV* 1838), which also appears in T. For texts and commentary, see Robbins, "Love Epistle," pp. 289–92; Wilson, "Five Unpublished Secular Love Poems," pp. 399–418; and Person, *Cambridge Middle English Lyrics*, pp. 14–16.

16   *intemerate jenypere*. The juniper is known for its ability to withstand fire and its berries were used for medicinal purposes; see Trevisa, *On the Properties of Things*, 17.84. Kooper points out that the juniper is often associated with the Virgin Mary in religious lyrics. The burning bush of the Old Testament (Exodus 3:2) was a Marian symbol anticipating the Virgin Birth. See Chaucer's Prioress' Tale: "O bussh unbrent, brennynge in Moyses sighte" (*CT* VII[B²]468); see also Lydgate, *Life of Our Lady* (lines 281–87) in *John Lydgate: Poems*, ed. Norton-Smith.

18   *infirmynat langoures*. T (*sores langorous*) is clearly the easier reading, reflecting this scribe's practice of sometimes emending for clarity. This word appears to be an aureate coinage, making it difficult to choose between H and A (*infirmatyf*). Although a show of hands is not the best guide, I have sided with H since in *Lady of Pité*, which incorporates this stanza, the reading is also "infyrmynat." The adjective is related to "infirm," "infirmate," that is, weakening or debilitating.

22   *peynted eloquence*. Skillful and/or deceptive rhetoric. Green notes that "The lady here is not ridiculing the artificiality of her lover's language in itself . . . merely seeking to discover what truth lies behind it" ("*Craft of Lovers*," p. 116).

24   *Dame Prudence*. A possible allusion to Chaucer's Tale of Melibee. Dame Prudence is known for her prolix sententiousness.

30–31   As a last resort, in order to make sense of these lines, I have transposed the first halves of the two lines. H reads, *O clarified cristal of worldly portreature, / O korven figure resplendent of glorye*.

         clarified cristal. "Clarified" suggests both illuminating or brightening and clarifying or cleansing.

32   *charbuncle*. A precious stone that shines in the dark. See Trevisa, *On the Properties of Things*, 16.25.

53   *vayne delectacioun*. The context suggests that *delectacioun* is used here in the intellectual sense, that is, a worthless or pretentious intellectual exercise in seductive rhetoric. However, another connotation, suggesting sensual pleasure, and more specifically, the second stage of sin — the pleasure in contemplating a sin — may also be inferred. See Chaucer's Parson's Tale (*CT* X[I]350–56).

57   Kooper notes, "The lover claims that he is attracted by the lady's inward, or essential, beauty. Such beauty springs from virtue and spiritual uprightness, as in the case of Mary, the virgin *plena gracia*" ("Slack Water Poetry," p. 486).

67   *O Vulcanus*. Vulcan, in Roman mythology, is the god of fire and metalworking and married to Venus. Known for his lameness and as a public cuckold. Vulcan's corruption perhaps refers to Venus (amorous love) herself or to his jealousy and vindictiveness following his discovery of her affair with Mars. Note that here the lady herself indulges in a bit of rhetorical excess.

88   *Desidery*. Kooper suggests a neologism: "it is a good example of what a skilled rhetorician can do: by using this self-coined word he can 'hide' his intentions behind a facade of completely diaphanous material" ("Slack Water Poetry," p.

487). However, the *OED* cites the OF *desiderie* from the L *desiderium*, "longing" or "desire."

Triewe Love. I have added capitals here and at lines 92 and 175. Both the lover and the lady appear to refer to a personified abstraction.

89 *Of mannys copulacioun the verray exemplary.* The lover's frank, if not crude, avowal of his sexual intentions is somewhat surprising given his earlier circumlocutions.

This may be one of the first uses of the term *copulacioun* in its modern sense. Kooper notes that although according to the *OED* this word is not used in the sexual sense until 1483, "ever since Alanus de Insulis's *De planctu Naturae* grammatical terms had been known to have sexual overtones" ("Slack Water Poetry," p. 487).

99–105 The so-called catalogue of worthies is common; Green cites the allusions in this stanza as an example of the "pretentious classical and biblical name-dropping" common to the second rhetoric tradition ("*Craft of Lovers*," p. 107). *Tullius* (line 99) is the common medieval name for Marcus Tullius Cicero; the Old Testament Absalon (line 102) was a conventional example of male beauty.

103 *Jobis.* Job is usually invoked as an emblem of patience rather than wealth. Kooper notes that Job's riches "are emphasized especially in texts that stem from folk-tale versions of his life. . . . The confusion in HA [which reads "robis"] is more easily understood if we bear in mind that the version of Job's life best known to medieval man was the one contained in the Office for the Dead" ("Slack Water Poetry," pp. 487–88).

118 *Grene flowryng age and manly countenaunce.* This can be taken in two senses. On the one hand it appears to be the conventional *carpe diem* argument: green age — that is, pale or sickly — and the concomitant manly (not feminine) features cause women to reconsider appropriate sexual behavior. However, the line may also suggest that in the vital prime of their age, which brings a mature attitude, women more wisely weigh (i.e., favorably consider) a suitor's case. Kooper suggests a somewhat different reading: "In spite of [the warnings of] Dame Prudence, desire for worldly concupiscence [or 'their lusty age' and men's attractive appearance] will occupy ladies' thoughts" ("Slack Water Poetry," p. 488).

127–33 This stanza and lines 169–75 are incorporated into *O Merciful and O Mercyable.*

131 *knyt the knot of excersise.* Playing on the term "losed" (loosened) in line 127, the lover suggests that she end this "exercise," in the sense of either a trial or a ritual. There might well be sexual implications to the suggestion as well.

132–33 *Both lok and key . . . emprinte.* This image has possible sexual overtones and brings to mind the "clyket" and "wyket" of Chaucer's Merchant's Tale (*CT* IV[E] 2045–46).

139 Green notes that here the lady "presumably means the dangers of *male bouche* and the loss of her good reputation" ("*Craft of Lovers*," p. 120).

155   *Phebus*. Phoebus, or Apollo, the sun god; also, appropriately, the genius of poetry.

159   *fifty and nine*. The discrepancy in dates found in HA (1459) and T (1458) has not been satisfactorily explained and may simply be an early mechanical error (confusing *viiii* and *viii*), although both H and A do use the form *ix*. In T, Stow adds in the margin, "Chaucer died 1400" and, believing the poem to be Chaucerian, indulges in some conscious variation of his own and changes the date to 1348 in his 1561 print of the poem.

160   *prepotent princess*. Moore suggests that this refers to Venus. Kooper notes that the term is also applied to the Virgin Mary "and thus the poet keeps up the fiction of decency to the very end" ("Slack Water Poetry," p. 489).

162 ff.   The final three stanzas do not appear in T. Since lines 169–75 also appear in *O Merciful and O Mercyable*, it is quite likely that the envoy is part of the original text.

169–75   Note the juridical language in this stanza. *Distrayned*: "To constrain or force (a person) by the seizure and detention of a chattel or thing, to perform some obligation" (*OED*); *maynprise*: A legalistic term; the action of securing the release of a prisoner by becoming surety for his appearance in court (*MED*).

176   *Salamon*. Solomon, known for his wisdom but, in the popular imagination, also for his predilection for amorous dalliance. See 3 Kings 11 where Solomon is said to have had seven hundred wives and three hundred concubines.

177   *sang in his trace*. *Trace*, a series of steps in dancing; a measure; a dance (*OED*). The metaphor suggests active and intimate involvement in the "dance" of love; compare *O Merciful and O Mercyable*: "For in thys case came I never, or now, / In loves daunce so fer in the trace" (lines 43–44).

180   *Quia amore langueo*. "I am faint with love" (Canticle of Canticles 2:5, 5:8). This popular refrain is also found in *Quia Amore Langueo* (*In a Valley of the Restless Mind*) and *In a Tabernacle of a Tower*; see Fein, ed., *Moral Love Songs and Laments*.

181   *joy ye*. Kooper ("Slack Water Poetry," p. 489) suggests *joy* is a variant of *joinen* (to fasten or unite) and translates the final sentence as, "Come on, my dear spouse, join me / Unite yourself with me [and say] . . ." However, *joien* (to enjoy, delight, take pleasure in) is another possibility.

TEXTUAL NOTES TO *THE CRAFT OF LOVERS*

ABBREVIATIONS: see p. 63.

1	*To moralise.* T: *Moralyse.*
	these. T: *theyr.*
2	*argument.* T: *argumentes* (plural also in lines 4 and 5).
3	*ben.* T: *be foundyn.*
5	*These.* T: *Thus.*
6	*can.* T: *they can.*
8	*list.* T: *lyst unto*; A: *list to.*
9	*loves lordshippe.* H: *lovers lordshippe*; T: *loves lordshippes.*
12	*that the maker be nat.* H: *that the maker be*; T: *the maker that he be.*
14	*spirites.* H: *spirit.*
15	*in.* T: *your.*
18	*to.* H: *and.*
	myn infirmynat langoures. T: *sores langorous*; A: *myn infirmatyf langoures.*
19	*amours.* T: *amerous.*
23	*eke.* A omits.
26	*curiously your eloquence.* T: *gloryously glad langage.*
28	*or than.* T: *for drede or.*
29	*the.* H omits.
30–31	I have transposed the second half of each line in order to keep the rhyme scheme consistent.
31	*of.* T: *with.*
32	*beauté.* A: *bounté.*
	or. T: *O.*
34	*in.* T: *your lovely.*
35	*Wherfor ye do.* T: *Ye.*
36	*suche demonstracioun.* T: *proclamacion.*
38	*and.* H omits.
39	*cogitaciouns.* T: *thought.*
40	*distresse.* T: *febylnes.*
42	*for drede that.* T: *of drede or.*
43	*myn.* H: *my.*
44	*lady.* T: *my lady.*
46	*nat disdayne.* T: *dedeyne.*
	that. A omits.
49	*your.* T omits.

50	*that ye.* T: *ye do.*
51	*maketh.* A: *maketh thus.*; T: *maketh hys.*
	glosed. T omits.
52	*briefly.* T omits.
53	*right.* T omits.
56	*in lesse that.* T: *for drede syr or.*
57	*in substaunce.* T: *and countenaunce.*
58	*to enclyne.* T: *enclyne.*
	yow. A: *youre.*
59	*wommanly.* T: *glorious.*
60	*spirit.* T: *spirytes.*
62	*suppliaunt.* T: *servaunt.*
63	*ones.* T omits.
67	*O Vulcanus.* T: *Of womens*; H: *Of vlcanus*; A: *Of.*
	erbe. A: *anerbe*
68	*helth.* H: *help*; T: *Remember man what chaunge ys perylouse.*
69	*the virgynal.* T: *virgines.*
70	*lesse that ye.* T: *or thow.*
72	*cast in mournyng.* T: *castyng mornyng.*
73	*whiche sittith.* T: *Jhesu sittyng.*
74	*conveyeth.* T, A: *convert.*
	this lady yeng. T: *my swete thyng.*
76	*youre.* A: *thy.*
78	*Me semes by your.* T: *Mesemeth by.*
80	*mekely.* A: *meke.*
	make. H: *may.*
81	*craftes.* T: *craft.*
83	*please shuld.* H: *please*; T: *shuld be to.*
84	T: *Wherfore I wyll be ware or I be shent.*
85	*O.* T omits.
86	*most is.* T: *ys most.*
87	*yow.* H, A: *my.*
	certificacioun. H, A: *trewe certificacioun.*
88	*Desidery.* H: *desiderary.*
90	*servaunts.* H: *servauaunts.*
91	*Wherfor I must be registred in your.* T: *I must be chyef callyd to.*
92	*yeeres grete excesse.* T: *of yeres gret processe.*
93	*hym never.* T: *never love.*
94	*be.* H: *by.*
96	*in som.* T: *and som men.*
97	*by avisement.* H: *bavisement*; A: *be avisement.*
98	*also.* T: *ever.*
	in lesse. T: *for drede.*
99	*of.* T omits.
101	*Salamons sapience.* H: *Salamon his sapience*; T: *Salamons prudence.*
103	*Jobis.* A, H: *robis.*
105	*wold.* T: *shuld.*

	I. H omits.
106	*it.* T: *yef that.*
107	*to.* A, T: *unto.*
108	*worldly.* T omits.
110	*man.* H: *mannes.*
112	*and ye shul nat.* T: *or drede syr ye.*
114	*desire.* A: *the desire.*
119	*hem.* T: *hit.*
120	*answers so benyngne.* T: *answere so notable.*
123	*wold be.* T: *wold fayne be.*
125	*virgyns.* H: *vyrgynite.*
126	*stonde in feere lesse that.* T: *am aferde or.*
	lesse. H: *lasse.*
127	*lovers.* T: *love.*
130	*cordial.* T: *amyable.*
133	*Wherfor.* T omits.
	me. T: *my love.*
134	*Of.* T: *O.*
135	*hert.* T: *hertes.*
138	*me.* T omits.
139	*froward.* T: *fraude.*
140	*my virgynite were.* T: *maydenhode shuld be.*
142	*stones.* H: *stone.*
143	*of comparison.* A: *comparisound.*
144	*Of al creatures.* T: *Above all creature.*
146	*resemblaunce.* T: *dissemblaunce.*
147	*fynally registre and take me in.* T: *graciously take me to.*
148	*manly.* T: *womanly.*
152	*shal.* T: *shall endure.*
153	*This confideracy.* T: *The federasy.*
	by. T: *wyth.*
155	*first.* T: *fresshe*
	his. T omits.
157	*dispute.* T: *profer.*
158	*of God.* T: *our lord.*
159	*fifty and nine.* T: *xl and viii.*
161	*of this terestry vale the.* T: *hem thy Region and.*
162 ff.	T omits.
164	*loke ye.* A omits.
165	*thens.* H: *thense.*
176	*in loves.* A: *my lovers.*
179	*am.* A: *all be.*
181	*my.* A omits.

John Lydgate, The Floure of Curtesye

1	In Feverier, whan the frosty moone	*February*
	Was horned, ful of Phebus firy lyght,	*crescent-shaped*
	And that she gan to reyse her streames sone,	*rays soon*
	Saynt Valentyne, upon thy blisful nyght	
5	Of dutie whan glad is every wight,	*person*
	And foules chese, to voyde her olde sorowe,	*birds choose, to relieve their*
	Everyche his make, upon the next morowe,	*Each; mate*
	The same tyme, I herde a larke synge	
	Ful lustely, agayne the morowe gray:	*anticipating; morning*
10	"Awake, ye lovers, out of your slombringe,	
	This glad morowe, in al the haste ye may!	
	Some observaunce dothe unto this day,	
	Your choyse agen of herte to renewe,	
	In confyrmyng forever to be trewe.	
15	"And ye that be, of chosyng, at your large	
	This lusty day, by custome of nature,	
	Take upon you the blisful holy charge	
	To serve love, whyle your lyfe may dure,	*last*
	With herte, body, and al your besy cure,	*diligent attention*
20	Forevermore, as Venus and Cipride	
	For you disposeth, and the god Cupyde.	*arrange*
	"For joye owe we playnly to obey	*ought*
	Unto this lordes mighty ordynaunce,	
	And, mercylesse, rather forto dye,	*without mercy*
25	Than ever in you be founden varyaunce;	
	And though your lyfe be medled with grevaunce,	*infused*
	And, at your herte, closed be your wounde,	*healed*
	Beth alway one, there as ye are bounde."	
	That whan I had herde and lysted longe,	*listened*
30	With devoute herte, the lusty melodye	
	Of this hevenly comfortable songe,	*comforting*
	So agreable as by ermonye,	*harmony*
	I rose anon, and faste gan me hye	*hasten*

Towarde a grove, and the way take,
35   Foules to sene everyche chose his make.   *each; mate*

And yet I was ful thursty in languisshyng;
Myn ague was so fervent in his hete,   *fever [of lovesickness]*
Whan Aurora, for drery complaynyng,   *Dawn*
Can distyl her chrystal teeres wete   *Began to*
40   Upon the soyle with sylver dewe so swete;
For she durste, for shame, not apere   *dared*
Under the lyght of Phebus beames clere.

And so, for anguysshe of my paynes kene,   *sharp pains*
And for constraynte of my sighes sore,
45   I set me downe under a laurer grene   *laurel*
Ful pitously; and alway more and more,
As I behelde into the holtes hore,   *dark grove*
I gan complayne myn inwarde deedly smerte,   *began; pain*
That aye so sore crampisshed myn herte.   *cramped*

50   And whyle that I, in my drery payne
Sate and behelde, aboute on every tre
The foules sytte, alway twayne and twayne,   *always two by two*
Than thought I thus: "Alas, what may this be,
That every foule hath his lyberté
55   Frely to chose, after his desyre,
Everyche his make thus, fro yere to yere?   *Each; mate*

"The sely wrenne, the tytemose also,   *insignificant; titmouse*
The lytel redbrest, have free election   *robin; free choice*
To flyen yfere and togyther go   *together (in company); together*
60   Where as hem lyst, aboute envyron,   *it pleases them, all around*
As they of kynde have inclynacion,   *nature; instinct*
And as Nature, empresse and gyde   *guide*
Of every thyng, lyst to provyde.   *chooses*

But man alone, alas, the harde stounde!   *condition*
65   Ful cruelly, by kyndes ordynaunce,   *nature's*
Constrayned is, and by statute bounde
And debarred, from al suche plesaunce.
What meneth this? What is this purveyaunce   *providence*
Of God above, agayne al right of kynde,   *law of nature*
70   Without cause, so narowe man to bynde?

"Thus may I sene, and playne, alas!   *say, and lament*
My woful houre and my disaventure,   *misfortune*
That doulfully stonde in the same caas   *miserably stand*
So ferre behynde from al helth and cure.   *far*

75 My wounde abydeth lyke a sursanure;   *waits; superficially healed wound*
 For me fortune so felly lyste dispose,   *cruelly chooses*
 My harme is hyd, that I dare not disclose.

 "For I my herte have set in suche a place
 Where I am never lykely forto spede,   *succeed*
80 So ferre I am hyndred from her grace
 That, save Daunger, I have none other mede;   *except for Aloofness; reward*
 And thus, alas, I not who shal me rede,   *do not know; advise*
 Ne for myne helpe shape remedye,
 For Male Bouche, and for false Envye.   *Wicked Tongue*

85 "The whiche twayne aye stondeth in my wey
 Malyciously, and false Suspection   *Suspicion*
 Is very cause also that I dey,   *die*
 Gynnyng and rote of my distruction,   *The beginning and root*
 So that I fele, in conclusyon,
90 With her traynes that they wol me shende   *their tricks; [so] rob (deny)*
 Of my labour, that dethe mote make an ende.   *might*

 "Yet or I dye, with herte, wyl, and thought,   *before*
 To God of Love this avowe I make: *vow*
 As I best can, howe dere that it be bought,   *however dearly*
95 Where so it be that I slepe or wake,
 Whyle Boreas dothe the leaves shake,   *the North Wind*
 As I have heyght plainly, tyl I sterve,   *promised; die*
 For wel or wo, that I shal her serve.

 "And for her sake, nowe this holy tyme,
100 Saynt Valentyne, somwhat shal I write;
 Although so be that I cannot ryme,
 Nor curyously by no crafte endyte,   *compose [a poem]*
 Yet lever I have that she put the wyte   *I would rather; blame*
 In unconnyng than in neglygence,   *ignorance*
105 Whatever I saye of her excellence.

 "Whatever I say, it is of duté,   *courtesy*
 In sothfastnesse, and no presumpcion;
 This I ensure to you that shal it se,
 That it is al under correction,
110 What I reherce in commendacion
 Of her, that I shal to you, as blyve,   *at once*
 So as I can, her vertues here discryve.

 "Ryght by example as the somer sonne
 Passeth the sterre with his beames shene,   *bright*
115 And Lucyfer, amonge the skyes donne,   *the morning star; dark*

A-morowe sheweth to voyde nyghtes tene,   *In the morning; affliction*
So verily, withouten any wene,   *truly; doubt*
My lady passeth, whoso taketh hede,
Al tho alyve, to speke of womanhede.   *those*

120   "And as the ruby hath the soveraynté
Of ryche stones and the regalye,   *pre-eminence*
And the rose of swetenesse and beauté
Of fresshe floures, without any lye,
Ryght so, in sothe, with her goodly eye,
125   She passeth al in bountie and fayrenesse,   *benevolence*
Of maner eke, and of gentylnesse.   *manners*

"For she is bothe the fayrest and the beste,
To reken al, in very sothfastnesse,   *All in all; truthfulness*
For every vertue is in her at reste;   *fixed*
130   And furthermore, to speke of stedfastnesse,
She is the rote, and of semelynesse   *graciousness*
The very myrrour, and of governaunce,
To al example, withouten varyaunce.

"Of porte benygne, and wonder glad of chere,   *deportment*
135   Havyng evermore her trewe advertence   *attention*
Alway to reason, so that her desyre
Is brideled aye by wytte and provydence;   *reason; discretion*
Thereto of wytte and of hye prudence
She is the welle, aye devoyde of pride,
140   That unto vertue her selven is the gyde.

"And over this, in her dalyaunce   *social interactions*
Lowly she is, discrete and secree,   *Gracious*
And goodly gladde by attemperaunce,   *temperament*
That every wight, of hygh and lowe degré,
145   Are glad in herte with her forto be;
So that, shortly, if I shal not lye,
She named is The Floure of Curtesye.

"And there to speke of femynyté,
The leste mannysshe in comparyson,   *mannish (masculine)*
150   Goodly abasshed, havyng aye pyté   *Courteously humble*
Of hem that ben in trybulacion;
For she alone is consolacion
To al that arne in mischefe and in nede,
To comforte hem of her womanhede.

155   "And aye in vertue is her besy charge,   *attentive care*
Sadde and demure, and but of wordes fewe;

	Dredful also of tonges that ben large,	*unrestrained (untruthful)*
	Eschewyng aye hem that lysten to hewe	*desire; strike*
	Above her heed, her wordes for to shewe;	*reveal*
160	Dishonestly to speke of any wight —	
	She deedly hateth of hem to have a syght.	

"The herte of whom so honest is and clene,
And her entent so faythful and entere   *sincere*
That she ne may, for al the worlde, sustene
165 To suffre her eeres any worde to here
Of frende nor foe, neyther ferre ne nere,
Amysse resowning that hynder shulde his name;[1]
And if she do, she wexeth reed for shame.   *waxes red*

"So trewely in menyng she is in-sette,   *purpose; set*
170 Without chaungyng or any doublenesse,
For bountie and beautie are together knette   *virtue; joined*
In her persone, under faythfulnesse;
For voyde she is of newfanglenesse,   *fickleness*
In herte aye one, forever to persever
175 There she is sette, and never to dissever.   *fall away*

"I am to rude her vertues everychone
Connyngly to discryve and write;
For wel ye wote, colour have I none,   *know; literary skill*
Lyke her discrecion craftely to endyte,   *describe*
180 For what I say, al it is to lyte;   *too little*
Wherfore to you thus I me excuse,
That I aqueynted am not with no muse.

"By rethorike my style to governe
In her preise and commendacion,
185 I am to blynde so hylye to discerne   *carefully*
Of her goodnesse to make discrypcion,
Save thus I say, in conclusyon,
If that I shal shortly her commende,
In her is naught that Nature can amende.   *improve upon*

190 "For good she is, lyke to Polycene,
And in fayrenesse to the quene Helayne,
Stedfast of herte, as was Dorigene,
And wyfely trouthe, if I shal not fayne,   *lie*
In constaunce eke and faythe, she may attayne

---

[1] *Wrongly conveying [an impression] that should damage his name*

195   To Cleopatre, and therto as secree   *discreet*
       As was of Troye the whyte Antygoné.

       "As Hester meke, lyke Judith of prudence,
       Kynde as Alcest or Marcia Catoun,
       And to Grisylde lyke in pacience,
200   And Ariadné of discrecioun,
       And to Lucrece, that was of Rome toun,
       She may be lykened as for honesté,
       And for her faythe, unto Penelopé.   *faithfulness*

       "To fayre Phyllis and to Hipsyphilee,
205   For innocence and for womanhede,
       For semelynesse unto Canacé;   *comeliness*
       And over this, to speke of goodlyhede,   *excellence*
       She passeth al that I can of rede,
       For worde and dede, that she naught ne fal,
210   Acorde in vertue, and her werkes al.

       "For though that Dydo with wytte sage   *mature judgment*
       Was in her tyme stedfast to Enee,
       Of hastynesse yet she dyd outrage,   *From*
       And so for Jason dyd also Medee;
215   But my lady is so avysee   *prudent*
       That, bountie and beautie bothe in her demeyne,   *possession*
       She maketh bountie alway soverayne.   *virtue*

       "This is to meane, bountie gothe afore,
       Lad by prudence, and hath the soveraynté,
220   And beautie foloweth, ruled by her lore,   *instruction*
       That she ne fende her in no degré;   *does not offend*
       So that, in one, this goodly fresshe fre,
       Surmountyng al, withouten any were,   *without doubt*
       Is good and fayre in one persone yfere.   *together*

225   "And though that I, for very ignoraunce,
       Ne may discryve her vertues by and by,   *one after another*
       Yet on this day, for a remembraunce,   *memento*
       Onely supported under her mercy,
       With quakyng honde, I shal ful humbly
230   To her hynesse, my rudenesse forto quyte,   *exonerate*
       A lytel balade here byneth endyte,

       "Ever as I can supprise in myn herte,   *endeavor*
       Alway with feare, betwyxt drede and shame,
       Leste out of lose any worde asterte   *loosely; slip out*
235   In this metre, to make it seme lame;

Chaucer is deed, that had suche a name   *dead*
Of fayre makyng, that was, without wene,   *doubt*
Fayrest in our tonge, as the laurer grene.

"We may assay forto countrefete
240 His gay style, but it wyl not be!
The welle is drie with the lycoure swete,
Bothe of Clye and of Caliopé;
And, first of al, I wol excuse me
To her that is grounde of goodlyhede,
245 And thus I say untyl her womanhede: *unto*

BALADE SYMPLE

"'With al my might and my best entent,
With al the faythe that mighty God of kynde
Me gave syth he me soule and knowyng sent,   *gave since*
I chese, and to this bonde ever I me bynde,
250 To love you best whyle I have lyfe and mynde.
Thus herde I foules in the daunynge   *dawn*
Upon the day of Saynte Valentyne synge.

"'Yet chese I, at the begynnyng, in this entent,
To love you, though I no mercy fynde,
255 And if you lyste I dyed, I wolde assent,
As ever twynne I quicke out of this lynde;   *depart; tree*
Suffyseth me to sene your fethers ynde.   *indigo (blue)*
Thus herde I foules in the mornynge
Upon the daye of Saynte Valentyne synge.

260 "'And over this, myne hertes luste to bente,   *direct*
In honour onely of the wodde-bynde,   *woodbine*
Holy I geve, never to repente   *give*
In joye or wo, where so that I wynde   *go*
Tofore Cupyde, with his eyen blynde.   *Before*
265 The foules al, whan Tytan dyd springe,   *the Sun*
With devoute hert, me thought I herde synge.'"

LENVOYE

Princesse of beautie, to you I represent
This symple dyté, rude as in makynge,   *poem*
Of herte and wyl faythful in myn entent,
270 Lyke as this day foules herde I synge.

Here endeth the Floure of Curtesy.

2	*Phebus*. Phoebus (Apollo); the sun.
4–7	*Saynt Valentyne . . . Everyche his make*. Lydgate is almost certainly situating himself in relation to Chaucer's *Parliament of Fowls*, lines 309–10: "Seynt Valentynes day, / Whan every foul cometh there to chese his make."
20	*Cipride*. "Cypriot," another name for Venus derived from Cyprus, a center for Venusian worship. The "doubling" of Venus here perhaps derives from a misunderstanding of Chaucer's *Parliament of Fowls*, lines 260–79, where the goddess is first called "Venus" (line 261) when seen, then called "Cypride" in a later reference (line 277).
27	*closed*. Thynne: *closet*.
33–35	*faste gan me hye . . . to sene everyche chose his make*. The narrator's eagerness to see nature in operation echoes the dreamer's eagerness in Chaucer's *Parliament of Fowls* and *Legend of Good Women* to see and hear the birds choose their mates and see the flowers open.
45	*laurer grene*. A tree for poets and lovers, where Daphne, Apollo's first love, was preserved against the eager god's assault by being turned into a laurel tree. Feeling her heart beating still beneath the bark, Apollo even so still loved her and made the laurel his sacred tree as the leaves of the laurel crown perpetually proclaim her beauty (see Ovid's *Metamorphoses* 1.452–567).
49	*crampisshed*. Thynne: *crampessh at*. Both MacCracken and Skeat emend Thynne's reading.
84	*Male Bouche*. An allegorical figure, in English known as Wicked Tongue or Foul Mouth (i.e., slander or gossip); this figure, as well as "Daunger" (line 81) and *Envye* (line 84), all representing impediments to successful courtship, are originally found in *The Romance of the Rose*.
96	*shake*. Thynne: *slake*.
142	*secree*. So Skeat. Thynne reads "wyse"; MacCracken supplies "fre."
157	*tonges that ben large*. Cp. *Troilus and Criseyde* 5.804, where Diomede is said by some to be "of tonge large" (i.e., deceitful, dishonest). See *Floure of Curtesye*, line 160.
158	*hem that lysten to hewe*. Skeat (*Chaucerian*, p. 509) notes an allusion to the proverb, "He that hews above his head, the chip falls in his eye," a warning to men who attack their betters. See Whiting C235 and Tilley C357.

188   *her commende*. Thynne: *commende*.

190ff.   A very similar list of exemplary female worthies is found in Lydgate's *A Valentine to Her that Excelleth All* (*IMEV* 3065), though both seem mainly to be echoing the dreamer's spontaneous song when he first meets Alceste, who exceeds in beauty Esther, Penelope, Marcia Cato, Adriane, Phyllis, Canace, Dido, Hypsipyle, and others (*LGW* F249–69). See various notes below.

190–96   *Polycene . . . Antygoné*. Polyxena (*Polycene* [line 190]), the daughter of Priam of Troy and, by some accounts, betrothed to Achilles, was sacrificed on Achilles' tomb in order to appease his ghost. See Lydgate, *Troy Book* 4.6640–6893, and Ovid, *Metamorphoses* 13.448–80. Helen of Troy (*Helayne* [line 191]) was, of course, proverbially beautiful. Dorigen (*Dorigene* [line 192]), the heroine of Chaucer's Franklin's Tale, considers suicide when her wifely fidelity is threatened. In Chaucer's version of the legend, in the wake of Anthony's suicide, the despondent Cleopatra (*Cleopatre* [line 195]) throws herself into a snake-pit (*LGW* 580–705). As Skeat notes (*Chaucerian*, p. 509), in Chaucer's *Troilus and Criseyde*, "fresshe Antigone the white" (2.876) is Criseyde's circumspect niece.

195   *secree*. Thynne: *setrone*.

197   *Hester . . . Judith*. In the Old Testament Book of Esther, Esther's meek and humble supplications to her husband, King Assuerus, saved the Israelites from massacre (15:1–19). Her meekness was proverbial; see Lydgate, *A Valentine to Her That Excelleth All* (lines 36–42), and Chaucer, The Merchant's Tale (*CT* IV[E] 1744–45). As described in the Book of Judith, the eponymous heroine beheads Holofernes and helps to deliver the Israelites from the Assyrians. Chaucer regularly lists her, along with Esther, Sarah, Rebecca, and Abigail, as an exemplary figure for wives.

198–99   *Alcest . . . Marcia Catoun . . . Grisylde*. Alceste is the heroine of Chaucer's *Legend of Good Women*, who, "for hire housbonde chees to dye, / And eke to goon to helle, rather than he" (*LGW* F513–14). For the story of Alceste and Admetus see also *Confessio Amantis* 7.1917–43. Marcia Cato is perhaps either the wife of Marcus Cato Uticensis who remained devoted to her husband even after his divorce, or their daughter, who remained faithful to her first love. She is also mentioned by Chaucer (*LGW* F252). Griselda is the patient and obedient heroine of Chaucer's Clerk's Tale.

200–03   *Ariadné . . . Lucrece . . . Penelopé*. Ariadne is deserted on an island after Theseus absconds with her sister (*LGW* 1886–2227, Ovid's *Heroides* 10, *Confessio Amantis* 5.5231–5495). Lucretia commited suicide after being raped by Tarquin (*LGW* 1680–1885, *Confessio Amantis* 7.4754–5130). Penelope is Ulysses' patient and faithful spouse (*Confessio Amantis* 4.146–233, *Heroides* 1).

204–06   *Phyllis . . . Hipsyphilee . . . Canacé*. Phyllis hanged herself after being abandoned by Demophon (*LGW* 2394–2561, *Heroides* 2, *Confessio Amantis* 4.731–878). Jason deserted Hipsyphilee and their two children (*LGW* 1368–1579; *Heroides* 6). Canacee most likely refers to the comely heroine of Chaucer's Squire's Tale.

211–14   *Dydo . . . Medee.* Dido committed suicide after Aeneas departed for Italy (*LGW* 924–1366, *Heroides* 7). Medea, having been spurned by Jason, killed their two children (*Confessio Amantis* 5.3227–4222, *Heroides* 12, *LGW* 1580–1670).

220–21   *And beautie foloweth . . . That she ne fende.* That is, beauty is ruled so completely by virtue that she does not offend or fight virtue in any way.

232   *supprise.* Skeat (*Chaucerian*, p. 510) suggests "undertake, endeavor to do," which the *MED* tentatively accepts.

234   *out of lose.* Skeat (*Chaucerian*, p. 510) suggests the phrase means "out of praise, discreditable," but the phrase appears to mean something closer to "out of turn; loosely." The claim of poetic ineptitude, itself a rhetorical trope, is common both with Lydgate and among many fifteenth-century writers. See Lawton, "Dullness."

236–38   *Chaucer is deed . . . / Of fayre makyng . . . / Fayrest in our tonge, as the laurer grene.* Compare the naming of the death of "Fraunceys Petrak, the lauriat poete" in the Clerk's prologue — "He is now deed" (*CT* IV[E]29–38).

237   *that was.* Thynne: *that.* I have followed Skeat's emendation.

242   *Clye and Caliopé.* Chaucer invokes both Clio (the muse of history) and Calliope (muse of epic poetry) in *Troilus and Criseyde* (2.8 and 3.45).

256   *lynde.* Thynne: *lyne.*

257   *ynde.* Blue is the color of constancy.

261   *wodde-bynde.* Skeat (*Chaucerian*, p. 510) notes that the woodbine "is an emblem of constancy, as it clings to its support."

THE LOVERS' MASS

INTROIBO

1	Wyth all myn hool herte enter,
	Tofore the famous riche auter
	Of the myghty God of Love,
	Whiche that stondeth high above,
5	In the chapel of Cytheron,
	I will, wyth gret devocion,
	Go knele and make sacrifyse,
	Lyke as the custom doth devyse,
	Afor that God preye and wake,
10	Of entent I may be take
	To hys servyse, and there assure,
	As longe as my lyf may dure,
	To contune as I best kan,
	Whil I lyve, to ben hys man.

entire
Before; altar

Venus (Citherea)

keep vigil
taken

last
continue
servant

CONFITEOR

15	I am aknowe and wot ryght well,
	I speke pleynly as I fel,
	Touchynge the grete tendyrnesse
	Of my youthe, and my symplesse,
	Of myn unkonyng and grene age,
20	Wil lete me han noon avantage;
	To serve Love I kan so lyte,
	And yet myn hert doth delyte
	Of hys servauntys forto here,
	By exaumple of hem I myghte lere
25	To folowe the wey of ther servyse,
	Yif I hadde konnyng to devyse,
	That I myght a servant be,
	Amongys other in my degré;
	Havynge ful gret repentaunce
30	That I non erste me gan avaunce
	In Love court, myselfe to offre,
	And my servyse forto profre,

I confess and know
feel
Concerning
simplicity
naiveté
have no
know so little

them; learn

skill

before

	For fer of my tender youthe;	*fear*
	Nouther be Est, nouther by Southe,	*Neither by*
35	Lyst Daunger putte me abake,	
	And Dysdeyn to make wrake,	*discord*
	Wolde hyndre me in myn entente;	
	Of al this thyng I me repente	
	As my conscience kan recorde,	
40	I sey lowly, Myserycorde.	*humbly, Mercy*

MISEREATUR

	By God of Lovys ordynaunce,	
	Folkys that have repentaunce,	
	Sorowful in herte, and nothyng lyght,	
	Whiche ha nat spent ther tyme aryght,	
45	But wastyd yt in ydelnesse,	
	Only for lake of lustynesse,	*vitality*
	In slep, slogardye, and slouthe,	*indolence; sloth*
	Of whom ys pyté and gret routhe;	
	But when they repente hem ageyn	
50	Of al ther tyme spent in veyn,	
	The God of Love thorgh hys myght —	
	Syth that mercy passeth ryght —	
	Ther mot acceptyd be to grace,	*must*
	And pute daunger out of place;	*disdain*
55	This, the wyl of Dame Venus	
	And of hyr bisshop, Genius.	

OFFICIUM

	In honour of the god Cupide,	
	First that he may be my guyde;	
	In worshepe eke of the pryncesse,	*also*
60	Whyche is lady and maystresse:	
	By grace they may for me provyde,	
	Humble of herte, devoyde of pryde,	
	Envye and rancour set asyde,	
	Withoute change or doubilnesse.	
65	In honour of the [god Cupide,]	
	first that he [may be my guyde.]	

	Joye and welfare in every tyde	*at all times*
	Be gove to hem, wherso they byde,	*given; reside*
	And give to hem grace on my dystresse,	
70	To have pyté of ther hyghnesse,	*because of; high rank*
	For in what place I go or ryde.	

In honour [of the god Cupide,]
　　　first that [he may be my guyde.]

KYRIE

Mercy, mercy, contynuely I crye,
75　In gret disjoynt, upon the poynt to deye,　　　　　　　*distress; just about*
　　For that pyté ys unto me contrayre,
　　Daunger my fo, Dysdeyn also, whylk tweye　　　　　　　*which two*
　　Causen myn herte, of mortal smert, dyspeyre,　　　　　*anguish*
　　For she that ys fayrest, ywys, of fayre,
80　Hath gladnesse of my syknesse to pleye,
　　Thus my trouble, double and double, doth repayre.　　　*return*

CHRISTE

　　Repeyreth ay, which, nyght nor day, ne cesseth nought,　*Return always*
　　Now hope, now dred, now pensyfhede, now thought,　　　　*anxiety*
　　As thyse yfere palen myn chere and hewe,　　　　　*together make pale*
85　Yet to hyr grace, ech hour and space, I ha besought;　　*have*
　　Hyr lyst nat here for hyr daunger doth ay renewe[1]
　　Towardys me, for certys, she lyst nat rewe　　　*deserves not [to have] pity*
　　Up on my peyne, and thus my cheyne ys wrought,
　　Which hath me bounde never to be founde untrewe.

KYRIE

90　Untrewe, nay, to se that day, God forbede!
　　Voyde slouthe, kepe my trouthe in dede,　　　　　　　　*Avoid*
　　Eve and morowe, for joye or sorowe, I have behyght,　　*promised*
　　Til I sterve, evere to serve hir womanhede;　　　　　　*die*
　　In erthe lyvynge ther is nothyng maketh me so lyght.　*cheerful*
95　For I shal dye ne but wer hir mercye mor than ryght,
　　Of no decertys, but mercy certys, my journé spede.　　*Of no merit*
　　Adieu al play, thus may I say, I, woful wyght.　　　*Goodbye*

GLORIA IN EXCELSIS

　　Worsshyppe to that lord above
　　That callyd ys the God of Love;
100　Pes to hys servantes everychon,
　　Trewe of herte, stable as ston,
　　　　　That feythful be.

---

[1] *It pleases her not to listen for her aloofness ever increases*

	To hertes trewe of ther corage,	*intention*
	That lyst chaunge for no rage,	*passion*
105	But kep hem in ther hestys stylle	*promises continually*
	In all maner wedris ylle,	*weathers ill (bad)*
	Pes, concord, and unyté.	*unity*
	God send hem sone ther desyrs,	
	And reles of ther hoote fyrs	*release from their hot fires*
110	That brenneth at her herte sore,	*burn*
	And encresseth more and more,	
	This my prayere.	
	And aftyr wynter wyth hys shourys	*showers*
	God send hem counfort of May flourys,	*flowers*
115	After gret wynd and stormys kene,	
	The glade sonne with bemys shene	*bright*
	May appere.	
	To give hem lyght after dyrknesse,	*give them*
	Joye eke after hevynesse,	*also*
120	And after dool and ther wepynge,	*torment*
	To here the somer foulys synge,	*hear; birds*
	God give grace.	
	For ofte sythe man ha seyn	*many times; has seen*
	A ful bryght day after gret reyn,	
125	And tyl the storme be leyd asyde,	
	The herdys under bussh abyde,	*herds*
	And taketh place.	
	After also the dirke nyght,	
	Voyde of the mone and sterre lyght,	*Devoid*
130	And after nyghtys dool and sorowe,	*doleful*
	Folweth ofte a ful glade morowe,	
	Of aventure.	*By chance*
	Now lorde that knowest hertys alle	
	Of lovers that for helpe calle,	
135	On her trouthe of mercy rewe,	
	Namely on swyche as be trewe,	
	Helpe to recure.	*restore*
	Amen.	

THE ORYSON

	Most myghty and most dredful lord,	
140	That knowest hertys fals and trewe,	*Who*
	As wel ther thynkyng as ther word,	
	Bothe of lovers olde and newe,	
	Of pyté and of mercy, rewe	*From; have pity*
	On thy servauntes that be stable,	
145	And make ther joye to renewe,	
	Swich as wyl never be chaungable.	

THE EPYSTEL IN PROSE

From the party of the por plentyf in love, wyth many yers of probacon pro-
fessyd to be trewe, to all the holy fraternite and confrary of the same bretherhede;
and to alle hospytlerys and relygious, nat spottyd nor mad foul wyth no cryme of
150   apostasye, nouthyr notyd nor atteynt with no double face of symulacon, nor con-
streyned countenaunce of ypocrysé: to alle swiche chose chyldre of stabylnesse —
wyth oute variaunce of corage or of herte — joye, elthe, and long prosperyte, wyth
perfeccon of perseveraunce in ther trouthe perpetually t'abyde.

Experyence techeth that pilgrymes and folkes customable to vyage, whan they
155   underfange any long weye wiche that ys laboryous, somwhile of consuetude and
custom they use a maner to reste on ther wey, of entent to wypé and wasshe away
the soot of ther vysages. And sum also usen to ley adoun the hevy fardellys of ther
bake forto alleggen ther wery lemys of her grete berthene. And some outher usen
to gadryn wyne; and some to drynken outher water or wyn of ther botell or goordys
160   to asswage the grete dryhnesse of ther gredy thruste. And somme of hem somwhile
rekne and accounten how myche they ha passyd of ther journe; and sodeynly
tourne ageyn ther bakkys towardys som notable seteys, which they of newe be par-
tyd fro. And therwyth al recorden and remembren hem of cytes, castelles, and
touns which they ha passyd by, and nat forgete hylles, ne valeys, dygne to be put
165   in remembraunce of hyt for a memoryal. Some entytlen hem in smale bookes of
report or in tabylys to callen hem to mynde whan they sene her tyme. And som
ought callen to mynde grete ryvers and smale, and pereylles of the see that they
ha passyd by. And whan they han alle accountyd and ageyn relatyd the partyes
passyd of her journé, of newe they take to hem force, vigour, and strengthe
170   myghtyly, wythoute feyntyse, to performe and manly to acomplysshe the resydue
and the remnaunt of her labour.

147 **plentyf**, plaintiff; **probacon**, proof. 148 **confrary**, confraternity. 149 **hospytlerys**,
members of a religious order that cared for the sick. 150 **nouthyr**, neither; **notyd**, no-
torious, stigmatized; **atteynt**, convicted; **symulacon**, dissimulation. 151 **ypocrysé**, hy-
pocrisy; **chose**, chosen. 152 **elthe**, health. 153 **t'abyde**, to abide. 154 **customable to**,
accustomed to. 155 **underfange**, undertake; **consuetude**, tradition. 157 **fardellys**, packs.
158 **alleggen**, relieve. 159 **gadryn**, acquire; **goordys**, gourds. 160 **thruste**, thirst. 161
rekne, reckon (count); **myche**, much. 162 **seteys**, cities. 164 **dygne**, worthy. 165 **entytlen**,
record. 168 **partyes**, regions. 170 **wythoute feyntyse**, without delay.

And thus I, in semblable wyse, al the tyme of my lyf, from my grene tendre youthe and tyme that I hadde yerys of dyscrecon, beynge, and contynuynge as an errynge pylgrym in the servyse of the myghty and dredful God of Love, how many perylous passages and wayes that I ha passyd by! How ofte, in compleynynge, I have setyn don to wypen away the soot of myn inportable labour, and dronken ever among of my botell and goordes the bytter drynkes of drerynesse and, ofte sythes, assayed to casten adoun the inportable fardel of myn hevy thoughtys. And amongys al this thyngys, lookyd bakward to consydren and sen the fyn and the ende of my worthy bretheren and predecessours in love that ha passyd the same pilgrymage toforn. And ther I ha founden and seyn the grete trouthe of Troylus, perseverant to hys lyves ende, the trewe, stable menyng of Penalope, the clennesse of Polycene, the kyndenesse of Dydo, quen of Cartage, and rad also ful often in my contemplatyf medytacons, *The Holy Legende of Martyrs of Cupydo*, the secre trouthe of Trystram and Ysoude, and the smale gerdouns of woful Palamydes. All thyse, and an hondryd thousand mo, callyd to mynde me semeth amonges all I am on of the most forsake, and ferthest set behynde of grace, and moste hyndred to the mercy of my lady dere, nat wythstondynge the grete party of my pilgrymage that I ha don. But that I shal evere, for lyfe or deth, contynue and persevere, trewe to my lyves ende, besechynge ful lowly to alle yow my brethere unto whom thys lytel epystel ys dyrect, that yt lyke yow of pyté amonge your devout observaunces to han me recomendyd with som especial memorye in your prayers that yet, or I dye, I may sum mercy fynde, or that the God of Love enspyre my ladyes herte, of hys grace, what I endure for hyr sake.

---

172 semblable, similar. **176 inportable**, unbearable. **177 ofte sythes**, often times. **178 fardel**, burden. **179 fyn**, conclusion. **182 menyng**, purpose; **clennesse**, purity. **185 gerdouns**, rewards. **193 enspyre**, inspire.

1–14   *Introibo.* Immediately following the initial sign of the Cross, the priest begins the Latin Mass by saying "Introibo ad altare Dei" ("I will go to the altar of God"), to which the congregation responds "Ad Deum qui laetificat juventutem meam" ("To God who gives joy to my youth"). The *Introibo, Confiteor,* and *Misereatur* are in tetrameter couplets.

15–40   *Confiteor.* The Confession, beginning "Confiteor Deo omnipotenti" ("I confess to Almighty God"). Here, his sin is not only his youth and inexperience but also his tardiness in seeking out Love's court.

41–56   *Misereatur.* The Absolution: "Misereatur vestri omnipotens Deus" ("Almighty God have mercy on you"). Rather than life everlasting, mercy in the form of his lady's grace is hoped for here.

44   *ther.* MS: *hys.* The context seems to require a plural pronoun.

53   *Ther.* MS: *The.* Hammond suggests the emendation I have adopted.

56   *Genius.* The god or force associated with reproduction, regeneration, and natural inclination. Descending ultimately from Alain de Lille's *De planctu naturae* (*The Complaint of Nature*), Genius acts as Nature's priest (and bishop) in *The Roman de la Rose* (lines 16272–20704), and as Venus' priest and the Lover's confessor in John Gower's *Confessio Amantis.*

57–73   *Officium.* The *Officium* (the Introit or entrance hymn) is a roundel, a short poem based on two rhymes in which the opening lines serve as a refrain in the middle and at the end.

65–66   The antiphon (from lines 57–58) is abbreviated here. Hammond notes that "Scribes often write only the first word or two of the repeated lines" (*English Verse,* p. 466).

72–73   The antiphon is abbreviated here. See note to lines 65–66.

74–97   *Kyrie.* The *Kyrie,* composed of three lines which alternate "Kyrie eleison / Christe eleison / Kyrie eleison" ("Lord have mercy / Christ have mercy / Lord have mercy"), is the first invocation after the Introit in the Ordinary of the Mass. Each of the three 8-line stanzas is in pentameter and has double internal assonant rhymes which change with each line. For another parody of the *Kyrie* see *Kyrie, so Kyrie* (also known as the "Kyrie Alison") in *Middle English Lyrics,* ed. Luria and Hoffman, pp. 84–85.

98–138   *Gloria in excelsis.* "Gloria in excelsis Deo" ("Glory to God in the highest"). Tetrameter quatrains with dimeter bob.

124   *A ful bryght day after gret reyn.* Proverbial; see Whiting D41 and Tilley R8.

139–46   *Oryson.* The prayer or "Collect" for the day preceding the Epistle.

144   *thy servauntes that be stable.* In keeping with the blurring of the secular and the religious throughout, the phrase suggests not only those who are steadfast in love but also, in an ecclesiastical sense, those who persevere in monastic life.

147 ff.   *The Epystel in Prose.* The first reading, from either the Old or the New Testament. This Epistle, which compares courtship to a touristic pilgrimage, draws freely from Laurent de Premierfait's French prose translation (c. 1409) of Boccaccio's *De Casibus Virorum Illustrium*, Book 3 (see Hammond, *English Verse*, p. 467). On the "at once commonplace and curiously elusive" motif of the pilgrimage in the Middle Ages, see Dyas, *Pilgrimage*.

          The author omits the rest of the Mass, including, for instance, the Gospel, Homily, Nicene Creed, Offertory, *Sanctus*, and *Agnus Dei*.

181–89   *And ther I . . . that I ha don.* Our amorous pilgrim is indeed in a bad way if he is "on of the most forsake" of this group of exemplary lovers. *The Holy Legende of Martyrs of Cupydo* (i.e., Chaucer's *Legend of Good Women*, which is referred to as "the Seintes Legende of Cupide" in the Introduction to the Man of Law's Tale — *CT* II[B^1]61) demonstrates that faithful love is usually both unrewarded and cruelly abused. Although Penelope's steadfast rejection of her predatory suitors is rewarded with Odysseus' return, in Chaucer's *Troilus and Criseyde*, Criseyde remains in the Greek camp with Diomede despite Troilus' "grete trouthe"; Aeneas abandons Dido despite her "kyndenesse" (Chaucer, *LGW* F924–1367); Polixena (Priam's daughter), sacrificed on Achilles' tomb to appease either his desire or his vengeance, modestly covers her exposed breast as she dies (Ovid, *Metamorphoses* 13.475–82); the "secre trouthe" of Tristram and Isolde causes both the illicit lovers only misery; and Palamides, Isolde's unrequited lover, has few rewards for his faithful service — see Lydgate, *The Complaint of the Black Knight*, lines 330–43 (Symons, ed., *Chaucerian Dream Visions*).

THE ANTIFEMINIST TRADITION

INTRODUCTION

The four antifeminist poems printed here, first introduced to the Chaucer canon in John Stow's 1561 edition of his works, may strike some readers as distinctly un-Chaucerian given the poet's reputation, dating back to the sixteenth century, as "wemenis frend."[1] Yet Chaucer's genuine works do have their fair share of antifeminist sentiments, usually with comic effect: the ironic encomiums to wedded bliss in The Merchant's Tale, the heavily ironic defense of archwives at the end of The Clerk's Tale, Chaunticleer's cynical observations on the efficacy of women's counsel in The Nun's Priest's Tale, and the ambiguous portrayal of the Wife of Bath who, for all her defiant vitality, is nonetheless the textual embodiment of Jerome's wicked wife. However, only one poem today printed as Chaucer's — *Against Women Unconstant* — dips as deeply into the trenchant antifeminist strain as that which is found in these poems that Stow introduced to the canon.

While Carolyn Ives and David Parkinson demonstrate that in the fifteenth century Chaucer does appear to have had some reputation in Scotland as a misogynist authority,[2] Stow's additions (including *Against Women Unconstant*) may have been dictated less by a desire to compile an authorial oeuvre than by his desire to complement Chaucer's image with poetry that was currently fashionable. Indeed, in *The Crooked Rib*, Francis Lee Utley demonstrates the popularity of the "querelle des femmes" in the mid-sixteenth century, calling the Renaissance the "most prolific age of English satire on women" and "a century when satires on women were pouring off the presses in a quantity unimagined in the times of Chaucer or Charlemagne."[3] Although demonstrating that the subject of female perfidy is an "age-old controversy," Utley suggests that contemporary political events, including "the long succession of Henry's queens, the dissolution of the monastic life, the quarrels over the legitimacy of Mary and Elizabeth, and the Statute of the Six Articles (1539), which hampered the reforming tendency by reaffirming the celibacy of the priesthood," sharpened the "perennial taste for satire."[4]

Although to modern readers these antifeminist lyrics may seem to violate a more refined and restrained courtly sensibility, in *Medieval Misogyny and the Invention of Western Romantic Love* R. Howard Bloch suggests that misogyny, by logical necessity, accompanies the idealization of the feminine found in courtly discourse. Bloch demonstrates that the paradoxical

---

[1] Spurgeon, *Five Hundred Years*, 1.72.

[2] See Ives and Parkison, "Scottish Chaucer."

[3] Utley, *Crooked Rib*, pp. 4–5.

[4] Utley, *Crooked Rib*, p. 73.

Western view of women as "Devil's Gateway" and "Bride of Christ" dates back to the asceticism of the early Christian era.[5] Due to a variety of social and cultural factors, including the increasing economic and matrimonial power of women, this dichotomy is revived in the early Middle Ages, and Bloch suggests that the treacherous, duplicitous female is a necessary corollary to the inaccessible, idealized courtly lady.[6] The posturing of the impotent and exasperated lover or spouse could then, as now, be grounded in conviction or experience, but by the late Middle Ages such poems, circulating in secular miscellanies, appear to have become a rhetorical game or exercise. The wimpy, inept, mentally self-castrated male, so prominent in courtly poems, is matched by the virago who beats him, tricks him, and cuckolds him. These poems perhaps provided a corrective to the idealizing rhetoric of courtly discourse, and were intended to be humorous rather than simply vituperative and cantankerous. That is, these poems perhaps represent an aspect of the gamesmanship that John Stevens detects in courtly love lyrics: "One of the delights of the 'fiction' consisted . . . in reacting against it with every possible coarseness and vulgarity."[7] Linda Woodbridge suggests that antifeminist verse in part served as an intellectual game for the practice of rhetoric, and for Elizabeth Clarke this game "is obviously played at an elite level": "Men and, it seems, sometimes women, wishing to establish a reputation for wit at various levels, find plenty of stock in the apothegms about women circulating in the period."[8] Taking a somewhat different approach in her study of early Tudor poetry, Elizabeth Heale reads the "discourse of misogyny" as primarily a male domain, meant to foster "male solidarity": "By strenuously asserting his own masculine trustiness in the face of feminized treachery and betrayal, the courtier could display his own reliability and virtue. In such ways a poetic discourse of misogyny could displace into safer forms the frustrations and resentments of courtly life."[9] But we should also remember the squeamish Absalom in Chaucer's Miller's Tale, who is much more the object of ridicule than Alisoun, as is old Januarie, rather than May, in The Merchant's Tale. The knife of satire has two edges, and so, too, the *querelle des femmes*.

   I Have a Lady and *O Mosy Quince*, both satirical descriptions of a mistress, represent parodies of the courtly panegyric which catalogue a lady's deficiencies rather than her charms. Although Utley describes some of the poems in this genre as "comic valentines," he nonetheless suggests that "the malice of most of these poems comes from the anger of a rebuffed lover."[10] I would suggest, however, that part of the point is the art of the insult; these poems appropriate and invert conventional courtly rhetoric and appreciation depends upon a knowledge of both secular and religious panegyrics, and perhaps "flyttings," insult poems affiliated with the legal profession . Indeed, Utley and Ziolkowski suggest that *I Have a Lady* may be considered a prototype for both Shakespeare's deft treatment of this genre in *Sonnet 130*, "My mistress' eyes are nothing like the sun," and John Donne's *Elegie II: The*

---

[5] Bloch, *Medieval Misogyny*, pp. 65–91.

[6] Bloch, *Medieval Misogyny*, pp. 143–64.

[7] Stevens, *Music and Poetry*, p. 223.

[8] Woodbridge, *Women in the English Renaissance*, p. 44; Clarke, "Anne Southwell," pp. 41–42.

[9] Heale, *Wyatt, Surrey*, p. 48.

[10] Utley, *Crooked Rib*, p. 213.

Anagram.[11] The author of *O Mosy Quince*, inspired perhaps by the proverbial adage that wine, women, honor, and age make men fools — which he incorporates into his poem — depends upon mundane metaphors to describe his "lovely lewde masterasse" (line 22), comparing her not only to old fruit but also, in the last stanza, to an animal that has been slaughtered, smoked, tanned, and turned to leather. This is no flower of courtesy or feminine deportment but the flower of the tanning vat, the "fowlyst of all the nacion" (line 24). Both *O Mosy Quince* and *I Have a Lady* parody conventional antiseptic descriptions of a woman's beauty (bright eyes, radiant skin, snowy breasts, long fingers, slender waist) by describing their mistresses in quite colorful terms: the "Fayre Lady" of *I Have a Lady*, for instance, has skin as smooth as an "oxys tong" (line 21) and the "Mosy Quince" has breasts that are both orange and "satournad" ("sagging" — line 18). Both poems, however, possess a surprising tenderness; despite each lady's ostensible defects, the authors nonetheless betray their affection: the author of *O Mosy Quince* intends to love his lady but "a lytyll" (line 25), but of all women, he loves her best (line 29).

Beware (now attributed to Lydgate) and *Of Theyre Nature* (also called *Balade against Hypocritical Women*), both marked by proverbial lore and pastiche, warn readers of the atavistic deceptiveness, fickleness, and treachery of women. On another level, these poems may reflect what Daniel Javitch calls the courtly "cult of dissimulation";[12] while women are denounced for their duplicitous artifice, such dissembling behavior was nonetheless recognized — and admired — as a necessary strategy for self-promotion and social advancement. *Beware*, which Utley accurately describes as "a skillful use of proverbial libels,"[13] is an especially interesting poem because it appears to have been repeatedly ransacked: its refrain, "Beware therfore; the blynde eteth many a flye," also appears in *Of Theyre Nature* and remained extant throughout the sixteenth century (see Whiting B348 and Tilley B451); and the final stanza (beginning "thogh al the erthe so wan / Were parchemyn smothe" — lines 36–37) is incorporated into *The Remedy of Love* (*IMEV* 3084) and is found as an independent poem (*IMEV* 1409.3) in both Edinburgh, National Library of Scotland MS Advocates' 1.1.6 (the Bannatyne manuscript, where it is marked "Chaucer") and London, British Library MS Additional 17492 (the Devonshire manuscript). *Of Theyre Nature*, inspired, no doubt, by the pessimistic musings in Lydgate's *Pain and Sorrow of Evil Marriage* from which the poet lifts seven lines, *in toto*, for his initial stanza, is somewhat pedestrian; indeed, even the poet himself appears to weary of his misogynist posturing. The poem is saved, however, by the felicitous expansion on the "blind eat many a fly" refrain: "But whether that the blynde ete flessh or fyssh, / I pray God kepe the fly out of my dyssh!" (lines 20–21).

THE TEXTS

O Mosy Quince (*IMEV* 2524) and *Of Theyre Nature* (*IMEV* 2661) are extant only in **T** (Cambridge, Trinity College MS R.3.19, fols. 205v–206r and 156v); *I Have a Lady* (*IMEV* 1300) appears in both T (fols. 205r–205v), and **L** (Leiden University, MS Vossius 9, fol. 110v). For a description of the Leiden manuscript (c. 1470–1500) and a transcript of the

---

[11] Utley, *Crooked Rib*, p. 213; Ziolkowski, "Avatars of Ugliness," p.19.

[12] Javitch, *Poetry and Courtliness*, p. 79.

[13] Utley, *Crooked Rib*, p. 180.

poem, see van Dorsten, "The Leyden 'Lydgate Manuscript,'" pp. 315–25. The L variants are found in the Notes.

Beware (*IMEV* 1944), also known as *Beware of Deceitful Women*, *Against Women*, or *The Blynde Eteth Many a Flye*, is now attributed to Lydgate. The poem, with various alterations, is extant in four manuscript miscellanies: T (fols. 207r–207v), **H** (British Library, MS Harley 2251, fols. 149v–150r), **O** (Cambridge, Trinity College MS O.9.38, fols. 28r–28v), and **R** (Rome College MS English 1405 *olim* 1306, fol. 75v). For a description of R, see Klinefelter, "Newly Discovered," pp. 3–6; and Robbins, "Middle English Diatribe," pp. 131–46. Since the version in R has not yet been published, I have provided a transcription here with the variants contained in the Textual Notes.

I HAVE A LADY (THE DESCRYVYNG OF A FAIR LADY)

1   I have a Lady, whereso she be,   *wherever*
      That seldom ys the soverayn of my thought;
      On whos beawté when I beholde and se,   *beauty*
      Remembryng me how well she ys wrought,   *fashioned*
5   I thanke fortune that to hyr grace me brought,
      So fayre ys she but nothyng angelyke —   *angelic*
      Hyr bewty ys to none other lyke.

      For hardely, and she were made of brasse,   *assuredly, even if*
      Face and all, she hath ynowgh fayrenesse:
10   Hyr eyen byn holow and grene as any grasse,   *sunken*
      And ravynnysshe yelow ys hyr sonny tresse.   *dark blond*
      Thereto she hath of every comlynesse
      Such quantyté gevyn hyr by nature,
      That with the leest she ys of hyr stature.

15   And as a bolt hyr browes byn y-bent,   *arched*
      And byttyl-browyd she ys also withall,   *beetle-browed*
      And of hir wytte as sympyll and innocent
      As ys a chylde that can no good at all.   *knows*
      She ys nat thyk; hyr stature ys but small.
20   Hyr fyngers byn lytyll and nothyng long,
      Hyr skyn ys smothe as any oxys tong.   *ox's tongue*

      Therto she ys so wyse in dalyaunce,   *Also; conversation*
      And besette hyr wordes so womanly,   *employs*
      That hyr to here hit doth me dysplesaunce.   *hear*
25   For that she seyth ys sayde so connyngly,
      That when that there be mo then she and I,   *more*
      I had lever she were of talkyng styll,   *quiet*
      Then that she shuld so goodly speche spyll.

      And slowth noone shall have in her entresse,   *sloth; entry*
30   So dylygent ys she and vertulesse,
      And so besy ay all good to undresse,
      That as a she-ape she ys harmelese,   *innocent*
      And as an hornet meke and pytelesse;

With that she ys so wyse and circumspecte,
35   That prudent noon hyr foly can infecte.   *prudence*

Ys hit nat joy that suche oone of hyr age,
Withyn the boundys of so gret tendyrnesse,
Shuld in her werke be so sad and sage,   *steadfast and wise*
That of the weddyng sawe all the noblesse   *splendor*
40   Of quene Jane, and was tho, as I gesse,   *then*
But of the age of yeres ten and fyve?
I trowe ther ar nat many suche alyve!   *believe*

For as Jhesu my synfull sowle save,
There nys creature in all thys world lyvyng   *is not*
45   Lyke unto hyr that I wold gladly have,
So pleseth myn hert that goodly swete thyng,
Whos sowle in haste unto hys blysse bryng,
That furst hyr formyd to be a creature.
For were she wele, of me, I dyd no cure.   *do not care*

Explicit the dyscryvyng of a fayre lady.

NOTES TO *I HAVE A LADY*

ABBREVIATIONS: see p.103.

1   The subtitle is taken from the explicit in T. Stow calls the poem "A balade pleasaunte" (p. 344r).

4   *wrought*. L: *i wrouht*.

7   *ys*. L: *as*.

11   *yelow*. L: *yyleve*.

15   *And as a bolt hyr browes byn y-bent*. Her brows are arched like an arrow or a bolt for fastening; i.e., her brows are straight, not arched. Arched brows were then, as now, a conventional sign of beauty.

         hyr. T: *hys*.

16   *byttyl-browyd*. Shaggy, prominent brows.

         ys. L omits.

26   *That*. T: *Then*.

30   *vertulesse*. "Lacking the quality of moral excellence; also, lewd, lecherous" (*MED*).

31   *ay all good*. L: *al good ay*.

32   *as a she-ape she ys harmelese*. Although sometimes a byword for a dupe, an ape is also often associated with trickery; therefore, she is not innocent at all.

35   *That*. T: *Than*.

38   *werke*. L: *warkys*.

40   *quene Jane*. Utley (*Crooked Rib*, pp. 147–48) notes that *Jane* refers to Joan of Navarre who was married to Henry IV in 1403 when the subject of the poem was fifteen years old. To suggest that there are "nat many suche alyve" that witnessed that event is a not very subtle way of saying that the fair lady is advanced in years. The allusion also allows editors to date the poem to the middle of the fifteenth century.

42   *ar*. L omits.

44   *There nys creature.* Satirical descriptions of a mistress sometimes close with similar, unusual benedictions. See, for instance, *The Lover's Mocking Reply* (*IMEV* 2437), printed in Robbins, *Secular Lyrics*, p. 220.

48   *be.* L: *ben.*

49   *I dyd.* L: *did I.*

❧ O MOSY QUINCE

O mosy quince, hangyng by your stalke,   *mossy fruit*
The whyche no man dar pluk away ner take,   *nor*
Of all the folk that passe forby or walke,
Your flowres fresshe be fallyn away and shake.   *scattered*
5   I am ryght sory, masteras, for your sake,   *mistress*
Ye seme a thyng that all men have forgotyn;
Ye be so rype ye wex almost rotyn.   *grow*

Wyne, women, worshyp, unweldy age,   *honor, enfeebled*
Make men to fonne for lak in theyr resons: *act foolishly*
10   Elde causeth dulnesse and dotage,   *senility*
And worshyp, chaunge of condicions;
Excesse of wyne blyndeth theyre dyscrecions,
And all bookes that poetes made and radde   *read*
Seyen women most make men madde!   *Say*

15   Youre ugly chere deynous and froward,   *scornful and bellicose*
Youre grene eyen frownyng and nat glad,   *eyes*
Yowre chekes enbolned lyke a melow costard,   *swollen; ripe apple*
Colour of orenge your brestys satournad,   *sagging*
Gylt, opon warantyse, the colour wyll nat fade;   *Painted, without fail*
20   Bawsyn-buttockyd, belyed lyke a tonne,   *Badger-assed, bellied; cask*
Men cry, "Seynt Barbara!" at lowsyng of your gonne.   *loosening; gown (gun or organ)*

My lovely lewde masterasse, take consideracion,
I am so sorowfull there as ye be absent;
The flowre of the barkfate, the fowlyst of all the nacion —   *tanning vat*
25   To love yow but a lytyll is myne entent.
The swert hath y-swent yow, the smoke hath yow shent;   *flame; struck; spoiled*
I trowe ye have be layde opon som kylne to dry.   *kiln*
Ye do me so moche worshyp there as ye be present;
Of all wemen I love yow best. A thowsand tymes fy!

ABBREVIATIONS: see p. 103.

1	*quince*. A yellow, acidic, pear-shaped fruit, used for preserves.
8–14	This inserted proverbial digression (*IMEV* 4230), sometimes known as *Four Things That Make a Man a Fool* and *Saying of Dan John*, is usually traced back to Lydgate. The popular rhyme royal stanza is extant in various forms, some lacking the antifeminist sting and counseling instead that one practice humility (see *Four Things That Make a Man a Fool* and *Yet of the Same*). Stow omits this stanza from his 1561 print of the poem.
16	*grene eyen*. Pale, colorless, or livid; the color green is often associated with inconstancy and envy.
17	*enbolned*. T: *enbonyd*. I have emended with Stow's correction, the past participle of *enbolnen*, to swell (with anger or pride); i.e., her cheeks are puffy or swollen like a ripe apple.
19	*gylt*. Covered with a thin coating of gold (and thus concealing defects).
	opon warantyse. For certain, without fail.
20	*bawsyn-buttockyd*. The "bawsyn" is a badger, but here the term implies fat or broad.
21	*Seynt Barbara*. Patron saint in times of danger from thunderstorms and fire and protector of artillery men, miners, firework makers, architects, builders. Therefore, an explosive declaration. Person (*Cambridge Middle English Lyrics*, p. 79) suggests a possible play on gown/gun (or, possibly, fart).
22	*lewde*. The adjective has several connotations, none complimentary: foolish, common, uneducated, unrefined, idle, dishonest, and lascivious.
24	*flowre of the barkfate*. A barkfat is a vat for tanning; therefore, odiferous and dried up or crusty. Note the unusual tanning metaphors throughout this stanza through which he compares his lady to a hide turned into leather.
25	*is*. T: *hit*. Stow's correction.

John Lydgate, Beware (The Blynde Eteth Many a Flye)

<table>
<tr><td>1</td><td>Loke wel aboute, ye that lovers bee,</td><td></td></tr>
<tr><td></td><td>Let not youre lustes lede you to dotage.</td><td>desires; folly</td></tr>
<tr><td></td><td>Be not anamoured on al thing that ye see:</td><td></td></tr>
<tr><td></td><td>Sampson the fort and Salomon the sage,</td><td>strong; wise</td></tr>
<tr><td>5</td><td>Deceyved were for al thaire grete courage.</td><td>valor</td></tr>
<tr><td></td><td>Men deeme it right that they see at eye,</td><td></td></tr>
<tr><td></td><td>But ever beware: the blynde eteth many a flie!</td><td>eat; fly</td></tr>
<tr><td></td><td></td><td></td></tr>
<tr><td></td><td>I meen in women, for all thaire cheres queynt,</td><td>attractive looks</td></tr>
<tr><td></td><td>Trust not to moche; thaire trouthe is but geson.</td><td>scarce</td></tr>
<tr><td>10</td><td>The fairest outward wel can they peynt;</td><td></td></tr>
<tr><td></td><td>Thayre stedfastnesse endureth but a seson.</td><td></td></tr>
<tr><td></td><td>They fayne frendlynes and worchen treson,</td><td>work</td></tr>
<tr><td></td><td>And sith thay be chaungeable naturally,</td><td></td></tr>
<tr><td></td><td>Beware, therfore: the blynde eteth many a flye.</td><td></td></tr>
<tr><td></td><td></td><td></td></tr>
<tr><td>15</td><td>Thogh all this world doo his besy cure</td><td>careful effort</td></tr>
<tr><td></td><td>To make women stande in stablenesse,</td><td></td></tr>
<tr><td></td><td>It may not be, it is ageyne nature:</td><td>against</td></tr>
<tr><td></td><td>The world is doo whan thay lak doublenesse.</td><td></td></tr>
<tr><td></td><td>They lagh and love not, this know men expresse;</td><td></td></tr>
<tr><td>20</td><td>In theyme to trust, it is but fantasie.</td><td>delusion</td></tr>
<tr><td></td><td>Therfore, beware: the blynde eteth many a flie.</td><td></td></tr>
<tr><td></td><td></td><td></td></tr>
<tr><td></td><td>What wight on lyve that trusteth on thaire cheres,</td><td>person; faces</td></tr>
<tr><td></td><td>Shal have at last his guerdon and his mede.</td><td>reward; compensation</td></tr>
<tr><td></td><td>They shave nerer than doth rasour or sheres;</td><td>razor or scissors</td></tr>
<tr><td>25</td><td>Al is not gold that shineth, men take hede!</td><td></td></tr>
<tr><td></td><td>Thaire galle is hid under a sugred wede;</td><td>bile; garment</td></tr>
<tr><td></td><td>It is ful queynte thaire fantasies to aspie.</td><td>clever; lies; detect</td></tr>
<tr><td></td><td>Beware, therfore: the blynde eteth many a flye.</td><td></td></tr>
<tr><td></td><td></td><td></td></tr>
<tr><td></td><td>Women of kynde have condicions thre:</td><td>by nature</td></tr>
<tr><td>30</td><td>The first is thay be full of deceite;</td><td></td></tr>
<tr><td></td><td>To spynne also is thaire propreté;</td><td>dissemble</td></tr>
<tr><td></td><td>And women have a wonderful conceite:</td><td></td></tr>
<tr><td></td><td>They wepen oft, and all is but a sleight;</td><td>trick</td></tr>
</table>

And whan hem lust, the teere is in the eye.   *desire*
35   Therfore, beware: the blynde eteth many a flye.

In sothe to sey, thogh al the erthe so wan   *ashen*
Were parchemyn smothe, white, and scribable,   *parchment*
And the grete see, called occian,   *ocean*
Were turned ink, blacker than is sable,
40   Eche stikk a penne, ech man a scrivener able,   *scribe*
Nought coude thay write womens trecherie.
Beware, therfore: the blynde eteth many a flye!

Explanatory Notes to *Beware*

Abbreviations: see p. 103.

1   R titles the poem "The blynde eteth many a flye"; similarly, O reads "Beware the blynd etyth meny flye." Skeat adopts Stow's title, "A balade, warnyng men to beware of deceiptfull women."

4   *Sampson the fort and Salomon the sage.* The proverbial models of strength and wisdom, combining the ideals of *fortitudo et sapientia.*

7   *the blynde eteth many a flie.* Proverbial; see Whiting B348 and Tilley B451. This line is also incorporated into *Of Theyre Nature* (lines 14, 20–21).

24   *They shave nerer than doth rasour or sheres.* Perhaps related to the saying, "To make one's beard" (i.e., "to trick"). See Whiting B116, and Chaucer, *House of Fame* (lines 689–91).

25   *Al is not gold that shineth.* Proverbial; see Whiting G282.

26   *Thaire galle is hid under a sugred wede.* Proverbial; see Whiting G12.

29–34   *Women of kynde have condicions thre / . . . in the eye.* From the Latin "Fallere, flere, nere, tria sunt hec in muliere." Proverbial; see Whiting D120. A variation appears in Chaucer's Wife of Bath's Prologue: "For al swich wit is yeven us in our byrthe; / Deceite, wepyng, spynnyng God hath yive / To wommen kyndely, whil that they may lyve" (*CT* III[D]400–02).

33   *but a sleight.* Variants include *asceyte* (T), which Robbins, *Secular Lyrics*, reads as *as teyte* ("cheerful"), and *but dysceyte* (O).

36–41   *thogh al the erthe so wan / . . . womens trecherie.* Linn ("If All the Sky Were Parchment," pp. 951–70) traces the literary history of this formula back at least two thousand years. It has been adapted to praise the glory and power of God, to describe the misfortunes of the Jews, to describe the joys of the saints, and, by Oliver Wendell Holmes, to satirize the human compulsion "to write, and write, and write."

TEXTUAL NOTES TO *BEWARE*

ABBREVIATIONS: see p. 103.

1	*Loke.* O: *Lokyth.*
6	*Men deeme.* H: *Myndemyth.*
	it. O: *hit ys.*
	that. O: *as.*
	at. T, H: *with.*
	O adds an extra line: *Be thynk yow well on thys passage.*
7	*But ever beware.* T, H: *Beware therfore*; O: *Byware.*
8	*in.* T: *of.*
9	*Trust.* T, H: *Trust hem.*
	geson. H: *a geson.*
10	*wel.* O: *full well.*
12	*They fayne frendlynes and worchen treson.* T: *For they feyne frendlynes and worchen treson*; H: *For they can feyne friendles and worche by treason*; O: *For and hyt schuld it were agayn reson.*
13	*And sith.* T, H: *And for*; O: *Syth.*
	be. T, H: *are.*
	O adds an extra line: *Salomon seyth all thyng hath seson.*
14	*therfore.* O omits.
15–28	Stanzas 3 and 4 are transposed in T.
15	*this.* T, O: *the.*
16	*stande.* O: *to stonde.*
17	*may.* T: *woll.*
18	*doo whan.* H: *doubteful.*
	lak. H: *lak no.*
19	*They.* T, H: *For they can.*
	not. H omits.
	know men. T, H: *ys.*
20	*In theyme to trust.* T: *To trust on theym*; H, O: *To trust in hem.*
	but. O: *but a.*
	O adds an extra line: *Y warne yow all both more and lasse.*
21	*Therfore beware.* T, H: *Beware therfore*; O: *Beware.*
22	*on lyve.* O: *a lyve.*
	that. T, O omit.
	on. O: *yn.*
23	*last.* H: *lust.*

24	*They* T, H: *For wemen can.*
	nerer. H: *more nere*; O: *nere.*
	doth. T, H omit.
	rasour. T: *rasours.*
	sheres. H: *sheere.*
27	*fantasies.* T, H: *fantasy.*
	queynte thaire fantasies. O: *harde theyr queyntesye.*
	to. H: *for to.*
	O adds an extra line: *Thow schalt not forthynk and thow do by rede.*
28	*therfore.* O omits.
29–42	Stanzas 5 and 6 transposed in O.
30	*is.* O: *ys that.*
31	*spynne.* H: *spyen.*
	is. O: *hyt ys.*
33	*They wepen.* T, H: *For they can wepe.*
	but a sleight. T: *asceyte*; O: *but dysceyte.*
34	*And.* T, H: *And ever.*
	teere is in the. O: *tyrys beth yn here.*
	O adds an extra line: *Full hard ys here cherys truly to aweyte.*
35	*Therfore beware.* T, H: *Beware therfore*; O: *Beware.*
36	*In sothe.* O: *Yn schorte.*
	thogh al the erthe so wan. H: *the erthe so broode and wane.*
38	*called.* T: *that callyd ys the*; H: *that clepid is*; O: *that clepyd ys the.*
39	*ink.* T: *in to ynke*; H: *to ynke*; O: *yn yngke.*
	is. T: omits.
40	*Eche.* T: *Every.*
	ech man. H: *echema.*
41	*Nought coude thay write.* T: *Nat cowde then wryte*; H: *Nat cowde write*; O: *They cowde nat wrytyn.*
	O adds an extra line: *They beth fayre fals and unstabyll.*
42	*eteth.* H: *ete.*
	therfore. O omits.
	O adds a seventh stanza:

What thyng than eyr is lyghter and meveabyll
The lyght men say that passyth yn a trowth
All yf the lyght be not so waryabyll
As ys the wynde that every weye blowth
And yut of reson sum men deme and trowe
Wymmen be lyghtyst of thes company
Let passe over yn ese and let the wynd blow
Beware the blynde ettyth many a flye

OF THEYRE NATURE

1	Of theyre nature they gretly theym delyte,	*themselves*
	Wyth holy face feynyd for the nones,	*occasion*
	In sayntwary theyre frendys to vysyte,	*church*
	More for reliques than for seyntes bones,	
5	Though they be closyd undyr precyous stones;	
	To gete hem pardon lyke theyr olde usages,	*customs*
	To kys no shrynes but lusty quyk ymages.	*live*
	Whan maydons ar weddyd and householdys have take,	
	All theyre humylyté ys exylyd awey,	
10	And the cruell hertes begynneth to awake;	
	They do all the besy cure that they can or may,	*effort*
	To wex theyr housholdes maisters, the soth forto sey;	*vex*
	Wherfore, ye yong men, I rede yow forthy,	*advise; therefore*
	Beware alwey, the blynde eteth many a fly.	
15	Of thys matyer I dar make no lengor relacion,	*report*
	For in defaute of slepe my spyrytes wexen feynt;	*absence; grow*
	In my study I have had so long an habitacion,	
	That my body and my gost ar grevously atteynt;	*spirit; exhausted*
	And therfore of thys proces I make no lengor compleynt.	
20	But whether that the blynde ete flessh or fyssh,	
	I pray God kepe the fly out of my dyssh!	
	Now I make an ende and ley me downe to rest,	
	For I know by experience verament,	*truly*
	Yef maydones and wyfes knew and wyst	
25	Who made the mater he shuld be shent;	*ruined*
	Wherfore I pray God omnipotent,	
	Hym save and kepe both nyght and day;	
	Wretyn in the lusty season of May.	

NOTES TO *OF THEYRE NATURE*

ABBREVIATIONS: see p. 103.

1–7   These lines are from Lydgate's *The Pain and Sorrow of Evil Marriage* (*IMEV* 919). In this satire warning against marriage, the speaker, about to take a wife, is warned in a vision of three angels about the evil nature of women. This stanza, extant in only one manuscript of the poem (Bodleian Library MS Digby 181), occurs at the end of a long exposé of women's atavistic sensuality and duplicity. See Salisbury, ed., *Trials and Joys*, and Lydgate, *Minor Poems*, ed. MacCracken.

4   *reliques*. A double entendre suggesting either sacred objects (i.e., "seyntes bones") or beloved persons. Fletcher suggests that the term refers to lovers' tokens ("Edition of MS R.3.19," p. 348). The sense of the line seems to be that women visit church more for their lovers (or lovers' tokens) rather than to worship saints' bones. The reading in Digby 181 is a bit different: "In seynuaries ther frendes to visite, / More than for relikkes or any seyntis bones."

14   This popular proverb counseling male vigilance (Whiting B348) is also found in *Beware*.

20   *flessh or fyssh*. T: *fyssh or flessh*. I have followed Stow's change which preserves the rhyme.

Good Counsel, Wisdom, and Advice

Introduction

Many of the poems that circulated with Chaucer's poetry in manuscript and print consist of proverbial wisdom, public counsel, and princely advice. Given the preponderance of *sententiae*, adages, and aphorisms in Chaucer's own poetry,[1] it is not surprising that Chaucer would have some perceived reputation as a fount of worldly wisdom and courtly counsel. Indeed, Richard Firth Green suggests that in the late fourteenth century, for the ambitious courtier or poet, literature of instruction and advice was likely to "attract a more favorable reception from their masters than they were by contributing to the literary tradition of the courtly 'game of love.'"[2] The ability to fashion oneself "as a practical and moral mentor" was necessary for any writer who desired recognition beyond the limited role as courtly minstrel: "if [Chaucer's] literary attainments had any effect at all upon his career as a courtier, it was probably to such works as *Boethius* and *Melibee* rather than love-allegories like the *Parliament of Fowls* that Chaucer would have owed his advancement."[3] Seth Lerer demonstrates that in the fifteenth century, Chaucer's "socially attuned" readers, including the scribe John Shirley, continued to imagine Chaucer as a poet of "courtly politics and royal diplomacy."[4] Given the number of proverbs and "*sententiae* of different sorts" that became attached to Chaucer's name in fifteenth-century manuscripts, Julia Boffey suggests that "[i]n addition to the association of Chaucer with Boethius, there are hints of a more general tendency to regard Chaucer as a source of wisdom."[5] In the sixteenth century, Chaucer's folio print editors, particularly Thynne and Stow, continued to add poems dispensing good counsel and advice, both domestic and political. In her study of humanist commonplace books, Mary Hart Crane suggests that during the reigns of both Henry VIII and Elizabeth, the command of good counsel became of a form of cultural capital and "the central credential" for those outside aristocratic circles seeking political advancement: "[t]he skillful citation of maxims and commonplaces became a way of displaying the fruits of humanist education when seeking preferment."[6] Humanist courtiers did not necessarily dis-

---

[1] Whiting counts 186 proverbs and 630 sententious phrases (*Chaucer's Use of Proverbs*, p. 10).

[2] Green, *Poets and Princepleasers*, p, 161.

[3] Green, *Poets and Princepleasers*, p. 166.

[4] Lerer, *Chaucer and His Readers*, pp. 124–25.

[5] Boffey, "Proverbial Chaucer," pp. 46–47.

[6] Crane, *Framing Authority*, p. 93.

play their wisdom to actually advise their sovereign; rather, "[t]he giving of such advice was . . . itself a sophisticated maneuver in the game of courtly power" maintaining the illusion of social mobility and allowing the monarch to avoid the appearance of tyranny.[7]

Eight Goodly Questions with Their Aunswers, Duodecim Abusiones, Prophecy, and *Four Things That Make a Man a Fool* each dispense conservative, proverbial advice that seems concerned with dissuading dissimulation and duplicity and reinforcing the social and cultural hierarchy. For instance, although some versions of *Four Things That Make a Man a Fool* and *Yit of the Same*, which weigh the relative dangers of women, honor, age, and wine, conclude with a misogynist sting, in this case the remedy for folly is "With thyne estate have humylytee" (line 14). *Eight Goodly Questions with Their Aunswers*, distinguished as the first item to appear in all the folio editions until the eighteenth century, consists of a series of pithy questions and answers about ideal social types ostensibly handed down by sage Greek philosophers. Skeat describes the poem as an expansion upon the first lines of Ausonius' *Septem Sapientum Senteniae Septenis Versibus Explicatae*: "Quis dives? Qui nil cupiet. quis pauper? Avarus" ("Who is a rich man? He who has no desires. Who is a pauper? The avaricious man"). This Latin poem (ostensibly a simplistic summary of Ausonius' *Ludus Septem Sapientum*), extant in numerous medieval manuscripts, is now considered spurious.[8] Similarly, *Duodecem Abusiones*, which some scholars attribute to Lydgate and which is known by several different titles (*Go Forth King, Advice to the Several Estates, Instructions to the Estates*) is derived from a popular Latin treatise used by medieval preachers called "On the Twelve Abuses" (*De duodecim abusiuis*) which "teaches morality" by discussing twelve social types "whose essential moral characteristics are concentrated in a single virtue that is expressed by its opposite."[9] Wenzel describes this genre (which he classifies as a "Type A" complaint) as a type of versified lament "at the decay or disappearance or perversion of virtues." In this case, the primary complaint is the apparent widespread transgression of traditional estate-specific social expectations. Similarly, *Prophecy*, a snapshot of social chaos, was first printed by Caxton at the end of his 1478 edition of *Anelida and Arcite* — probably as what Boffey calls a "makeweight" or "programme filler" to utilize extra page space.[10] Lesley A. Coote categorizes this type of poem, which lists four moral and social evils followed by a prophetic final couplet, as an example of the "world-upside-down formula" of the Thomas Erceldoune variety, noting that such simple prognostics share characteristics with moralizing discourse and acted as a "means of expressing fundamental beliefs about the relationship of king, people, and nation."[11] Although England's imminent ruin is predicted, because the poem chronicles how vices have become virtues, Wenzel classifies *Prophecy* as a type of complaint lyric ("Type B") that witnesses the evils of the age: "the old virtues have passed away, vices are now triumphant, what used to be prized highly is nowadays scorned, and the like."[12]

John Gower's *In Praise of Peace* and *Scogan's Morale Balade*, both in the tradition of advice to princes and both formally addressed to royalty, provide good examples of "the

---

[7] Crane, *Framing Authority*, p. 95.

[8] See Shenkl, Appendix; and Green, *Works of Ausonius*, pp. 674–76.

[9] Wenzel, *Preachers*, p. 177.

[10] See, for instance, Boffey, "Manuscripts of English Courtly Love Lyrics," p. 12.

[11] Coote, *Prophecy*, p. 237.

[12] Wenzel, *Preachers*, p. 182.

generous qualities of flattery, programmatic conciliation, wary evasion, and self-protective equivocation" that Paul Strohm finds "common to most advice-giving to medieval kings."[13] Gower's *In Praise of Peace*, variously dated between the years 1399 and 1404, is addressed to Henry IV following his usurpation of Richard II in the fall of 1399. Gower begins by reiterating some of the official Lancastrian claims to the crown (divine election, hereditary right, popular sanction), heavily emphasizing the role of divine providence — rather than Lancastrian malfeasance — in Richard's deposition. The body of the poem — which contrasts the political benefits of peace with the social instability occasioned by wars of conquest — is a distillation or pastiche of themes explored more fully elsewhere in Gower's poetry, especially Book VII of the *Confessio Amantis*.[14] Against the background of the Hundred Years' War with France and continuing hostilites with Scotland, Wales, and Ireland, Gower asserts that in the Christian era, rulers should be constrained to follow the law of charity, even in the absence of ecclesiastical example. Belligerent action is permissible in only two cases: to defend one's "rightful heritage" (lines 50–70) and against the Saracens, in the defense of the Church (lines 244–52): in the first case alluding obviously to Henry's usurpation of Richard II, and the second perhaps to his participation in the Lithuanian crusade. Given the lack of Church leadership and internecine warfare as a result of the Great Schism, it falls to secular rulers to follow natural law and reason in establishing and maintaining peaceful community. Gower closes with an encomium to Henry's pity, patience, and "pris" ("excellence" — line 3721) which he enjoins all men to commend.

R. F. Yeager suggests that *In Praise of Peace* represents the logical conclusion of a "pacifistic" trend that Gower adopted toward the end of his life, "in the doctrinal mode of Augustine, with its strong position against all but the most limited wars of defense."[15] On the other hand, John Fisher reads the poem as a propagandistic justification for Henry's administration, reflecting Gower's role as "an apologist for the Lancastrian usurpation of Richard."[16] In either case, Gower faced, as Frank Grady contends in a sophisticated reading of the numerous conventional exempla used to put forth his case, some "manifest contradictions" in addressing Henry IV on the theme of peace. Describing *In Praise of Peace* as "a poem of exasperation and a valediction to the mirror-for-princes genre" Grady argues that both the exempla (Solomon, Constantine, Alexander) and current events, including the numerous uprisings and rebellions at the beginning of Henry's reign, serve to undermine Gower's sanguine panegyric; Gower provides no "topical allusions" because "there simply wasn't much peace or pity to describe."[17] As such, Gower's mirror for princes provides a good example of what Judith Ferster calls the "dance of deference and delicate challenge" that marks the literature of counsel in the late Middle Ages.[18]

According to the scribe John Shirley, *Scogan's Moral Balade* is an occasional piece, reportedly written for the entertainment and edification of Henry IV's four sons, to be read at a supper at the house of a prominent citizen, Lewis John, and critics have imagined

---

[13] Strohm, *England's Empty Throne*, p. 175.

[14] See Peck, *Kingship*, pp. 142–59.

[15] Yeager, *John Gower's Poetic*, p. 241.

[16] Fisher, *John Gower*, p. 133.

[17] Grady, "Lancastrian Gower," p. 572.

[18] Ferster, *Fictions of Advice*, p. 88.

similar privileged and convivial circumstances for Chaucer's own minor poems. Henry Scogan (1361?–1407) served in Richard II's household and later as tutor to the sons of Henry IV. He is perhaps best known to Chaucerians as the well-placed friend addressed in the *Envoy to Scogan*, and as part of the group of successful civil servants and courtiers who comprised the "inner circle" of Chaucer's original audience. Scogan's poem, chiefly valued by modern editors for its testimony to Chaucer's authorship of *Gentilesse*, which is quoted in full (lines 105–25), is marked by its modest and self-deprecating tone and by the thoroughly conventional and conservative nature of its advice. Expanding upon Chaucer's theme in *Gentilesse* — that the exercise of virtue is ennobling and that true nobility is derived from character, not birth — Scogan begins with a short prayer regretting his own misspent youth, then proceeds to urge the princes to cultivate virtue at an early age for both earthly honor and heavenly reward. Although Scogan does assert that even "folkes of poure degree" (line 89) have been set "in gret honnour" (line 90) through the exercise of virtue, the idea of "generositas virtus, non sanguis" ("nobility is virtue, not blood") is not necessarily democratic. The point is that those of high estate should, through the practice of a somewhat ill-defined "virtue," honor that station that God has conferred upon them. The consequence of sloth, which in this case seems to be set in opposition to vertuous "besynesse," is not simply a bad reputation but either divine retribution or, closer to home, loss of earthly prosperity: "Thenkthe also howe many a governour / Calde to estate hath offt be sette ful lowe / Thorughe misusing of right, and for errour" (lines 93–95). Scogan provides only legendary and exemplary figures culled from Chaucer's Monk's Tale to support his case, but given the turbulence of their father's early reign, many contemporary examples would, no doubt, be close at hand. Indeed, A. J. Minnis wryly comments: "the sons of Henry IV would not have needed much reminding of what had happened to Richard II a few years earlier."[19]

THE TEXTS

In two cases there are no extant manuscripts so I have used the earliest print editions: *Eight Goodly Questions with Their Aunswers* (*IMEV* 3183) is from Thynne's 1532 edition, and *Duodecim Abusiones* (*IMEV* 920) is from Wynken de Worde's edition of Lydgate's *Temple of Glass* (London, 1498). Various versions of *Prophecy* (*IMEV* 3943) are extant in manuscript (see Robbins, "Chaucerian Apocrypha," 4.1292); I have used the text from Caxton's *Anelida and Arcite* (London, 1478), the text which was reprinted by later editors. *Four Things That Make a Man a Fool* and *Yit of the Same* (*IMEV* 3523 and 3521), which first appeared in Stow's 1561 edition, are based on Trinity College Cambridge R.3.20 (pp. 8–9) from which Stow derived his texts.

The text of Gower's *In Praise of Peace* (*IMEV* 2587) is a diplomatic transcription of British Library, MS Additional 59495, commonly called the Trentham Manuscript, fols. 5r–10v; I have supplied the variants found in Thynne's (**Th**)1532 text of the poem which is based on a different manuscript that is no longer extant. For a description of the contents of the Trentham Manuscript, see Macaulay (**Mac**), *Complete Works of John Gower*, 1.lxxix–lxxxiii.

Scogan's Moral Balade (*IMEV* 2264) is extant in two manuscripts, **A** (Bodleian Library, MS Ashmole 59, fols. 25r–28r) and **H** (British Library, MS Harley 2251, fols. 153v–156r),

---

[19] Minnis, Scattergood, and Smith, eds., *Oxford Guides to Chaucer*, p. 485.

and two prints, by Caxton (*Temple of Bras*, c. 1477) and Thynne (*Workes*, 1532). A disordered fragment (10 discontinuous stanzas) is also found in **Ff** (Cambridge University Library Ff.4.9, fols. 85r–86r); and Stow's copy of several lines from A is found in British Library, Harley 367, fol. 86b. I have based my text on A, correcting some of its obvious errors with readings from H. A transcription of A is available in Furnivall, ed., *Parallel-Text Edition of Chaucer's Minor Poems*, Part 3 (pp. 427–30). For a collation of Caxton's text and A, see Boyd, ed., *Chaucer according to William Caxton*.

Four Things That Make a Man a Fool and Yit of the Same

A Seying of Daun Johan

1	Ther beothe foure thinges that maketh man a fool:	*are*
	Honnour first putethe him in oultrage,	*in [a state of] intemperance*
	And alder nexst solytarye and sool;	*next; alone*
	The secound is unweldy crooked aage;	*infirm*
5	Wymmen also bring men in dotage,	
	And mighty wyne in many dyvers wyse	*different ways*
	Distempren folk wheche beon holden wyse.	*Impairs*

Yit of the Same

	Ther beon foure thinges causing gret folye:	
	Honnour first, and unweldy aage,	
10	Wymmen an wyne, I dare eeke specefye,	*and; also*
	Make wyse men fallen in dotage;	
	Wherfore, by counseyle of phylosofres saage,	
	In gret honnour lerne this of me:	
	With thyne estate have humylytee.	

1 Somtyme in Grece, that noble region,   *Once*
 There were eight clerkes of grete science,   *learning*
 Philosophers of notable discretion,   *moral discernment*
 Of whom was asked, to prove their prudence,
5 Eight questions of derke intellygence;   *difficult subject matter*
 To whiche they answered, after their entent,   *opinion*
 As here dothe appere playne and evydent.

 The fyrst questyon: What erthly thyng
 Is best, and to God moost commendable?
10 The first clerke answered without tarying:
 "A mannes soule ever ferme and stable
 In right, from trouthe nat varyable;
 But nowe, alas, ful sore may we wepe,
 For covetyse hath brought trouth a slepe."   *caused; to be neglected*

15 The seconde: What thyng is moost odious?
  "A double man," sayd the philosophre,
 "With a virgyn face and a tayle venomous,   *innocent*
 With a fayre vieu and a false profre;   *offer*
 A corrupte caryen in a golden coffour,   *decayed corpse; coffin*
20 It is a monster in natures lynage,   *family*
 One man to have a double vysage."

 The thirde: What is the best dower   *dowry*
 That maye be to a wyfe appropriate?
  "A clene lyfe," was the clerkes aunswer,   *pure*
25 "Without synne, chast, and invyolate
 From al disceytes and speches inornate,   *indecorous*
 Or countenaunce, whiche shal be to dispyse: *conduct*
 No fyre make and no smoke wol aryse!"

 The fourth questyon: What mayden may
30 Be called clene in chastyté?
  The fourth clerke answered: "Whiche alway
 Every creature is ashamed on to lye,   *to slander*
 Of whom every man reporteth great honesté;

Good maydens kepe your chastyté forthe,   *continuously*
35   And remembre that good name is golde worthe."

Who is a poore man, ever ful of wo?
     "A covetouse man whiche is a nygon,   *miser*
He that in his herte can never say 'ho';   *stop*
The more good, the lesse distributyon,   *spending*
40   The richer, the worse of condityon;
Men in this cost clepen him a nygarde;   *condition*
Sir Guy the bribour is his stewarde."   *swindler; overseer*

Whiche is a riche man withouten fraude?
     "He that can to his good suffyse,   *is able to be content with his prosperity*
45   Whatsoever he hath, he geveth God the laude,   *gives; praise*
And kepeth him clene from al covetyse;
He desyreth nothyng in ungoodly wyse;
His body is here, his mynde is above:
He is a riche man, for God doth him love."

50   Who is a foole, is the seventh demaunde.   *question*
     "He that wolde hurte and hath no powere,
Myght he, mykel moche wolde he commaunde,   *very*
His malyce great, his myght nought were;
He thretteth ful faste, ful lytel may he dere;   *threaten; injure*
55   Thynketh nat howe men have sayd beforne:
God sendeth a shreude cowe a shorte horne!"   *malicious*

Who is a wyse man, is the eight question:
     "He that myght noye and dothe no noyaunce,   *harm; injury*
Myght punysshe and leaveth punyssion;
60   A man mercyful without vengeaunce;
A wyse man putteth in remembraunce,
Sayeng, 'Had I venged al myne harme,   *avenged*
My cloke had nat be furred halfe so warme!'"

19	*coffour*. This scribal emendation is found in the Bannatyne manuscript. Thynne reads *tree*. See Fox and Ringler, eds., *Bannatyne Manuscript*.
32	*to lye*. Perhaps a double entendre suggesting both "to slander" and "to have intercourse with."
42	*Sir Guy*. This is either an idiomatic name for a swindler or is perhaps a reference to the villain Guy of Gisborne. In *Robin Hood and Guy of Gisborne*, Robin states, "Thou hast beene traytor all thy liffe, / Which thing must have an ende" (lines 165–66). The earliest extant version of this ballad dates from the seventeenth century, but the episode is thought to be based on a much older version. See Knight and Ohlgren, eds., *Robin Hood and Other Outlaw Tales*.
51	There is no indent in the print.
56	Proverbial; see Whiting G217 and C751.
58	There is no indent in the print.
62–63	*had I venged . . . furred halfe so warme*. In other words, "had I spent all my energy avenging my injuries, I would not be half as prosperous."

DUODECIM ABUSIONES (THE TWELVE ABUSES)

Rex sine sapientia.	*A king without wisdom*
Episcopus sine doctrina.	*A bishop without doctrine*
Dominus sine consilo.	*A lord without counsel*
Mulier sine castitate.	*A woman without chastity*
Miles sine probitate.	*A soldier without honesty (i.e., honor)*
Judex sine justicia.	*A judge without justice*
Dives sine elemosina.	*A rich man without pity (i.e., giving no alms)*
Populus sine lege.	*A people without laws*
Senex sine religiose.	*An old man without religion*
Servus sine timore.	*A servant without fear*
Pauper suberbus.	*An arrogant poor man*
Adolescens sine obedientia.	*A youth without obedience*

1   Go forth kynge, rule thee by sapyence.   *wisdom*
    Bysshop, be able to mynyster doctrine.
    Lorde, to trewe counsell gyve audyence.
    Womanhede, to chastyté ever enclyne.
5   Knyght, lette thy dedes worshyp determyne.   *honor*
    Be ryghtwyse juge, in savynge thy name.   *impartial*
    Ryche, do almes lest thou lese blysse with shame.   *works of charity*

    People, obeye your kynge and the lawe.
    Age, be thou ruled by good relygyon.
10 Trewe servaunt, be dredul and kepe thee under awe.   *respectful*
    And thou, poore, fye on presumpcyon.
    Inobedyence, to youth, is utter destruccyon.
    Remembre you howe God hath sette you, lo: *you [all]*
    And do your parte as ye are ordeyned to.

1   Each of the twelve Latin abuses is remedied in the ME verses by the assertion of its opposite.

13   *God hath sette you.* In essence, the poem recommends the status quo of medieval estates theory. Every person has been assigned a place in society, and that position requires certain behaviors in order for the whole of the society to function properly.

 **PROPHECY**

1	Whan feyth failleth in prestes sawes,	*teachings*
	And lordes hestes ar holden for lawes,	*commands*
	And robbery is holden purchas,	*legitimate acquisition*
	And lechery is holden solas,	*pleasure*
5	Than shal the lond of Albyon	
	Be brought to grete confusion.	

4   *solas*. Perhaps a double entendre, suggesting not only physical pleasure but also spiritual comfort.

5   *Albyon*. Another name for Britain, derived from the Latin *albus* ("white"), alluding to the white appearance of the coastal cliffs. Appropriately, in Shakespeare's *King Lear* the Fool parodies the medieval prophecy:

> When priests are more in word than matter;
> When brewers mar their malt with water;
> When nobles are their tailors' tutors;
> No heretics burn'd, but wenches' suitors;
> Then shall the realm of Albion
> Come to great confusion . . .
> This prophesy Merlin shall make, for I live before his time. (3.2.81–95)

For similar versions attributed to Merlin, see Dean, ed., *Medieval English Political Writings*.

JOHN GOWER, IN PRAISE OF PEACE

Electus Cristi, pie Rex Henrice, fuisti,
Qui bene venisti cum propria regna petisti,
Tu mala vicisti que bonis bona restituisti,
Et populo tristi nova gaudia contribuisti.
Est michi spes lata quod adhuc per te renovata
Succedent fata veteri probitate beata;
Est tibi nam grata gracia sponte data.[1]

1	O worthi noble kyng, Henry the ferthe,	*fourth*
	In whom the glade fortune is befalle	*On; has befallen*
	The poeple to governe uppon this erthe,	
	God hath thee chose, in comfort of ous alle:	*chosen*
5	The worschipe of this lond, which was doun falle,	*honor; had fallen down*
	Now stant upriht thurgh grace of thi goodnesse,	*stands*
	Which every man is holde forto blesse.	*obliged*

The highe God of His justice allone,
The right which longeth to thi regalie,   *royal status*
10 Declared hath to stonde in thi persone,   *uphold*
And more than God may no man justefie.   *adjudicate*
Thi title is knowe uppon thin ancestrie,   *recognized*
The londes folk hath ek thy riht affermed: *people of the land have also*
So stant thi regne of God and man confermed.   *your reign*

15 Ther is no man mai seie in other wise   *say to the contrary*
That God himself ne hath thi riht declared;   *has not*
Whereof the lond is boun to thi servise,   *By which; prepared for*
Which for defalte of help hath longe cared.   *lack; grieved*
Bot now ther is no mannes herte spared   *man's heart*
20 To love and serve and wirche thi plesance,   *work*
And al is this thurgh Godes pourveiance.   *providence*
In alle thing which is of God begonne

---

[1] *Pious King Henry, you were chosen by Christ, / Who rightfully came when you caught your own realms, / You conquered evils and restored property to good people, / And you bestowed new joys to a sorrowful people. / I have hope for what you have brought because what you have restored so far / Will raise up through honest blessing what was said of old; / And for you, grateful thanks are given freely.*

	Ther folwith grace, if it be wel governed;	*follows*
	Thus tellen thei whiche olde bookes conne,	*know*
25	Whereof, my lord, Y wot wel thow art lerned.	*Of which; I know*
	Axe of thi God, so schalt thou nought be werned	*Ask; refused*
	Of no reqweste whiche is resonable;	
	For God unto the goode is favorable.	
	Kyng Salomon, which hadde at his axinge	*request*
30	Of God what thing him was levest to crave,	*wished to ask for*
	He ches wisdom unto the governynge	*chose*
	Of Goddis folk, the whiche he wolde save:	*people, whom he would*
	And as he ches, it fel him forto have;	*chose, it came down [to] him to*
	For thurgh his wit, whil that his regne laste,	*reign lasted*
35	He gat him pees and reste unto the laste.	*won peace; until the end*
	Bot Alisaundre, as telleth his histoire,	*Alexander*
	Unto the God besoghte in other weie:	*entreated*
	Of all the world to winne the victoire,	
	So that undir his swerd it myht obeie.	*might obey [him]*
40	In werre he hadde al that he wolde preie;	*war*
	The myghti God behight him that beheste:	*granted; promise*
	The world he wan and had it of conqweste.	
	Bot thogh it fel at thilke time so,	*happened at that*
	That Alisandre his axinge hath achieved,	*request*
45	This sinful world was al paiene tho,	*pagan then*
	Was non which hath the hihe God believed.	*high*
	No wondir was thogh thilke world was grieved:	*then that*
	Thogh a tiraunt his pourpos myhte winne,	
	Al was vengance and infortune of sinne.	*misfortune*
50	Bot now the feith of Crist is come a place	*into place*
	Among the princes in this erthe hiere,	*here*
	It sit hem wel to do pité and grace.	*causes them (i.e., the princes)*
	Bot yit it mot be tempred in manere:	*moderation*
	For as thei finden cause in the matiere	
55	Uppon the point, what aftirward betide,	*whatever [may] afterward occur*
	The lawe of riht schal noght be leid aside.	*laid*
	So mai a kyng of werre the viage	*war; enterprise*
	Ordeigne and take, as he therto is holde,	
	To cleime and axe his rightful heritage	*claim and ask [for]*
60	In alle places wher it is withholde.	*withheld*
	Bot other wise if God himsilve wolde	
	Afferme love and pes betwen the kynges,	
	Pes is the beste, above alle erthely thinges.	*Peace*

         Good is t'eschue werre, and natheles   *to avoid war*
65   A kyng may make werre uppon his right,
         For of bataile the final ende is pees.   *combat; peace*
         Thus stant the lawe, that a worthi knyght   *stands*
         Uppon his trouthe may go to the fight;   *honor*
         Bot if so were that he myghte chese,   *choose*
70   Betre is the pees, of which may no man lese.   *lose*

         Sustene pes oghte every man alyve: *Keep [the] peace ought*
         First for to sette his liege lord in reste,
         And ek these othre men that thei ne stryve,   *also; they might not fight*
         For so this world mai stonden ate beste.
75   What kyng that wolde be the worthieste,
         The more he myghte oure dedly werre cesse,   *cease*
         The more he schulde his worthinesse encresse.   *increase*

         Pes is the chief of al the worldes welthe,
         And to the Heven it ledeth ek the weie;
80   Pes is of soule and lif, the mannes helthe
         Of pestilence, and doth the werre aweie.   *From plague*
         My liege lord, tak hiede of that Y seie: *take heed of what I say*
         If werre may be left, tak pes on honde,   *ceased; in hand*
         Which may noght be withoute Goddis sonde.   *God's dispensation*

85   With pes stant every creature in reste;   *stands*
         Withoute pes ther may no lif be glad;
         Above alle othre good, pes is the beste;
         Pes hath himself whan werre is al bestad;   *beset (distressed)*
         The pes is sauf, the werre is ever adrad: *safe; afraid*
90   Pes is of al charité the keie,   *key*
         Which hath the lif and soul forto weie.   *weigh*

         My liege lord, if that thee list to seche   *wish to seek*
         The sothe essamples that the werre hath wroght,   *true examples*
         Thow schalt wiel hiere of wisemennes speche,   *shall well hear*
95   That dedly werre turneth into noght;   *turns [all things] into nothing*
         For if these olde bokes be wel soght,
         Ther myght thou se what thing the werre hath do,   *has done*
         Bothe of conqueste and conquerer also.

         For vein honour or for the worldes good,   *vain; goods (wealth)*
100 Thei that whilom the stronge werres made,   *once the great wars*
         Wher be thei now? Bethenk wel in thi mod,   *Consider; mind*
         The day is goon, the nyght is derk and fade;   *gone*
         Her crualté, which mad hem thanne glade,   *Their cruelty*
         Thei sorwen now and yit have noght the more;   *They regret*
105 The blod is schad which no man mai restore.

     The werre is modir of the wronges alle: *mother*
It sleth the prest in Holi Chirche at Masse,   *slays*
Forlith the maide and doth here flour to falle;   *Rapes; flower (virginity)*
The werre makth the grete citee lasse,   *less*
110   And doth the Lawe his reules overpasse.   *transgress*
There is no thing wherof meschef mai growe,
Which is noght caused of the werre, Y trowe.   *I believe*

The werre bringth in poverté at hise hieles,   *its heels*
Wherof the comon poeple is sore grieved.
115   The werre hath set his cart on thilke whieles   *those wheels*
Wher that Fortune mai noght be believed;
For whan men wene best to have achieved,   *assume; succeeded*
Ful ofte it is al newe to beginne:
The werre hath no thing siker, thogh he winne.   *certain*

120   Forthi, my worthi prince, in Cristes halve,   *Therefore; behalf*
As for a part whos feith thou hast to guide,
Leie to this olde sor a newe salve,   *sore; remedy*
And do the werre awei, what so betide.   *whatsoever happens (i.e., regardless of cost)*
Pourchace pes and sette it be thi side,   *Acquire*
125   And suffre noght thi poeple be devoured;
So schal thi name ever after stonde honoured.

If eny man be now, or ever was,
Agein the pes thi prevé counseillour,   *Against; personal*
Lete God ben of thi counseil in this cas,
130   And putte awei the cruel werreiour;
For God, which is of man the creatour,
He wolde noght men slowe His creature   *would not [have] men kill*
Withoute cause of dedly forfeture.   *reason of; crime*

Wher nedeth most, behoveth most to loke: *it is necessary*
135   Mi lord, how so thi werres ben withoute,   *although; external*
Of time passed who that hiede toke,   *heed*
Good were at hom to se riht wel aboute;   *home*
For everemor the werste is forto doute.   *worst is to be uncertain*
Bot if thou myghtest parfit pes atteigne,   *perfect peace attain*
140   Ther schulde be no cause forto pleigne.   *complain*

Aboute a kyng good counseil is to preise
Above alle othre thinges most vailable;   *beneficial*
Bot yit a kyng withinne himself schal peise,   *consider*
And se the thinges that ben resonable,
145   And ther uppon he schal his wittes stable,   *establish*
Among the men to sette pes in evene,   *to settle peace*
For love of Him which is the Kyng of Hevene.   *(i.e., Christ)*

	Ha, wel is him that schedde never blod,	*Ah, well*
	Bot if it were in cause of rihtwisnesse;	*righteousness*
150	For if a kyng the peril undirstod	
	What is to sle the poeple, thanne Y gesse,	*slay the people, then I suppose*
	The dedly werres and the hevynesse,	
	Wherof the pes distourbid is ful ofte,	
	Schulde at som time cesse and wexe softe.	*grow soft*

	O kyng, fulfild of grace and of knyghthode,	*full; nobility*
155	Remembre uppon this point for Cristes sake:	
	If pes be profred unto thi manhode,	*offered*
	Thin honour sauf, let it noght be forsake,	
	Though thou the werres darst wel undirtake;	*wars did*
160	Aftir reson yit tempre thi corage,	*temper; valor*
	For lich to pes ther is non avantage.	*no benefit*

	My worthi lord, thenke wel, how so befalle,	
	Of thilke lore, as holi bokes sein:	*lesson*
	Crist is the heved and we ben membres alle,	*head; limbs*
165	Als wel the subgit as the sovereign.	*As well*
	So sit it wel that charité be plein,	*complete*
	Which unto God himselve most acordeth,	
	So as the lore of Cristes word recordeth.	

	In th'Olde Lawe, er Crist Himself was bore,	*Old Testament, before; born*
170	Among the Ten Comandementz Y rede	
	How that manslaghtre schulde be forbore;	*abstained from*
	Such was the will that time of the Godhede.	
	And aftirward, whanne Crist tok His manhede,	*achieved; humanity*
	Pes was the ferste thing He let do crie	
175	Agein the worldes rancour and envie.	*against*

	And er Crist wente out of this erthe hiere,	
	And stigh to hevene, He made His testament,	*ascended*
	Wher He beqwath to His disciples there	*bestowed*
	And gaf His pes, which is the foundement	*gave; foundation*
180	Of charité, withouten whos assent	
	The worldes pes mai never wel be tried,	*tested*
	Ne love kept, ne lawe justefied.	

	The Jewes with the paiens hadden werre,	*pagans*
	Bot thei among hemself stode evere in pes;	*themselves*
185	Whi schulde thanne oure pes stonde oute of herre,	*out of kilter*
	Which Crist hath chose unto His oghne encres?	*benefit*
	For Crist is more than was Moises,	
	And Crist hath set the parfit of the lawe,	*perfection*
	The which scholde in no wise be withdrawe.	

190   To give ous pes was cause whi Crist dide;   *died*
      Withoute pes may no thing stonde availed;   *strong*
      Bot now a man mai sen on everi side   *see*
      How Cristes feith is every dai assailed,
      With the paiens destruid, and so batailed   *pagans devastated; beset*
195   That for defalte of help and of defence,   *lack*
      Unethe hath Crist His dewe reverence.   *Hardly*

      The righte feith to kepe of Holy Chirche,
      The firste point is named of knyghthode,   *principle*
      And everi man is holde forto wirche   *work*
200   Uppon the point which stant to his manhode.   *principle; attests to*
      Bot now, helas, the fame is sprad so broode,   *alas*
      That everi worthi man this thing compleigneth,   *appeals to*
      And yit ther is no man which help ordeigneth.   *provides*

      The worldes cause is waited overal;   *attended to everywhere*
205   Ther ben the werres redi to the fulle.   *fully*
      Bot Cristes oghne cause in special,
      Ther ben the swerdes and the speres dulle;   *spears*
      And with the sentence of the popes bulle   *pronouncement; edict*
      As forto do the folk paien obeie,   *pagan folk*
210   The chirche is turned al an other weie.

      It is to wondre above a mannys wit,
      Withoute werre, how Cristes feith was wonne;
      And we that ben upon this erthe yit,
      Ne kepe it noght as it was first begonne.
215   To every creature undir the sonne
      Crist bad Himself how that we schulden preche,
      And to the folk His evangile teche.   *message*

      More light it is to kepe than to make;   *easy; acquire*
      Bot that we founden mad tofore the hond,   *made beforehand*
220   We kepe noght, bot lete it lightly slake.   *lessen*
      The pes of Crist hath altobroke his bond;   *completely broken*
      We reste ourselve and soeffrin every lond   *allow*
      To slen ech other as thing undefendid: *slay; not forbidden*
      To stant the werre, and pes is noght amendid.   *established*

225   Bot thogh the Heved of Holy Chirche above   *Head (i.e., Christ)*
      Ne do noght al His hole businesse
      Among the men to sette pes and love,
      These kynges oughten of here rightwisnesse,   *their righteousness*
      Here oghne cause among hemself redresce;   *repair*
230   Thogh Petres schip as now hath lost his stiere,   *Peter's ship (i.e., the Church); rudder*
      It lith in hem that barge forto stiere.   *falls to them; steer*

If Holy Cherche, after the dueté   *duty*
Of Cristes word, ne be noght al avysed
To make pes, acord, and unité
235   Among the kinges that ben now devised,   *divided*
Yit natheles the lawe stant assised   *ordained*
Of mannys wit to be so resonable,
Withoute that, to stonde hemselve stable.

Of Holy Chirche we ben children alle,
240   And every child is holden forto bowe
Unto the modir, how that ever it falle,
Or elles he mot reson desalowe;   *must; repudiate*
And for that cause a knyght schal ferst avowe   *first swear*
The right of Holi Chirche to defende,
245   That no man schal the previlege offende.   *violate*

Thus were it good to setten al in evene,   *to settle calmly*
The worldes princes and the prelatz bothe,   *prelates*
For love of Him which is the King of Hevene;
And if men scholde algate wexe wrothe,   *nevertheless; grow angry*
250   The Sarazins, whiche unto Crist be lothe,   *are hateful*
Let men ben armed agein hem to fighte,   *against*
So mai the knyht his dede of armes righte.   *direct*

     Uppon thre pointz stant Cristes pes oppressed:
Ferst Holy Cherche is in hersilf divided,
255   Which oughte of reson first to be redresced;   *repaired*
Bot yit so highe a cause is noght decided.
And thus whan humble pacience is prided,
The remenant, which that thei schulden reule,   *remnant*
No wondir is though it stonde out of reule.   *in disorder*

260   Of that the heved is siek, the limes aken: *Because; head; ache*
These regnes that to Cristes pes belongen,   *reins*
For worldes good, these dedly werres maken,   *worldly possessions*
Whiche helpples as in balance hongen;
The heved above hem hath noght undirfongen   *undertaken*
265   To sette pes, bot every man sleth other,   *kills*
And in this wise hath charité no brother.

The two defaltes bringen in the thridde,   *failures; third*
Of mescreantz, that sen how we debate;   *infidels*
Betwene the two thei fallen in amidde,   *the middle*
270   Wher now aldai thei finde an open gate.   *all day (i.e., always)*
Lo, thus the dedly werre stant algate.   *always*
Bot evere Y hope of Kyng Henries grace,
That he it is which schal the pes embrace.

My worthi noble prince and kyng enoignt, *anointed*
275 Whom God hath of His grace so preserved,
Beholde and se the world uppon this point, *attend to*
As for thi part, that Cristes pes be served;
So schal thin highe mede be deserved *your high reward*
To Him which al schal qwiten ate laste, *From; requite*
280 For this lif hiere mai no while laste.

See Alisandre, Ector, and Julius,
See Machabeu, David, and Josue, *[Judas] Maccabeus; Joshua*
See Charlemeine, Godefroi, Arthus, *Godfrey [of Bouillon]*
Fulfild of werre and of mortalité. *Too full*
285 Here fame abit, bot al is vanité; *Their; abides*
For deth, which hath the werres under fote,
Hath mad an ende of which ther is no bote. *remedy*

So mai a man the sothe wite and knowe, *truth recognize*
That pes is good for every king to have;
290 The fortune of the werre is evere unknowe,
Bot wher pes is, ther ben the marches save. *territories safe*
That now is up, to morwe is under grave;
The mighti God hath alle grace in honde,
Withouten Him pes mai nought longe stonde.

295 Of the tenetz to winne or lese a chace, *tennis*
Mai no lif wite er that the bal be ronne; *person; played out*
Al stant in God what thing men schal pourchace: *receive*
Thende is in him er that it be begonne. *The end; before*
Men sein the wolle, whanne it is wel sponne, *say the wool; spun*
300 Doth that the cloth is strong and profitable, *serviceable*
And elles it mai never be durable. *otherwise*

The worldes chaunces uppon aventure *events; chance*
Ben evere sett, bot thilke chaunce of pes *opportunity*
Is so behoveli to the creature, *beneficial*
305 That it above alle othre is piereles. *peerless*
Bot it mai noght be gete, natheles, *gotten*
Among the men to lasten eny while,
Bot wher the herte is plein withoute guyle. *sincere; guile*

The pes is as it were a sacrement
310 Tofore the God, and schal with wordes pleine, *before*
Withouten eny double entendement, *meaning*
Be treted, for the trouthe can noght feine. *dissemble*
Bot if the men withinne hemself be veine, *deficient of virtue*
The substance of the pes may noght be trewe,
315 Bot every dai it chaungeth uppon newe.

	Bot who that is of charité parfit,	*perfect*
	He voideth alle sleightes ferr aweie,	*removes; schemes*
	And sett his word uppon the same plit	*pledge*
	Wher that his herte hath founde a siker weie;	*secure*
320	And thus whan conscience is trewly weie,	*weighed*
	And that the pes be handlid with the wise,	
	It schal abide and stonde in alle wise.	*in all respects*

	Th'apostle seith ther mai no lif be good	*The apostle*
	Which is noght grounded uppon charité,	
325	For charité ne schedde nevere blod;	
	So hath the werre, as ther, no proprité.	
	For thilke vertu, which is seid pité,	*called*
	With charité so ferforth is aqweinted	*far*
	That in here may no fals semblant be peinted.	*her [pity]; resemblance*

330	Cassodre, whos writinge is auctorized,	*Cassiodorus; trustworthy*
	Seith wher that pité regneth ther is grace,	*reigns*
	Thurgh which the pes hath al his welthe assised,	*secured*
	So that of werre he dredeth no manace.	
	Wher pité dwelleth, in the same place	
335	Ther mai no dedly cruelté sojorne,	*reside*
	Wherof that merci schulde his wei torne.	

	To se what pité forth with mercy doth,	*further*
	The croniqe is at Rome, in thilke empire	*story*
	Of Constantin, which is a tale soth,	*true*
340	Whan him was levere his oghne deth desire	*would rather*
	Than do the yonge children to martire:	*martyr*
	Of crualté he lafte the querele;	*cause*
	Pité he wroghte, and pité was his hele.	*remedy*

	For thilke mannes pité which he dede,	*did*
345	God was pitous and mad him hol at al;	*healthy altogether*
	Silvestre cam, and in the same stede,	*immediately*
	Gaf him baptisme first in special,	
	Which dide awai the sinne original,	
	And al his lepre it hath so purified,	*leprosy*
350	That his pité forever is magnified.	*exalted*

	Pité was cause whi this emperour	
	Was hol in bodi and in soule bothe,	*healthy*
	And Rome also was set in thilke honour	
	Of Cristes feith, so that the lieve of lothe,	*enemies (disbelievers)*
355	Whiche hadden be with Crist tofore wrothe,	*before angry*
	Resceived were unto Cristes lore;	*faith*
	Thus schal pité be preised evermore.	

My worthi liege lord, Henri be name,   *by*
Which Engelond hast to governe and righte,   *direct*
360   Men oghten wel thi pité to proclame,
Which openliche, in al the worldes sighte,   *plainly*
Is schewed with the help of God almighte,
To give ous pes, which longe hath be debated,   *opposed*
Wherof thi pris schal nevere ben abated.   *fame; diminished*

365   My lord, in whom hath ever yit be founde
Pité, withoute spot of violence,
Kep thilke pes alwei withinne bounde
Which God hath planted in thi conscience;
So schal the cronique of thi pacience,   *record*
370   Among the seintz be take into memoire,   *remembrance*
To the loenge of perdurable gloire.   *praise; eternal*

And to thin erthli pris, so as Y can,   *excellence*
Which everi man is holde to commende,   *praise*
I, Gower, which am al thi liege man,
375   This lettre unto thin excellence Y sende,
As Y, which evere unto my lives ende,
Wol praie for the stat of thi persone   *welfare*
In worschipe of thi sceptre and of thi throne.

Noght only to my king of pes Y write,
380   Bot to these othre princes Cristene alle,
That ech of hem his oghne herte endite   *own heart examine*
And see the werre er mor meschief falle;   *deal with the war before*
Sette ek the rightful pope uppon his stalle,   *Set also; seat*
Kep charité and draugh pité to honde,
385   Maintene lawe, and so the pes schal stonde.

Explicit carmen de pacis commendacione, quod ad laudem et memoriam serenissimi principis domini Regis Henrici quarti suus humilis orator Johannes Gower composuit.

[Here ends the poem on the praising of peace, which his humble orator, John Gower, composed for the praise and memory of that most august prince of the Lord, King Henry the Fourth.]

EXPLANATORY NOTES TO *IN PRAISE OF PEACE*

4   *God hath thee chose.* In the opening stanzas, Gower repeats some standard justifications for Henry's usurpation of Richard II: the good fortune of divine sanction, hereditary right, and popular consent. Compare Chaucer, *The Complaint of Chaucer to His Purse*: "O conquerour of Brutes Albyon, / Which that by lyne and free eleccion / Been verray kyng" (23–24). It is only later in the poem (see below, lines 50–70) that Gower alludes to the martial component of Henry's accession to the throne. On both Chaucer's and Gower's poems as examples of Lancastrian propaganda, see Strohm, "Saving the Appearances: Chaucer's *Purse* and the Fabrication of the Lancastrian Claim" (chapter 4 in *Hochon's Arrow*).

25   *thow art lerned.* On Henry IV's books, see Doyle, "English Books"; Meale, "Patrons, Buyers and Owners"; and Summerson, "English Bible."

29   *Kyng Salomon.* This is an abbreviated version of Solomon's career. Although in *CA* Solomon is initially lauded for his wisdom (7.3891–3942), he is nonetheless later denounced for violating chastity, the fifth principle of kingship, since his polygamy and promiscuity lead to idolatry and the division of his kingdom (*CA* 7.4469–4545).

36   *Alisaundre.* See the tale of Alexander and the Pirate (*CA* 3.2361–2480), in which a pirate convinces Alexander that the nature of their exploits differs only in degree. The tale concludes with the consequences of Alexander's tyranny: "Thus was he slain that whilom slowh" (*CA* 3.2461). Although in some versions of Book 7 Gower includes an exemplum showing Alexander's pity (*CA* 7.3168–3181), Porter ("Gower's Ethical Microcosm") argues that Gower's Alexander represents the failure to achieve "ethical self-governance."

50–70 In these three stanzas, Gower reiterates four times that war is permissible only when one must defend "the lawe of riht" (line 56) and one's "rightful heritage" (line 59), echoing the official Lancastrian rhetoric used to defend the "naked illegality" (Pollard, *Late Medieval England*, p. 25) of Henry's usurpation of Richard II; see Barron, "Deposition of Richard II."

66   *For of bataile the final ende is pees.* The notion is Augustinian in origin; see Yeager, "Pax Poetica."

107–08 *It sleth the prest . . . Forlith the maide.* See *CA* 3.2275–6. Macaulay points out several other echoes: line 78 (*CA* 3.2265), line 113 (*CA* 3.2294), line 115 (*CA* Prol.444), and line 155 (*CA* Prol.89).

174   *Pes was the ferste thing.* See Matthew 5:9: "Blessed are the peacemakers, for they will be called the children of God."

178   *beqwath to His disciples there.* See John 14:27: "Peace I leave with you; my peace I give to you: not as the world giveth, do I give unto you. Let not your heart be troubled, nor let it be afraid."

250   *Sarazins.* Following an aborted attempt to aid Christians against Saracens in Africa, Henry did complete a campaign against the pagan Lithuanians in Prussia. See Du Boulay, "Henry of Derby's Expeditions."

        Although the crusade is here condoned as a legitimate outlet for chivalric bellicosity, in *CA* Genius condemns the activity as violating Christ's law of charity. See, for instance, 3.2481–2546 and 4.1679–81: "A Sarazin if I sle schal, / I sle the Soule forth withal, / And that was nevere Cristes lore."

254   *Holy Cherche is in hersilf divided.* A reference to the two papal courts — at Rome and Avignon — of the Great Schism, responsible, in Gower's view, for Lollardy and other heresies. See *CA* Prol.328–498.

267   *The two defaltes bringen in the thridde.* The first two faults or failures are the Great Schism (1378–1417) and the internecine wars between Christian powers; these lead to the third, the threat of non-Christians. In other words (line 260), the head is sick and the limbs ache, allowing the body of the Church to be attacked by either infidels or heretics.

281–83 The Nine Worthies, three pagan (Alexander, Hector, Julius Caesar), three Jewish (Judas Maccabeas, David, Joshua), and three Christian (Charlemagne, Godfrey of Boulogne, Arthur), are often cited as paragons of a transcultural nobility and chivalry, but also, as here, as exemplary victims of the power of transience and mortality. Godfrey of Boulogne, duke of Lorraine (1061–1100), was the leader of the First Crusade and king of Jerusalem (1099–1100). Judas Maccabeus (c. 2nd century BC), whose exploits are described in 1 and 2 Maccabees, led the Jewish revolt against the Hellenist Seleucids, restored the Temple, and established a period of self-rule.

295   *to winne or lese a chace.* In the medieval game of tennis, *chase* refers to the "second impact on the floor (or in a gallery) of a ball which the opponent has failed or declined to return; the value of which is determined by the nearness of the spot of impact to the end wall. If the opponent, on sides being changed, can 'better' this stroke (i.e., cause his ball to rebound nearer the wall) he wins and scores it; if not, it is scored by the first player; until it is so decided, the 'chase' is a stroke in abeyance" (*OED*). In other words, in tennis, as in life, the significance or meaning of a given action can be understood only in retrospect.

323   *Th'apostle.* St. Paul. See 1 Corinthians 13:1–13.

330   *Cassodre.* Cassiodorus was a sixth-century Roman statesman and monk. The reference is to his *Variarum Libri XII* (11.40). Also quoted in *CA*: "Cassodre in his apprise telleth, / 'The regne is sauf, wher pité duelleth'" (7.3161–62). See further Jones, "Influence of Cassiodorus."

auctorized. On the textual, literary, and cultural connotations of this term, see
Minnis, *Medieval Theory of Authorship*, pp. 73–159, and Scanlon, *Narrative, Authority, and Power*, pp. 37–54.

337–57   This version of Constantine's conversion is given more fully in *CA* 2.3187–3496.
As a cure for his leprosy, Constantine's physicians suggest that he bathe in the
blood of young children, but the emperor is moved to pity by their mothers'
grief. In a dream, he is directed by Peter and Paul to visit Silvester and after
having been instructed in the basic tenets of Christianity, he is baptized. The
"fisshe skales" of his malady fall away and he orders the baptism — upon pain of
death — of all of Rome. Genius tells his story in order to represent the efficacy
of charity in combating envy. Grady notes that the sanitized version of
Constantine's career found in *In Praise of Peace* is perhaps cleaned up "for the
king's consumption" ("Lancastrian Gower," p. 569). On the different versions of
Constantine current in the Middle Ages, see Webb, "Truth about Constantine."

❧ TEXTUAL NOTES TO *IN PRAISE OF PEACE*

Macaulay emends British Library MS Additional 59495 in four cases. 1) He elides the final *-e* in the following imperative forms: *Leie*, line 122; *sette*, line 124; *Lete*, line 129; *putte*, line 130; *thenke*, line 162; *Beholde*, line 276. 2) He changes the possessive pronoun of the feminine singular (*here*, *her*) to the more regular form (*hire*, *hir*) at lines 108, 254, and 329. 3) He adds *-e* to adverbial *ever* and *never* (lines 89, 126, 127, 148, 181, 241, 301, 350, and 365). 4) For the sake of meter, he sometimes elides (*Betwen*, line 269; line 384) or adds (*highe*, line 8; *alle*, line 90; *weie*, line 336; *more*, line 382) a final *-e*. I have let stand the scribal peculiarities that Macaulay finds contrary to Gower's practice, although in the fourth case his emendations surely help the meter.

In Thynne's version (titled "John Gower unto the Noble and Worthy Kynge Henry the Fourth"), the Latin epigraph is placed at the end of the poem, followed without a break by the Trentham version of Gower's Latin poem *Quicquid homo scribat*.

ABBREVIATIONS: see pp. 122–23.

1	*worthi noble*. Th: *noble worthy*.
3	*uppon this*. Th: *here upon*.
4	*chose*. Th: *chosen*.
16	*thi*. Th: *the*.
17	*boun*. Th: *bounde*.
21	*is this*. Th: *this is*.
27	*whiche*. Mac: *which*, from Th.
30	*to*. Th omits.
31	*the*. Th omits.
35	*unto the*. Th: *in to his*.
36	*histoire*. Th: *storie*.
38	*victoire*. Th: *vyctorie*.
39	*it*. MS: *itt*, with the second *t* canceled.
42	*he*. Th omits.
45	*paiene*. Th: *paynem*.
54	*as*. Th omits.
71	*Sustene*. So Mac. MS: *S*, followed by an erasure. Th reads *To stere*.
	every man alyve. Th: *everiche on lyve*.
74	*world mai stonden*. Th: *lande may stande*.
93	*that*. Th: *what*.
96	*soght*. Th: *ysought*.
121	*to*. Th: *be*.

144   *ben*. Th: *be*.

153   *the*. Th omits.

155   *and of*. Th: *of*.

164   *ben*. Th: *be*.

165   *the*. Th: *be*.

173   *And*. Th: *But*.

175   *Agein*. Th: *Ayenst*.

177   *stigh*. Th: *styghed*.

183   *paiens*. Th: *paynyms*. See also line 194.

185   *herre*. Th: *erre*.

200   *which*. Th: *that*.

202   *worthi*. Th omits.

203   *ther is*. Th: *is there*.

               which. Th: *that*.

205   *ben*. Th: *be*.

209   *paien*. Th: *payne*.

211   *to*. Th omits.

               a. Th: *any*.

213   *ben*. Th: *be*.

216   *how*. Th omits.

219   *the*. Th omits.

223   *slen*. Th: *slee*.

227   *men*. Th: *people*.

238   *hemselve*. Th: *him selfe*.

246   *setten*. Th: *sette*.

250   *be*. Th: *ben*.

251   *ben*. Th: *be*.

               agein. Th: *ayenst*.

254   *is*. Th omits.

263   *helpples*. Th: *helplesse*. Mac: *helpeles*.

265   *sleth*. Mac: *sleeth*, from Th.

272   *Kyng*. Mac: *King*, from Th.

278   *thin*. Th: *thy*.

283   *Arthus*. Th: *and A*.

288   *mai*. Th: *many*.

291   *ben*. Th: *is*.

294   *pes*. Th: *men*.

305   *it*. Th: *is*.

               is. Th omits.

306   *be gete*. Th: *begete*.

313   *be*. Th: *ben*.

321   *the pes*. Th: *these*.

331   *regneth*. Mac: *reigneth*, from Th.

               ther. Th omits.

342   *crualté*. MS: *y* inserted between *t* and *e* by later hand.

356   *were*. So MS, Th. Mac emends to *weren*: "However the case may be with
            Chaucer, there is no instance elsewhere in Gower of elision prevented by

caesura. The cases that have been quoted are all founded on mis-readings" (3.554).

360	*oghten*. Th: *ought*.
364	*schal*. So MS. Mac: *shal*, from Th.
371	*loenge*. Th: *legende*.
378	*of*. Th omits.
382	*see*. Stow: *sease*.

❦ SCOGAN'S MORAL BALADE

Here folowethe nexst a moral balade to my lord the Prince, to my lord of Clarence, to my lord of Bedford, and to my lorde of Gloucestre, by Henry Scogan, at a souper of feorthe merchande in the Vyntre in London, at the hous of Lowys Johan.

1	My noble sonnes and eke my lordes dere,	*also*
	I, youre fadre called, unworthely,	*father*
	Sende unto yowe this balade folowing here,	
	Writen of myne owen hande ful rudely;	*unskillfully*
5	Yitte howe it be that I not reverently	
	Have writen to yowre estates, yet I yowe prey,	*group [of high rank]*
	That myne unkonyng yee take benignely	*error (ignorance)*
	For Goddes sake, and herkyne what I seye.	*listen to*
	I compleye sore whane I remembre me	*grieve*
10	The sodeyne age that is upon me falle;	
	More I compleyne my mispent juventé,	*mourn; youth*
	The whiche is inpossible ageine to calle;	
	But comunely, the moste compleynte of alle	*commonly*
	Is foreto thenke that I have beon so nyce,	*Is to think; been so ignorant*
15	And that I wolde no vertue to me calle	
	In al my youthe, but vyces ay cheryce.	*always cherished*
	Of whiche I aske mercy of Thee, Lord,	
	That art Almighty Lorde in Magestee,	
	Byseching Thee to make so even acorde	*agreement*
20	Bytwene Thee and my soule, that vanytee	
	Of worldely louste ne blynde prosperitee	*lust (pleasure) nor*
	Have no lordship over my flesshe so freel:	*frail*
	Thou Lord of reste and parfite unitee,	*perfect*
	Putte fro me vyce and kepe my soules heel.	*health*
25	And gif me might, while I have lyf and space,	*give; time*
☞	Me to confourme fully to thy plesaunce;	*satisfaction (see note)*
	Shewe upon me th'aboundance of thi grace;	
	In gode werkis graunte me perseverance;	*good*
	Of al my youthe forgete the ignorance;	
30	Gyf me gode wille to serve Thee ay to qweme;	*always properly*

Sette ay my lyff affter Thy governaunce,
And able me to mercy or Thou deeme.   *enable; judge*

My lordes dere, why I this compleinte wryte
To yowe, alle whome I love entierely,
35   Is for to warne yowe, as I cane endyte,   *prescribe*
That tyme eloste in yowthe folely,   *lost; foolishly*
Grevethe a wight goostely and bodely,   *person spiritually*
I mene hem that to vyces list t'entende;   *choose to be inclined to*
Therfore I prey you lordes tendrely,
40   Youre youthe in vertue shapethe to dispende.   *spend*

Plantethe the roote of youthe in suche a wyse
That in vertue youre growing beo alweye;   *be*
Looke ay, goodenesse beo in youre excercyse,
That shal you mighty make, at eche assaye,
45   For to withstonde the feonde at eche affraye;   *fiend; attack*
Passethe wisely this paraillous pilgrymage;
Thenke on this worde and use it every daye:
That shal yowe gif a parfyte floured age.   *prosperous*

☞   Takethe heede alsoo, howe that theos noble clerkis   *(see note)*
50   Wrote in theire bookis of noble sapience,   *wisdom*
☞   Seying that feythe is ded withowten werkis;   *(see note)*
So is estate withoute intelligence   *noble rank*
Of vertue; therfore, with diligence,
Shapethe of vertue so to plante the roote,
55   That yee thereof have ful exparience,
To worship of youre lyf and soules boote.   *honor; benefit*

Thenkethe also that lordshipe ne estate,   *high rank*
Withoute vertue, may not longe endure;
Thenkethe also how vices and vertue at debate   *in opposition*
60   Have beon, and shal, whiles the worlde may dure;
And ay the vicyous, by aventure,
Is overthrowe; and thenkithe evermore
That God is lorde of vertue and figure   *embodiment*
Of alle godenes: loke that yee folowe His lore.   *teaching*

65   My maistre Chaucier, God his soule have,
That in his langage was so curyous,   *skillful*
He saide that the fader, nowe dede and grave,   *buried*
Beqwathe nothing his vertue with his hous   *Bestows*
Unto his sone; therfore, laborious
70   Aught you to beo, beseching God of grace,
To geve you might for to be vertuous,   *give*
Thorughe whiche yee might gete part of His feyre place.

Here may yee see that vertuous noblesse
Comthe not to yowe of youre auncestrye,
75   But it comthe thorugh leofful besynesse,   *proper*
Of honeste lyff, and noght of slougardery;   *idleness*
Wherfore, in youthe, I rede you edefye   *Therefore; advise*
The hous of vertue in sŏo wyse manere,
That in youre age it may you kepe and guye   *guide*
80   Frome the tempeste of worldly wawes here.   *waves*

Thenkethe how bytwene vertue and estate   *noble rank*
There is a perfite blessed mariage;
Vertue is cause of pees, vyce of debate   *conflict*
In mannes soule; for whiche, with full corage
85   Cherisshethe vertue, vyce to outrage,   *expel*
Dryveth awe, let hem have no wonnyng   *away; dwelling*
In youre soules; leese not the heritage   *inheritance*
Whiche God hathe give to vertuous living.

Takethe heede also howe folkes of poure degree
90   Thorughe vertue have be sette in gret honnour,
And ever have lyved in gret prosperitee
By cherisshinge of vertuous labour;
Thenkthe also howe many a governour
Calde to estate hath offt be sette ful lowe   *high office*
95   Thorughe misusing of right, and for errour;   *judgment*
Therfore, I counsayle yowe vertue to knowe.

By auncestrye thus may yee no thing clayme,
As that my maistre Chaucier dothe expresse,
But temporell thinge that man may hurte and mayme;
100   Thane is Gode stocke of vertuous noblesse.   *Therefore God is the source*
And sithe that He is Lord of blessednesse,
That made us alle and for mankynde that dyed,
Folowe His vertue with full besynesse,   *diligence*
104   And of this thinge herke howe my maistre seyde: *listen to*

☞   "The first fader and foundour of gentylesse,   *(see note)*
What man that claymethe gentyle for to be,
Moste felowe heos traas and alle heos wittes dresse,   *line*
Vertue to suwe and vyces for to flee;   *pursue*
For unto vertue longethe dignytee,
110   And nought the reverse, savely dar I deeme,
Al were he mytre, croune, or dyademe.   *Whether he wear miter*

"This first stocke was grounde of rightwysnesse,   *righteousness*
Truwe of his worde, sobur, pitous, and fre,   *generous*
Clene of his gooste, and loved besynesse,   *spirit*

115   Ageinst the vice of slouthe, in honestee;

    And but his heyre love vertue as did he,   *heir*

    He nys not gentyle, thaughe him ryche seeme,

    Al were he mytre, crowne, or dyademe.

    "Vyce may wele be an heyre til olde richchesse,   *heir to*

120   But there may noman, as thou maist wele se,

 ☞   Beqweythe his heyre his vertuous noblesse;   *(see note)*

    That is appropred unto no degree,   *appropriated to no rank*

    But to first fadre in magestee

    That mathe his heyre him that wol him qweme,   *makes; please*

125   Al were he mytre, crowne, or dyademe."

    Loo here, this noble poete of Brettayne

    Howe hyely he, in vertuous sentence,   *expression*

    The losse in youthe of vertue can compleyne;   *lament*

    Wherfore, I prey yowe, doothe youre diligence,

130   For youre estates and Goddes reverence,

    T'enprynte vertue fully in youre mynde,   *To imprint*

    That whane yee come into youre juges presence,

    Yee be not sette as vertulesse byhinde.

    For yee lordes, of coustume nowe adayes,   *custom*

135   Thaughe one of you here of a gode matere,

    Youre unsure youthe is of so fals alayes,   *alloying*

    That of suche artes you list not to here.   *desire; hear*

    But as a shippe that is withouten stere,   *rudder*

    Dryvethe up and doune, withouten variaunce,

140   Weoning the calme wol laste yeere by yeere,   *Assuming*

    Right so fare yee, thorughe veray ignoraunce.

    For verray shame, knowe yee not, by raisoun,

    That affter an ebbe there comethe a flode rage?   *raging*

    Right even so, whane youthe passethe his saysoun,

145   Comthe croked and unweldy palled age;   *infirm; impaired*

    Soone affter that komthe kalendes of dotage;   *comes the beginning*

    And of youre youthe no vertue have provyded,

    Alle folke wol seye: "Fye on youre vasellage!"   *knightly behavior*

    Thus hathe youre youthe and slouthe you al misgyded.   *sloth*

150   Boece, that clerk, as men may rede and see,   *Boethius*

    Seythe in his Booke of Consolacyoun

    What man desyrethe to have of vyne or tree

    Plenty of fruyt in the riping saysoun,

    Most ay eschuwe to doone oppressioun

155   Unto the roote whylest it is yonge and grene;

Yee may wele see by this conclusioun,
That youthe vertulesse dothe ay michil teene.   *much harm*

Sithe, there ageinst, that vertuous noblesse   *Since, on the contrary*
Rooted in youthe, with goode perseverance,
160   Dryvethe aweye al vyce and wrecchednesse,
Al slogardrye, al ryots, and dispence;   *idleness; debauchery; expense*
Seothe eke howe vertue causethe suffisaunce,   *self-sufficiency*
And suffisaunce exylethe coveityse:
Thus who hathe vertue hathe gret habondaunce
165   Of wele, als far as raison can devyse.   *well-being*

Takethe heede of Tulius Hastilius,
That came frome povertee to hye degré   *rank*
Thorughe vertue; eke redethe of Julius   *Julius Caesar*
The conquerrour, howe poure a man was he;
170   Yitte thorughe his vertue and humanyté,
Of many a lande hade he the governance:
Thus vertue bringethe unto gret degree
Eche wight that list do to him attendaunce.

Rede there ageine of Nero vertulesse,
175   Takethe heede also of proude Baltasare;   *Balthasar*
They hated vertue, equytee, and pees.   *justice*
Looke howe Anthyocus fel frome his chare,   *chariot*
That he his skyn and also heos boones totare;   *tore*
Looke what meschaunces they hade for theire vices!
180   Who so that wil not by theos signes beware,
I dare wele seye infortunate or nyce is.   *ignorant*

I cane more, but hereby may yee se,
Howe vertue causethe perfyte sikurnesse,   *security*
And vyces done exyle prosparitee;
185   The beste is eche to cheesen, as I gesse.
Dothe as yowe list, I me excuse expresse;   *openly*
I wil be sorye if that yee mischeese.
God you conferme in vertuous goodnesse,
So that thorughe necgligence yee nothing leese.   *lose*

EXPLANATORY NOTES TO *SCOGAN'S MORAL BALADE*

Before 1 The heading from Ashmole 59 contextualizes this piece as an occasional poem, sent to and read at a supper of the Merchants' Guild in the Vintry, in the presence of the four sons of Henry IV when they were teenagers. John was not created duke of Bedford until 1415; the other sons are Henry ("my lord the Prince"), Thomas (duke of Clarence), and Humphrey (duke of Gloucester). Skeat, who dates the poem c. 1406–07, probably correctly suspects that the biographical information was supplied by the scribe John Shirley, who is well-known for his personalized, chatty marginal notes. See Connolly, *John Shirley*, pp. 145–69.

On Henry Scogan, see Farnham, "John (Henry) Scogan"; Kittredge, "Henry Scogan"; and Hallmundsson, "Chaucer's Circle."

feorthe merchande. The fourth meeting of merchants or the fourth of four quarterly meetings of the guild (Skeat, *Chaucerian*, p. xlii).

Lowys Johan. Connolly describes the Welshman Lewis John, Esquire, who, among other things, served as steward to Henry IV's dowager queen, Joan of Navarre, and as chief butler under Henry V, as a "protégé of Thomas Chaucer" (*John Shirley*, p. 137). See Carr, "Sir Lewis John."

26 ☞ **Latin marginalia**: *Delicta juventutis mee et ignorancias meas ne memineris me domine* ["Lord, do not remember the sins of my youth and my idiocies"].

49 ☞ **Latin marginalia**: *nota per Shirley* ["written by Shirley"].

51 ☞ **Latin marginalia**: *fides sine operibus nihil est* ["Faith without works is nothing"], from James 2:17: "So faith also, if it have not works, is dead in itself."

67–68 *He saide that the fader . . . Beqwathe nothing*. The sentiment is found in both Chaucer's Wife of Bath's Tale (*CT* III[D]1121–22), and *Gentilesse* (lines 16–18).

97 *By auncestrye thus may yee no thing clayme*. The quotation is from Chaucer's Wife of Bath's Tale (*CT* III[D]1131–32): "For of oure eldres may we no thyng clayme / But temporel thyng, that man may hurte and mayme."

105 ☞ **Latin marginalia**: "Geffrey Chaucier made theos thre balades nexst that folowen." The poem is Chaucer's *Gentilesse*, which touches upon one of Chaucer's favorite Boethian themes: that nobility depends upon character, not birth. See also the "pillow sermon" in The Wife of Bath's Tale (*CT* III[D]1111–76).

112   *first stocke*. Variously interpreted by Chaucerians as referring to a first human an-
        cestor, to the first generation of nobles, to Adam, or to God. Scogan explicitly
        chooses a genealogical source of virtue: "Thane is Gode stocke of vertuous
        noblesse" (line 100). See Allen, "'Firste Stok.'"

119   *richchesse*. The doubling of the double consonant is a habit of the scribe, John
        Shirley.

121   ☞ **Latin marginalia** (in later hand): *Nam genus et proauos et quae non fecimus ipsi
        Vix ea nostra voco* ["For race and ancestors and whatever we ourselves have not
        made, those things I scarcely call ours"].

150   *Boece*. Anicius Manlius Severinus Boethius (c. 480–524). The allusion appears to
        be to 1.me.6.11–15, which, in Chaucer's translation of *Boece* reads:

> Yif thou desirest or wolt usen grapes, ne seek thou nat with a glotonos
> hand the streyne and presse the stalkes of the vyne in the first somer
> sesoun; for Bachus, the god of wyn, hath rather yyven his yiftes to au-
> tumpne (*the lattere ende of somer*).

162   *vertue causethe suffisaunce*. This is ultimately a Boethian notion. See *Consolation
        of Philosophy* 3.pr.9–11.

166   *Tulius Hastilius*. Tulius Hostillius (673–42 BC), the legendary third king of Rome
        popularly known for his humble origins and his charity to the poor. Also cited
        in Chaucer's Wife of Bath's Tale (*CT* III[D]1165–67): "Thenketh hou noble, as
        seith Valerius, / Was thilke Tullius Hostillius, / That out of poverte roos to heigh
        noblesse."

168–79 *eke redethe . . . what meschaunces they hade*. Scogan no doubt culled his exemplary
        figures — Julius Caesar (line 168), Nero (line 174), Balthasar (line 175), and
        Antiochus (line 177) — from Chaucer's Monk's Tale. Compare, for instance,
        Scogan's description of Antiochus (lines 177–78) to Chaucer's: "For he so soore
        fil out of his char / That it his limes and his skyn totar" (*CT* VII[B²]2610–11).

TEXTUAL NOTES TO *SCOGAN'S MORAL BALADE*

Skeat's text of the poem is based on Thynne, with some variants supplied from Caxton, A, and H. H lacks the text of *Gentilesse*; I have based my text on A, correcting some of its obvious errors with readings from H. Since the texts of H and Ff are not readily available, I have provided their significant variants here.

ABBREVIATIONS: see p. 120–21.

1–8	Ff omits.
	called. H omits.
	balade folowing. H: *litel tretice.*
	ful. H omits.
	Yitte howe. H: *Although.*
	estates. H: *estate.*
	yet. H omits.
	That. H omits.
	yee take. H: *takith.*
8	*herkyne.* H: *herk.*
9	*sore.* Ff: *me sore.*
10	*is upon me.* Ff: *uppon me is.*
11	*juventé.* H: *yong age.*
13	*comunely.* H, Ff: *certaynly.*
14	*beon.* H: *be.*
15	*And.* H, Ff omit.
	wolde. Ff: *ne wolde.*
	no. H: *never no.*
	to. H: *un to.*
17	*I aske.* H: *yowth* (error).
	of. Ff: *to.*
18	*lorde.* H, Ff: *god.*
20	*Bytwene.* H: *betwixt.*
	Thee. Ff: *me.*
21	*ne.* H: *nor*; Ff: *and.*
	blynde prosperitee. Ff: *parfyte unyte* (error).
22–23	Ff omits.
24	*vyce.* H: *vyces.*
25	*lyf.* H: *tyme.*
27	*me.* A: *thee* (error).

29	*Of.* Ff: *In.*
	forgete. Ff: *to f.*
32	*or Thou.* Ff: *or that you.*
33	*lordes.* Ff: *maysters.*
34	*alle whome.* H: *whiche that*; Ff: *whiche.*
36	*eloste.* H: *lost.*
38	*vyces list t'.* Ff: *lustes and vyces.*
39	*Therfore.* H: *Wherfor*; Ff: *Wherfore syrs.*
	lordes tendrely. H: *lordis especially*; Ff: *specyally.*
41	*Plantethe.* Ff: *And p.*
42	*vertue . . . beo.* H: *vertu yowre growyng be.*
43	*ay.* H: *alwey.*
44	*make.* Ff: *makyn.*
45	*For to withstonde . . . affraye.* H: *The fiende for to withstond and his affray*; Ff omits *for.*
47	*use it.* H: *werke it*; Ff: *worcheth.*
48	*That.* H: *And that.*
	yowe. H omits.
49	*heede alsoo.* H: *also heede*; Ff: *hede.*
50	*wrote.* H, Ff: *writen.*
	noble. H, Ff: *grete.*
52	*estate.* H: *eche estate.*
	withoute intelligence. H: *with necligence.*
53	Ff transposes with 129.
54–56	Ff transposes with 131–33.
56	*youre.* H omits.
57–88	Ff transposes with 134–65.
57	*ne.* H: *nor.*
59	*Thenkethe also.* H: *Thynk eke.*
	vertue. H: *vertues.*
60	*whiles.* H: *while.*
	beon. H: *be.*
64	*alle.* H omits.
	loke that yee folowe. H: *therfor folowith.*
65	*Chaucier.* H: *Chaunchier*; Ff: *Chauncer.*
66	*langage.* Ff: *longe age.*
67	*He.* H omits.
	that. H, Ff omit.
	nowe. H, Ff: *that is.*
68	*nothing.* Ff: *not.*
69	*Unto his sone; therfore.* Ff: *Therfore every wy ??? to be.*
70	*beseching.* H: *sechyng.*
	Ff transposes with 102.
71	*for.* H omits.
72	*feyre.* H omits.
	Ff transposes with 104.
73	*Here.* H: *Here by.*

74	*of youre.* H: *by wey of.*
76	*of.* H: *be.*
78	*soo wyse.* H: *suche a.*
80	*wawes.* H: *welthis.*
85	*vertue.* H: *the vertu.*
	vyce. H: *the vyces.*
86	*awe.* H: *hym away.*
87	*leese.* H: *lesith.*
88	*give.* H omits (error).
89–93	Ff transposes with 65–9.
89	*Takethe.* H: *Take.*
	folkes. H: *men.*
	poure. H: *yowre.*
92	*By.* H: *Thurgh.*
94	*Offt.* H omits.
	Ff transposes with 102.
95	*for.* H: *of.*
	Ff transposes with 71.
96	Ff transposes with 104.
97	*By auncestrye thus may yee.* H: *Thus by youre auncestris ye may.*
98	*my.* H omits.
	Chaucier. H: *Chauncer.*
	dothe. H: *sayde.*
102	*That.* H: *And.*
	mankynde that. H: *us al.*
	Ff: *Besychynge hym oft that for us all deyed.*
103	*his.* H: *hym in.*
105–25	H omits.
120	*se.* A: *seeme* (error).
127	*he.* H omits.
128	*losse.* A: *lesse.*
129	*Wherfore.* H: *Therfor*; Ff: *Wherfore syrs.*
130	*estates.* H: *estate.*
131	*T'enprynte.* Ff: *To plant.*
132	*into.* Ff: *in.*
134	*For.* H omits; Ff: *But.*
	lordes. Ff: *yonge men.*
	of coustume. H, Ff: *have a maner.*
135	*of you here of a gode.* H, Ff: *shewe you a vertuous.*
136	*unsure youthe.* H: *fervent love*; Ff: *fervent youthe.*
137	*Suche artes.* H, Ff: *that art.*
	list not. H, Ff: *have no joy.*
139	*variaunce.* H, Ff: *governaunce.*
140	*calme.* A: *worlde.*
	laste yeere. H: *laste.*
142	*not, by.* Ff: *not.*
143	*there.* H, Ff omit.

	rage. H, Ff: *full rage.*
144	*Right even so.* H, Ff: *In the same wise.*
	his. H omits.
145	*croked.* H: *febilnes.*
146	*Soone affter that.* H, Ff: *And sone after.*
	kalendes. H, Ff: *the k.*
147	*And of youre.* H: *And if*; Ff: *Yf ye in.*
148	*Alle folke.* H: *Thanne men*; Ff: *All men.*
149	*youthe and slouthe you al misgyded.* H: *yowth from worshyp yow devided*; Ff: *slouthe from worshyp yow devided.*
150	*that.* H, Ff: *the.*
	Boece. H: *Boys.*
153	*Plenty of.* H, Ff: *Plentyuous.*
155	*whylest.* H, Ff: *while.*
156	*Yee may wele.* Ff: *Thus may ye.*
157	*ay michil.* H, Ff: *moche.*
158	*Sithe, there ageinst, that.* H, Ff: *Seeth here ageyn how.*
161	*Al.* H, Ff: *As.*
	al ryots. H, Ff: *riot.*
163	H omits (error).
164	*Thus who.* H: *And who so.*
	gret. H, Ff: *al.*
167	*came frome povertee.* H: *from poverte cam.*
168	*eke redethe.* H: *redith eke.*
169	*poure.* A: *a poure* (error).
171	*lande.* H: *contre.*
	the. H omits.
172	*unto.* H: *us to* (error).
173	*do to.* H: *to do.*
174	*of.* A: *to.*
175	*heede also.* H: *also heede.*
177	*Looke.* H: *Lo.*
178	*That.* H: *There.*
	also heos. H omits.
	totare. H: *altotare.*
179	*meschaunces.* H: *mychaunce.*
180	*that.* H omits.
181	*is.* H: *he is.*
182	*more.* H: *no more.*
	hereby. H: *here*
184	*done exyle.* H: *exilen al.*
185	*eche to cheesen.* A: *dethe to cheesen*; H: *to chese.* I follow Skeat's emendation.
186	*Dothe as yowe.* H: *Do ye as ye.*
	me. H: *myn* (error).
187	*wil.* H: *wolde.*
188	*you conferme.* H: *conferme yow.*

 # EPIGRAPH

A BALADE IN THE PRAISE AND COMMENDACION OF
MASTER GEFFRAY CHAUSER FOR HIS GOLDEN ELOQUENCE

1 Maister Geffray Chauser, that now lithe in grave,   *who now lies in [his] grave*
  The noble rhetoricion and poet of Great Bretaine,
  That worthy was the laurer of poetry to have,   *laurel*
  For this, his labor, and the palme to atteine,
5 Whiche first made to dystil and reine
  The gold dewe dropes of speche and eloquence,
  Into English tong through his excelence.

From John Stow's *Workes of Geffrey Chaucer*, 1561 (fol. 337v). These seven lines served as an envoy to Chaucer's *Parliament of Fowls* in both Trinity College, Cambridge MS R.3.19 and British Library, MS Harley 7333. The extract from John Lydgate's *Life of Our Lady* (2. 1628–34). Described by Walter Skeat as "a poor imitation of the style of Lydgate" (*Chaucerian*, p. 554).

BIBLIOGRAPHY

Allen, Valerie. "The 'Firste Stok' in Chaucer's *Gentilesse*: Barking up the Right Tree." *Review of English Studies* 40 (1989), 531–37.

Ausonius. *The Works of Ausonius*. Ed. R. P. H. Green. Oxford: Clarendon Press, 1991.

Barron, Caroline M. "The Deposition of Richard II." In *Politics and Crisis in Fourteenth-Century England*. Ed. John Taylor and Wendy Childs. Gloucester: Alan Sutton, 1990. Pp. 132–49.

Bates, Catherine. *The Rhetoric of Courtship in Elizabethan Language and Literature*. Cambridge: Cambridge University Press, 1992.

Bayless, Martha. *Parody in the Middle Ages*. Ann Arbor: University of Michigan Press, 1996.

Bell, Robert, ed. *Poetical Works*. See Chaucer, Geoffrey.

Blamires, Alcuin, ed. *Woman Defamed and Defended: An Anthology of Medieval Texts*. Oxford: Clarendon Press, 1992.

Bloch, R. Howard. *Medieval Misogyny and the Invention of Western Romantic Love*. Chicago: University of Chicago Press, 1991.

Boffey, Julia. "Manuscripts of Courtly Love Lyrics in the Fifteenth Century." In *Manuscripts and Readers in Fifteenth-Century England*. Ed. Derek Pearsall. Cambridge: D. S. Brewer, 1981. Pp. 3–14.

———. "Proverbial Chaucer and the Chaucer Canon." In *Reading from the Margins: Textual Studies, Chaucer, and Medieval Literature*. Ed. Seth Lerer. San Marino, CA: The Huntington Library, 1996. Pp. 37–47.

Bonner, Francis W. "The Genesis of the Chaucer Apocrypha." *Studies in Philology* 48 (1951), 461–81.

Boyd, Beverly, ed. *Chaucer according to William Caxton*. See Chaucer, Geoffrey.

Brewer, Derek, ed. *The Works, 1532*. See Chaucer, Geoffrey.

Brown, Carleton, and Rossell Hope Robbins, eds. *The Index of Middle English Verse*. New York: Columbia University Press, 1943. [*IMEV.*]

Campbell, Gertrude H. "Chaucer's Prophesy in 1586." *Modern Language Notes* 29 (1914), 195–96.

Carlson, David R. "Chaucer, Humanism, and Printing: Conditions of Authorship in Fifteenth-Century England." *University of Toronto Quarterly* 64 (1995), 274–88.

Carr, A. D. "Sir Lewis John — A Medieval London Welshman." *Bulletin of the Board of Celtic Studies* 22 (1967), 260–70.

Chaucer, Geoffrey. *The Workes of Geffray Chaucer Newly Printed: With Dyvers Workes Whiche Were Never in Print Before*. Ed. William Thynne. London: Thomas Godfray, 1532. (*STC* 5068.)

———. *The Workes of Geffrey Chaucer, Newlie Printed, with Divers Addicions, whiche Where Never in Print Before*. Ed. John Stow. London: Jhon Kingston, 1561. (*STC* 5075.)

———. *The Poetical Works of Geoffrey Chaucer*. Ed. Robert Bell. The Annotated Edition of the English Poets 4. London: J. W. Parker, 1855.

———. *A Parallel-Text Edition of Chaucer's Minor Poems*, Part 3. Ed. Frederick J. Furnivall. Chaucer Society, First Series 58. London: N. Trübner and Co. for the Chaucer Society, 1879.

———. *The Complete Works of Geoffrey Chaucer*. Ed. W. W. Skeat. 7 vols. Second ed. Oxford: University Press, 1899. [See especially, for the Chaucerian apocrypha, Skeat, vol. 7, *Chaucerian and Other Pieces*.]

———. *The Works, 1532: With Supplementary Material from the Editions of 1542, 1561, 1598 and 1602*. Ed. Derek A. Brewer. Ilkley, UK: Scolar Press, 1976.

————. *Chaucer according to William Caxton: Minor Poems and Boece, 1478*. Ed. Beverly Boyd. Lawrence, KS: Allen Press, 1978.

————. *The Riverside Chaucer*. Third ed. Gen. ed. Larry D. Benson. Boston: Houghton Mifflin, 1987.

Clarke, Elizabeth. "Anne Southwell and the Pamphlet Debate: The Politics of Gender, Class, and Manuscript." In *Debating Gender in Early Modern England, 1500–1700*. Ed. Cristina Malcolmson and Mihoko Suzuki. New York: Palgrave, 2002. Pp. 37–53.

Connolly, Margaret. *John Shirley: Book Production and the Noble Household in Fifteenth-Century England*. Aldershot, UK: Ashgate, 1998.

Coote, Lesley A. *Prophecy and Public Affairs in Later Medieval England*. York: York Medieval Press, 2000.

————, and Tim Thornton. "Merlin, Erceldoune, Nixon: A Tradition of Popular Political Prophecy." *New Medieval Literatures* 4 (2001), 117–37.

The Court of Sapience. Ed. E. Ruth Harvey. Toronto: University of Toronto Press, 1984.

Crane, Mary Thomas. *Framing Authority: Sayings, Self, and Society in Sixteenth-Century England*. Princeton: Princeton University Press, 1993.

Dane, Joseph A. *Who Is Buried in Chaucer's Tomb? Studies in the Reception of Chaucer's Book*. East Lansing: Michigan State University Press, 1998.

Daniels, R. B. "Rhetoric in Gower's 'Henry IV, In Praise of Peace.'" *Studies in Philology* 32 (1935), 62–73.

Davenport, W. A. "Bird Poems from *The Parliament of Fowls* to *Philip Sparrow*." In *Chaucer and Fifteenth-Century Poetry*. Ed. Julia Boffey and Janet Cower. King's College London Medieval Studies 5. London: Centre for Late Antique and Medieval Studies, 1991. Pp. 66–83.

Davies, R. T. *Medieval English Lyrics: A Critical Anthology*. Chicago: Northwestern University Press, 1964.

Dean, James M., ed. *Medieval English Political Writings*. Kalamazoo, MI: Medieval Institute Publications, 1996.

Doyle, A. I. "English Books in and out of Court from Edward III to Henry VII." In *English Court Culture in the Later Middle Ages*. Ed. V. J. Scattergood and J. W. Sherborne. London: Duckworth, 1983. Pp. 163–82.

Du Boulay, F. R. H. "Henry of Derby's Expeditions to Prussia 1390–1 and 1392." In *The Reign of Richard II: Essays in Honour of May McKisack*. Ed. F. R. H. Du Boulay and Caroline M. Barron. London: Athlone Press, 1971. Pp. 153–72.

Dyas, Dee. *Pilgrimage in Medieval English Literature, 700–1500*. Woodbridge, UK: D. S. Brewer, 2001.

Edwards, A. S. G., and J. Hedley. "John Stowe, *The Craft of Lovers*, and T. C. C. R.3.19." *Studies in Bibliography* 28 (1975), 265–68.

Farnham, W. E. "John (Henry) Scogan." *Modern Language Review* 16 (1921), 120–28.

Fawtier, E. C., and R. Fawtier. "From Merlin to Shakespeare: Adventures of an English Prophecy." *Bulletin of the John Rylands University Library of Manchester* 5 (1918–20), 388–92.

Fein, Susanna Greer, ed. *Moral Love Songs and Laments*. Kalamazoo, MI: Medieval Institute Publications, 1998.

Ferster, Judith. *Fictions of Advice: The Literature and Politics of Counsel in Late Medieval England*. Philadelphia: University of Pennsylvania Press, 1996.

Fisher, John H. *John Gower: Moral Philosopher and Friend of Chaucer*. New York: New York University Press, 1964.

————. *The Importance of Chaucer*. Carbondale: Southern Illinois University Press, 1992.

————. "A Language Policy for Lancastrian England." *PMLA* 107 (1992), 1168–80. Rpt. in *Writing after Chaucer: Essential Readings in Chaucer and the Fifteenth Century*. Ed. Daniel J. Pinti. New York: Garland, 1998. Pp. 81–100.

Fletcher, Bradford Y. "An Edition of MS R.3.19 in Trinity College, Cambridge: A Poetical Miscellany of c. 1480." Ph.D. Dissertation: University of Chicago, 1973.

————. "Printer's Copy for Stow's *Chaucer*." *Studies in Bibliography* 31 (1978), 184–201.

————. *Manuscript Trinity R.3.19: A Facsimile*. The Facsimile Series of the Works of Geoffrey Chaucer, vol. 5. Norman, OK: Pilgrim Books, 1987.

Forni, Kathleen. *The Chaucerian Apocrypha: A Counterfeit Canon*. Gainesville: University Press of Florida, 2001.

Foucault, Michel. "What Is an Author?" Trans. Josue V. Harari. In *Contemporary Literary Criticism: Literary and Cultural Studies*. Fourth ed. Ed. Robert Con Davis and Ronald Schleifer. New York: Longman, 1998. Pp. 364–76.

Fox, Denton, and William F. Ringler, eds. *The Bannatyne Manuscript: National Library of Scotland Advocates' MS 1.1.6*. London: Scolar Press, 1980.

Friedman, Bonita. "In Love's Thrall: *The Court of Love* and Its Captives." In *New Readings of Late Medieval Love Poems*. Ed. David Chamberlain. Lanham, MD: University Press of America, 1993. Pp. 173–90.

Furnivall, Frederick J., ed. *Parallel Text Edition*. See Chaucer, Geoffrey.

Gower, John. *The Complete Works of John Gower*. Ed. G. C. Macaulay. 4 vols. Oxford: Clarendon Press, 1899–1902. Vols. 2 and 3 rpt. as *The English Works of John Gower*. EETS e.s. 81–82. London: Oxford University Press, 1900–01; rpt. 1957.

———. *Confessio Amantis*. Ed. Russell A. Peck, with Latin translations by Andrew Galloway. 3 vols. Kalamazoo, MI: Medieval Institute Publications, 2000–04.

Grady, Frank. "The Lancastrian Gower and the Limits of Exemplarity." *Speculum* 70 (1995), 552–75.

Graybill, Robert V. "Courts of Love: Challenge to Feudalism." *Essays in Medieval Studies* 5 (1988), 93–101.

Green, Richard Firth. *Poets and Princepleasers: Literature and the English Court in the Late Middle Ages*. Toronto: University of Toronto Press, 1980.

———. "The *Craft of Lovers* and the Rhetoric of Seduction." *Acta* 12 (1988), 105–25.

Hallmundsson, May Newman. "Chaucer's Circle: Henry Scogan and His Friends." *Medievalia et Humanistica* 10 (1981), 129–139.

Hammond, Eleanor Prescott. "Two British Museum Manuscripts." *Anglia* 28 (1905), 1–28.

———. *Chaucer: A Bibliographical Manual*. New York: Macmillan, 1908.

———. *English Verse between Chaucer and Surrey*. 1927. Rpt., New York: Octagon Books, 1969.

———. "Chaucer's 'Book of the Twenty-five Ladies'." *Modern Language Notes* 48 (1933), 514–16.

Heale, Elizabeth. *Wyatt, Surrey, and Early Tudor Poetry*. New York: Longman, 1998.

———. "Misogyny and the Complete Gentleman in Early Elizabethan Printed Miscellanies." *Yearbook of English Studies* 33 (2003), 233–47.

Huot, Sylvia. "The Daisy and the Laurel: Myths of Desire and Creativity in the Poetry of Jean Froissart." In *Contexts: Style and Values in Medieval Art and Literature*. Ed. Daniel Poirion and Nancy Freeman Regalado. Special edition of *Yale French Studies*, 1991. Pp. 240–51.

———. *Allegorical Play in the Old French Motet: The Sacred and the Profane in Thirteenth-Century Polyphony*. Palo Alto, CA: Stanford University Press, 1996.

Ives, Carolyn, and David Parkinson. "Scottish Chaucer, Misogynist Chaucer." In *Rewriting Chaucer: Culture, Authority, and the Idea of the Authentic Text, 1400–1602*. Ed. Thomas A. Prendergast and Barbara Kline. Columbus: The Ohio State University Press, 1999. Pp. 186–202.

Javitch, Daniel. *Poetry and Courtliness in Renaissance England*. Princeton: Princeton University Press, 1978.

Jones, Leslie W. "The Influence of Cassiodorus on Medieval Culture." *Speculum* 20 (1945), 433–42.

Kelly, Henry Ansgar. *Chaucer and the Cult of St. Valentine*. Leiden: E. J. Brill, 1986.

Kittredge, George L. "Henry Scogan." *Harvard Studies and Notes* 1 (1892), 109–17.

Klinefelter, Ralph A. "A Newly Discovered Fifteenth–Century English MS." *Modern Language Quarterly* 14 (1953), 3–6.

Knight, Stephen, and Thomas H. Ohlgren, eds. *Robin Hood and Other Outlaw Tales*. Kalamazoo, MI: Medieval Institute Publications, 1997.

Kooper, Erik. "Slack Water Poetry: An Edition of the *Craft of Lovers*." *English Studies* 68 (1987), 473–89.

Lawton, David. "Dullness and the Fifteenth Century." *English Literary History* 54 (1987), 761–99.

Leonard, Frances McNeely. *Laughter in the Courts of Love: Comedy in Allegory, from Chaucer to Spenser*. Norman, OK: Pilgrim Books, 1981. Pp. 97–103.

Lerer, Seth. *Chaucer and His Readers: Imagining the Author in Late-Medieval England*. Princeton: Princeton University Press, 1993.

———. "Medieval English Literature and the Idea of the Anthology." *PMLA* 118 (2003), 1251–67.

Lewis, C. S. *The Allegory of Love: A Study in Medieval Tradition*. Oxford: Clarendon Press, 1936.

———. *English Literature in the Sixteenth Century excluding Drama*. Oxford: Clarendon Press, 1954. Rpt. 1966.

Linn, Irving. "If All the Sky Were Parchment." *PMLA* 53 (1938), 951–70.

Lounsbury, Thomas Raynesford. *Studies in Chaucer: His Life and Writings*. 3 vols. New York: Harper, 1892.

Luria, Maxwell S., and Richard L. Hoffman, eds. *Middle English Lyrics*. New York: W. W. Norton, 1974.

Lydgate, John. *Lydgate's Temple of Glas*. Ed. J. Schick. EETS e.s. 60. London: K. Paul, Trench, Trübner & Co., 1891. Rpt., New York: Kraus Reprint, 1973. Pp. cxxix–cxxxi.

———. *The Minor Poems of John Lydgate, Part II: Secular Poems*. Ed. Henry Noble MacCracken. EETS o.s. 192. London: Humphrey Milford, Oxford University Press, 1934.

———. *John Lydgate: Poems*. Ed. John Norton-Smith. Oxford: Clarendon Press, 1966.

Manning, Stephen. "Game and Ernest in Middle English and Provençal Love Lyrics." *Comparative Literature* 18 (1966), 225–41.

Marotti, Arthur. *Manuscript, Print, and the English Renaissance*. Ithaca, NY: Cornell University Press, 1995.

Maximianus. *The Elegies of Maximianus*. Ed. Richard Webster. Princeton: Princeton University Press, 1900.

McGann, Jerome. *A Critique of Modern Textual Criticism*. Charlottesville: University of Virginia Press, 1983.

Meale, Carol M. "Patrons, Buyers and Owners: Book Production and Social Status." In *Book Production and Publishing in Britain, 1375–1475*. Ed. Jeremy Griffiths and Derek Pearsall. Cambridge: Cambridge University Press, 1989. Pp. 201–28.

Middle English Dictionary. Gen. eds. Hans Kurath and Sherman M. Kuhn. Ann Arbor: University of Michigan Press, 1952–2003.

Minnis, A. J. *Medieval Theory of Authorship: Scholastic Literary Attitudes in the Later Middle Ages*. Second ed. Philadelphia: University of Philadelphia Press, 1988.

Minnis, A. J., V. J. Scattergood, and J. J. Smith, eds. *Oxford Guides to Chaucer: The Shorter Poems*. Oxford: Clarendon Press, 1995.

Miskimin, Alice S. *The Renaissance Chaucer*. New Haven: Yale University Press, 1975.

Mooney, Linne R. "Scribes and Booklets of Trinity College, Cambridge, Manuscripts R.3.19 and R.3.21." In *Middle English Poetry: Texts and Traditions*. Ed. A. J. Minnis. York: York Medieval Press, 2001. Pp. 241–66.

Moore, Arthur K. "Some Implications of the Middle English *Craft of Lovers*." *Neophilologus* 35 (1951), 231–38.

Murphy, James Jerome, ed. *Three Medieval Rhetorical Arts*. Berkeley: University of California Press, 1971.

Murphy, James Jerome. *Rhetoric in the Middle Ages: A History of the Rhetorical Theory from Saint Augustine to the Renaissance*. Medieval & Renaissance Texts & Studies 227. Tempe: Arizona Center for Medieval and Renaissance Studies, 2001.

Neilson, William Allan. *The Origins and Sources of the Court of Love*. Boston: Ginn, 1899. Rpt., New York: Russell and Russell, 1967.

Norton-Smith, John. Introduction to *Bodleian Library, MS Fairfax 16*. [Facsimile.] London: Scolar Press, 1979.

Nouvet, C. "'The 'Marguerite': A Distinctive Signature." In *Chaucer's French Contemporaries: The Poetry/Poetics of Self and Tradition*. Ed. R. Barton Palmer. New York: AMS Press, 1999. Pp. 251–76

Oruch, Jack B. "St. Valentine, Chaucer, and Spring in February." *Speculum* 56 (1981), 534–65.

Oxford English Dictionary. Second ed. Ed. J. A. Simpson and E. S. C. Weiner. Oxford: Clarendon Press, 1989.

Peck, Russell A. *Kingship and Common Profit in Gower's Confessio Amantis*. Carbondale: Southern Illinois University Press, 1978.

———. *Chaucer's Romaunt of the Rose and Boece, Treatise on the Astrolabe, Equatorie of Planetis, Lost Works and Chaucerian Apocrypha: An Annotated Bibliography 1900–1985*. Toronto: University of Toronto Press, 1988.

Person, Henry A., ed. *Cambridge Middle English Lyrics*. Seattle: University of Washington Press, 1953. Rev. ed. New York: Greenwood Press, 1969.

Pollard, A. J. *Late Medieval England, 1399–1509*. London: Longman, 2000.

Porter, Elizabeth. "Gower's Ethical Microcosm and Political Macrocosm." In *Gower's Confessio Amantis: Responses and Reassessments*. Ed. A. J. Minnis. Cambridge: D. S. Brewer, 1983. Pp. 135–62.

Prokosch, Frederick. "The Chaucerian Apocrypha." Ph.D. Dissertation, Yale University, 1932.

Robbins, Rossell Hope, ed. *Secular Lyrics of the Fourteenth and Fifteenth Centuries*. Oxford: Clarendon Press, 1952.

———. "A Love Epistle by 'Chaucer.'" *Modern Language Review* 49 (1954), 289–92.

———. "A Middle English Diatribe against Philip of Burgundy." *Neophilologus* 39 (1955), 131–46.

———. "The Chaucerian Apocrypha." In *A Manual of the Writings in Middle English 1050–1500*. Ed. J. Burke Severs and Albert E. Hartung. 10 vols. New Haven: Connecticut Academy of Arts and Sciences, 1967–. Vol. 4, pp. 1061–1101 and 1285–1306.

Robbins, Rossell Hope, and John L. Cutler. *Supplement to the Index of Middle English Verse*. Lexington: University of Kentucky Press, 1965. [*SIMEV.*]

Salisbury, Eve, ed. *The Trials and Joys of Marriage*. Kalamazoo, MI: Medieval Institute Publications, 2002.

Salomon, L. B. *The Devil Take Her!: A Study of the Rebellious Lover in English Poetry*. Second ed. New York: Barnes and Noble, 1961.

Scanlon, Larry. *Narrative, Authority, and Power: The Medieval Exemplum and the Chaucerian Tradition*. Cambridge: Cambridge University Press, 1994.

Schenkl, Karl. *D. Magni Ausonii Opuscula*. Berlin: Weidmann, 1883. Appendix.

Seaton, Ethel. *Sir Richard Roos, c. 1410–1482: Lancastrian Poet*. London: Rupert Hart-Davis, 1961. Pp. 445–54.

Skeat, Walter W., ed. *Chaucerian and Other Pieces*. See Chaucer, Geoffrey, *Complete Works of Geoffrey Chaucer*.

Skeat, Walter W. *The Chaucer Canon: With a Discussion of the Works Associated with the Name of Geoffrey Chaucer*. Oxford: Clarendon Press, 1900.

Spurgeon, Caroline F. E. *Five Hundred Years of Chaucer Criticism and Allusion, 1357–1900*. 3 vols. Cambridge: Cambridge University Press, 1925.

Stemmler, Theo. "My Fair Lady: Parody in Fifteenth-Century Lyrics." In *Language and Literature*. Ed. Wolf Dietrich Bald and Horst Weinstock. Frankfurt: Lang, 1984. Pp. 205–13.

Stevens, John. *Music and Poetry in the Early Tudor Court*. Lincoln: University of Nebraska Press, 1963.

Stow, John. See Chaucer, Geoffrey.

Strohm, Paul. "Chaucer's Fifteenth-Century Audience and the Narrowing of the 'Chaucer Tradition.'" *Studies in the Age of Chaucer* 4 (1982), 3–32.

———. *Hochon's Arrow: The Social Imagination of Fourteenth-Century Texts*. Princeton: Princeton University Press, 1992.

———. *England's Empty Throne: Usurpation and the Language of Legitimation, 1399–1422*. New Haven: Yale University Press, 1998.

Summerson, Henry. "An English Bible and Other Books Belonging to Henry IV." *Bulletin of the John Rylands University Library* 79 (1997), 109–15.

Symons, Dana M., ed. *Chaucerian Dream Visions and Complaints*. Kalamazoo, MI: Medieval Institute Publications, 2004.

Thynne, William. See Chaucer, Geoffrey.

Tilley, Morris Palmer. *A Dictionary of the Proverbs in England in the Sixteenth and Seventeenth Centuries*. Ann Arbor: University of Michigan Press, 1950.

Trevisa, John. *On the Properties of Things: John Trevisa's Translation of Bartholomaeus Anglicus De proprietatibus rerum: A Critical Text.* Ed. M. C. Seymour et al. 3 vols. Oxford: Clarendon Press, 1975–88.

Utley, Francis Lee. *The Crooked Rib: An Analytical Index to the Argument about Women in English and Scots Literature to the End of the Year 1568.* Columbus: The Ohio State University, 1944.

van Dorsten, J. A. "The Leyden 'Lydgate Manuscript.'" *Scriptorium* 14 (1960), 315–25.

Wall, Wendy. *The Imprint of Gender: Authorship and Publication in the Renaissance.* Ithaca, NY: Cornell University Press, 1993.

Walsh, P. G., ed. and trans. *Love Lyrics from the Carmina Burana.* Chapel Hill: University of North Carolina Press, 1993.

Watkins, John. "'Wrastling for this world': Wyatt and the Tudor Canonization of Chaucer." In *Refiguring Chaucer in the Renaissance.* Ed. Theresa M. Krier. Gainesville: University Press of Florida, 1998. Pp. 21–39.

Webb, Diana M. "The Truth about Constantine: History, Hagiography and Confusion." In *Religion and Humanism: Papers Read at the Eighteenth Summer Meeting and the Nineteenth Winter Meeting of the Ecclesiastical Historical Society.* Ed. Keith Robbins. Oxford: Basil Blackwell, 1981. Pp. 85–102.

Wenzel, Siegfried. *Preachers, Poets, and the Early English Lyric.* Princeton: Princeton University Press, 1986.

Whiting, Bartlett Jere, with the collaboration of Helen Wescott Whiting. *Proverbs, Sentences, and Proverbial Phrases from English Writings Mainly before 1500.* Cambridge, MA: The Belknap Press of Harvard University Press, 1968.

Wilson, Kenneth G. "Five Unpublished Secular Love Poems from MS Trinity College Cambridge 599." *Anglia* 72 (1954) 399–418.

Wimsatt, James I. *Chaucer and the French Love Poets: The Literary Background of the Book of the Duchess.* Chapel Hill: University of North Carolina Press, 1968.

———. *The Marguerite Poetry of Guillaume de Machaut.* Chapel Hill: University of North Carolina Press, 1970.

Woodbridge, Linda. *Women in the English Renaissance.* Urbana: University of Illinois Press, 1984.

Yeager, R. F. "Literary Theory at the Close of the Middle Ages: William Caxton and William Thynne." *Studies in the Age of Chaucer* 6 (1984), 135–64.

———. "Pax Poetica: On the Pacifism of Chaucer and Gower." *Studies in the Age of Chaucer* 9 (1987), 97–121.

———. *John Gower's Poetic: The Search for a New Arion.* Woodbridge, UK: D. S. Brewer, 1990.

Ziolkowski, Jan. "Avatars of Ugliness in Medieval Literature," *Modern Language Review* 79 (1984), 1–20.

GLOSSARY

actual *real; vigorous*
affiaunce *confidence, trust*
afore *before*
agayn, ayein *against*
and *if, even if*
anon *immediately*
apace *promptly*
avisement *careful consideration*
ay(e) *constantly, all the time; always*

baiten *to feed*
balad(e) *a poem or stanza in rhyme royal*
be *by, through*
besy *diligent, attentive; anxious*
bidden *to ask; pray; demand*
biden *to stay, remain*
biteden *to happen, come to pass*
bill *a petition, letter, prayer*

careful *sorrowful; miserable, troubled*
chere *attitude; expression; behavior; mood; countenance*
chese *to choose*
clene *pure; bright; splendid*
comlynesse *fairness*
commendable *worthy of admiration*
conceite *idea; mental ability*
connyngly *skillfully*
contriven *to fashion; to devise*
councel *secret, confidence*
countenaunce *conduct, bearing; appearance*
curious *skillful; subtle; intricate*

daunger *resistance; disdain, arrogance*
debonayre *kind, courteous*
defaute *lack; absence*

degre *social rank; stage*
demaunde *question*
demen *to judge*
dispute *discuss*
dotage *folly; senility; infatuation*
drery *sorrowful, sad*
duren *to last, to remain*

eft *again, once more; after*
ek(e) *also; moreover*
er *before*
ese *comfort; pleasure; benefit*
estat(e) *rank; condition*
expresse *certainly; clearly*

fayne (adv.) *gladly*
feinen *to invent; disguise; dissemble*
feint *exhausted*
flour(e) *flower; model, paragon*
for *because, because of; since*
forby *past*
forthy *therefore*
forto *to*
fre *gracious; generous*
fro *from*
ful *very*
furious *unrestrained*
furth *forth, forward*

gan *began*
glose *explain; falsify; flatter*
grucchen *complain; annoy*

ha *have*
hele *health; happiness*
hem *them*
her *their; her*

holden *hold, maintain; obligated*
hole *wholly*
hoten *to be called*

ich(e) *I*
iwis *certainly*

joylof *joyful; vigorous; beautiful*

lawrer *laurel*
lesen *to lie; to lose; to set free*
list *wish*
longen *belong; desire*
lust *pleasure; sexual desire*

maner(e) *custom; manners*
manly *masculine; reliable; noble*
me *my*
mercyable *compassionate; compliant*
mot *must*
musen *to ponder*

nas *was not*
naught *nothing*
ne *nor, not*
nere *nearer*
none *not any, no*
nys *is not*

of *from*
on *for*
ones *at once*
other *or*
outrage *violence; excess*
owe *ought*

palme *palm branch*
pensifhede *anxiety; sorrow*
plesaunce *pleasure; politeness; desire; consent*
proces *discourse; activity; event*

quemen *to serve in an acceptable manner*
quod *said*

relacion *narration, report*

reserven *to keep*
resort *return*
reuth *pity*
rewen *have pity on; regret*

sad *steadfast; serious; prudent*
sanatyf *healing*
scribable *suitable for being written on*
shenden *ruin; harm; confound*
sith *since*
slaken *cease; diminish; alleviate*
sondry *various*
sothfastnesse *truth*
sothly *truly*
sownen *sound; incline to*
speden *prosper; succeed; assist; hasten*
spillen *to waste; to perish; to pine away (for love)*
stature *height, size*
straunge *aloof, reserved*
submyttyng *submitted for judgement*
swert *sword*

tendre *young; delicate*
thider *there, to that place*
tho *those; then*
thought *concern; plan, idea*
tofore *before*
touching *mentioning; alluding to*
trouthe *promise; loyalty*

ure *fate*

variaunce *inconstancy; change*
verray *true; certain*
vieu *gaze*
vowen *promise*

wele *(adj.) happy; healthy; (n.) prosperity*
welfare *well being, delight*
wight *person*
wise *manner, way*
withoute(n) *unless*
wonder *(adv.) extraordinarily*
wonderly *marvelously*

worship *honor*
wot(e) *know*

Y *I*
yfere *together*
yode *went*

MIDDLE ENGLISH TEXTS SERIES

Richard Maidstone, *Concordia (The Reconciliation of Richard II with London)*, edited by
David R. Carlson, with a verse translation by A. G. Rigg (2003)

Three Purgatory Poems: The Gast of Gy, Sir Owain, and The Vision of Tundale, edited by
Edward E. Foster (2004)

William Dunbar, *The Complete Works*, edited by John Conlee (2004)

Chaucerian Dream Visions and Complaints, edited by Dana M. Symons (2004)

Stanzaic Guy of Warwick, edited by Alison Wiggins (2004)

Saints' Lives in Middle English Collections, edited by E. Gordon Whatley, with Anne B.
Thompson and Robert K. Upchurch (2004)

Siege of Jerusalem, edited by Michael Livingston (2004)

The Kingis Quair and Other Prison Poems, edited by Linne R. Mooney and Mary-Jo Arn
(2005)

DOCUMENTS OF PRACTICE SERIES

Love and Marriage in Late Medieval London, selected, translated, and introduced by
Shannon McSheffrey (1995)

Sources for the History of Medicine in Late Medieval England, selected, introduced, and
translated by Carole Rawcliffe (1995)

A Slice of Life: Selected Documents of Medieval English Peasant Experience, edited, translated,
and with an introduction by Edwin Brezette DeWindt (1996)

Regular Life: Monastic, Canonical, and Mendicant Rules, selected with an introduction by
Douglas J. McMillan and Kathryn Smith Fladenmuller (1997); second edition,
selected and introduced by Daniel Marcel La Corte and Douglas J. McMillan (2004)

Women and Monasticism in Medieval Europe: Sisters and Patrons of the Cistercian Reform,
selected, translated, and with an introduction by Constance H. Berman (2002)

Medieval Notaries and Their Acts: The 1327–1328 Register of Jean Holanie, introduced,
edited, and translated by Kathryn L. Reyerson and Debra A. Salata (2004)

COMMENTARY SERIES

Commentary on the Book of Jonah, Haimo of Auxerre, translated with an introduction by
Deborah Everhart (1993)

Medieval Exegesis in Translation: Commentaries on the Book of Ruth, translated with an intro-
duction by Lesley Smith (1996)

Nicholas of Lyra's Apocalypse Commentary, translated with an introduction and notes by
Philip D. W. Krey (1997)

*Rabbi Ezra Ben Solomon of Gerona: Commentary on the Song of Songs and Other Kabbalistic
Commentaries*, selected, translated, and annotated by Seth Brody (1999)

John Wyclif: On the Truth of Holy Scripture, translated with an introduction and notes by
Ian Christopher Levy (2001)

Second Thessalonians: Two Early Medieval Apocalyptic Commentaries, translated with an
introduction by Steven R. Cartwright and Kevin L. Hughes (2001)

The Glossa Ordinaria *on the Song of Songs*, translated with an introduction and notes by
Mary Dove (2004)

MEDIEVAL GERMAN TEXTS IN BILINGUAL EDITIONS SERIES

Sovereignty and Salvation in the Vernacular, 1050–1150, introduction, translations, and notes by James A. Schultz (2000)

Ava's New Testament Narratives: "When the Old Law Passed Away," introduction, translations, and notes by James A. Rushing, Jr. (2003)

History as Literature: German World Chronicles of the Thirteenth Century in Verse, introduction, translations, and notes by R. Graeme Dunphy (2003)

VARIA

The Study of Chivalry: Resources and Approaches, edited by Howell Chickering and Thomas H. Seiler (1988)

Studies of British Library MS Harley 2253, edited by Susanna Fein (2000)

The Liturgy of the Medieval Church, edited by Thomas J. Heffernan and E. Ann Matter (2001); second edition (2005)

TO ORDER PLEASE CONTACT:

Medieval Institute Publications
Western Michigan University
Kalamazoo, MI 49008-5432
Phone (269) 387-8755
FAX (269) 387-8750

http://www.wmich.edu/medieval/mip/index.html

Medieval Institute Publications is a program
of The Medieval Institute, College of Arts
and Sciences, Western Michigan University

Typeset in 10/13 New Baskerville
with Golden Cockerel Ornaments display
Designed by Linda K. Judy
Manufactured by Cushing-Malloy, Inc. — Ann Arbor, Michigan

Medieval Institute Publications
College of Arts and Sciences
Western Michigan University
1903 W. Michigan Avenue
Kalamazoo, MI 49008-5432
http://www.wmich.edu/medieval/mip

 WESTERN MICHIGAN UNIVERSITY